Cultivating Imagination in Leadership

Transforming Schools and Communities

Gillian Judson and Meaghan Dougherty

Foreword by Scott Brandon

TEACHERS COLLEGE PRESS
TEACHERS COLLEGE | COLUMBIA UNIVERSITY
NEW YORK AND LONDON

Published by Teachers College Press,® 1234 Amsterdam Avenue, New York, NY 10027

Copyright © 2023 by Teachers College, Columbia University

Front cover by Holly Grundon / BHG Graphics. Image by Nongkran_ch / iStock by Getty Images.

This project was financially supported by the Centre for Imagination in Research, Culture, and Education (CIRCE) (www.circesfu.ca) and the Centre for the Study of Educational Leadership and Policy (CSELP) (https://www.sfu.ca/cselp.html).

All rights reserved. No part of this publication may be reproduced or transmitted in any form or by any means, electronic or mechanical, including photocopy, or any information storage and retrieval system, without permission from the publisher. For reprint permission and other subsidiary rights requests, please contact Teachers College Press, Rights Dept.: tcpressrights@tc.columbia.edu

Library of Congress Cataloging-in-Publication Data

Names: Judson, Gillian, editor. | Dougherty, Meaghan, editor.
Title: Cultivating imagination in leadership : transforming schools and communities / [edited by] Gillian Judson and Meaghan Dougherty; foreword by Brandon Scott.
Description: New York, NY : Teachers College Press, 2023. | Includes bibliographical references and index. | Summary: "Expanding on Kieran Egan's theory of Imaginative Education, this comprehensive book will help current and future leaders employ imagination to address day-to-day challenges and to support equity, diversity, and inclusion. The text includes discussion sections, easy-to-use activities, and guidelines for applying imagination to key leadership processes and practices"—Provided by publisher.
Identifiers: LCCN 2022044809 (print) | LCCN 2022044810 (ebook) | ISBN 9780807768044 (paperback) | ISBN 9780807768051 (hardcover) | ISBN 9780807781579 (ebook)
Subjects: LCSH: Educational leadership—Psychological aspects. | School improvement programs. | Social justice in education. | Community and school. | School environment. | Imagination.
Classification: LCC LB2806 .C843 2023 (print) | LCC LB2806 (ebook) | DDC 371.2/011—dc23/eng/20221109
LC record available at https://lccn.loc.gov/2022044809
LC ebook record available at https://lccn.loc.gov/2022044810

ISBN 978-0-8077-6804-4 (paper)
ISBN 978-0-8077-6805-1 (hardcover)
ISBN 978-0-8077-8157-9 (ebook)

Printed on acid-free paper
Manufactured in the United States of America

For Kieran Egan

Thank you for encouraging us to imagine the possible and inspiring us to situate imagination at the heart of educational leadership.

Contents

List of Tables ix

Foreword: Imagination and Educational Leadership *Scott Brandon* xi

Preface *Gillian Judson and Meaghan Dougherty* xiii

Introduction 1
  Gillian Judson and Meaghan Dougherty

PART I: EXPLORING POSSIBILITIES

Imagination in Action: A Leadership Story 15
  Lori Driussi

1. **Exploring the Possible in Leadership: Inviting Stories of Imagination** 19
   Gillian Judson, Craig Mah, Rose Pillay, Courtney Robertson, and Jonathan Sclater

   Cultivating Curiosity, Conversation, and Imagination 33

2. **Exploring Possibilities: How School Leaders Employ Imagination to Build Thriving School Communities** 37
   Tara Preston

   Cultivating Curiosity, Conversation, and Imagination 48

3. **A Leadership Journey Toward Innovation Through Wide-Awakeness, Curiosity, and Imagination** — 51
   Karen Steffensen

   Cultivating Curiosity, Conversation, and Imagination — 61

PART II: POETICS OF MEMORY

   Imagination in Action: A Leadership Story — 65
   Craig Mah

4. **A Bridge Across Our Fears: Poetic Imagination as a Catalyst for School Change** — 67
   Sarah Pazur

   Cultivating Curiosity, Conversation, and Imagination — 83

5. **Education Policy: Imagination, Creation, and Innovation** — 86
   Dan Laitsch and Gillian Judson

   Cultivating Curiosity, Conversation, and Imagination — 100

6. **Embodying Imagination: Creative Leadership in Compassionate Action** — 102
   Lynn Fels

   Cultivating Curiosity, Conversation, and Imagination — 113

PART III: IMAGINATION'S ROLE IN SOCIAL JUSTICE AND EQUITY

   Imagination in Action: A Leadership Story — 119
   Moraima Machado

7. **Troubling Educational Leadership: Exploring Influences of Imaginative Practices on Equity and Social Justice** — 123
   Zachary Thomas and James W. Koschoreck

   Cultivating Curiosity, Conversation, and Imagination — 132

8. **Rewilding Imagination: Reorienting Eco-Leadership in Education** — 135
Mark Fettes and Sean Blenkinsop
Cultivating Curiosity, Conversation, and Imagination — 149

9. **Disrupting Deficit Through Radical Reimaginings of Urban Student Subjectivities and Knowledges** — 152
Kathryn Strom, Kara Viesca, and Jessica Masterson
Cultivating Curiosity, Conversation, and Imagination — 167

Postscript and Possibilities — 171
Laurie Anderson

Appendix. Cultivate Leadership Imagination With Cognitive Tools — 179

Endnotes — 185

Index — 187

About the Editors and Authors — 195

List of Tables

Table 5.1—The Policy Cycle as a Gardening Cycle:
    The Metaphor Unearthed   98
Table A.1—Use Imagination to Deepen Understanding and
    Generate New Ideas   179
Table A.2—Use Imagination to Engage Others in
    Meaning-Making   181
Table A.3—Use Imagination for Equity, Diversity,
    and Inclusion   182

Foreword
Imagination and Educational Leadership[1]

There is a joke that education, as a field, is not rocket science—it is much more difficult. Many may dismiss this as sheer hyperbole and possibly even ill-informed, but after having the experience of starting new schools, redesigning existing schools, and serving as board chairman of others, I remain steadfastly convinced of its veracity.

Educational leadership bears the responsibility of imagining how keeping students and staff engaged is possible in the modern, post-COVID context. Leadership structures need to be designed so that they have form and outcomes that serve an aesthetic and imaginative goal, and must be enacted with flow and constructive meaning-making so that all the goals are within the reach of every student who educators so nobly serve.

As you read this book, written to inform and inspire ever more effective educational leadership strategies, I implore you to continually ask questions of yourself as an educator and as a human, starting with this: *What is educational leadership?*

The answer for me is: It is the curation of learning and the environmental conditions within which it exists. It is an active pursuit of pedagogical constants that again serve these goals. It is to act imaginatively, knowledgeably, and empathetically not just for oneself but for all.

There's that word. *Imagination.* While the meaning differs for each person, I would like to posit a few assumptions I hold regarding imagination and education:

1. Imagination and creativity can be taught to all students—in fact, to everyone.
2. There are strategies to grow imagination that can be used across subject areas, grounded in skills of perception, and adapted to the structures of each academic area.
3. The very same strategies that help students learn to take creative action can and must be used by teachers

and administrators as they change their schools to be more responsive to 21st-century needs and opportunities.

Imagination summons up visions of a better state of things, illuminates the deficiencies in existing situations, connects to the education of feeling, and is a part of intelligence. It allows us to perceive deeply, to reflect, to always work to avoid the numbness of apathy and futility.

So, why do we need more imaginative approaches in educational leadership today? And why now? Think what the impact on commerce, education, and culture could be if we focused on imagination, creativity, and innovation rather than economic drivers alone. Humans have always existed in complex systems; as thinking beings who have endless curiosity yet limited scope of vision, we have always asked questions and sought answers to life's imponderables. We also have consistently and fruitfully designed and created systems that advance our social, economic, and emotional well-being.

Yet somehow, we have also always created an inherently complex set of problems that serve to advance our conflicts, our relational differences. Add them to today's complex technological environment, one where advances to change the capacity of human thought and action happen almost in an instant. Without knowing the scope of challenges that will face the future of students of today, educational leaders need to apply imagination skills to every part of their strategies and plans.

I believe imagination—*the capacity to create, evolve, and exploit mental models of things or situations that do not yet exist*—is the crucial factor in seizing and creating new opportunities, and finding new paths to growth. As I see it, we live in an era defined by hypercomplexity and disruptive enterprise, where the task is to imagine and design social (media) networks; crowdsource thoughts into ideas; create new forms and structures that challenge the status quo; engage new cross-sectoral exploration; and enact concepts such as diversity, imagination, culture, and virtual enterprise.

How do you become an imaginative educational leader? Just like getting to Carnegie Hall, it takes practice, practice, practice. We need to enjoy swimming in the organic mush called life and be the catalyst for growth and change that is needed. To paraphrase John Dewey: The goal of education, of aesthetic literacy, is to enable students to live aesthetic lives rather than anesthetic ones, to awaken rather than numb. Educational leaders must harness the power of imagination to achieve this goal.

—Scott Brandon

Preface

Gillian Judson and Meaghan Dougherty

This scholarly and practical text explores the fertile terrain of imagination in the context of educational leadership. As defined in this text, imagination is *"the ability to envision the possible in all things; it is the generative feature of mind that enables understanding of the self, and others, and that fuels creativity and innovation"* (Judson, 2020, p. 8). This text is designed to provide theoretical understanding of how imagination contributes to effective leadership and to offer practical tools all educational leaders can employ to cultivate their imaginations and the imaginations of others in their communities. To support these goals, chapters offer a multiplicity of perspectives on what imagination is, why it is essential for educational leaders, and how it may be developed. Overall, this text creates a learning opportunity—it offers leaders the opportunity to both *understand* the contributions of imagination to leadership and *cultivate* their imaginative capacities.

Leaders require imagination to be adaptive in the face of uncertain futures and to create socially and ecologically just and inclusive communities. In addition, leader imagination helps create school cultures that embrace *the possible* for learners and educators. Overall, this book unearths the value of imagination for leadership in education and creates a space for readers to grow personally and professionally.

INTENDED AUDIENCE

Many educational leaders hold administrative positions; many do not. This book is for both formal leaders and for those educational stakeholders who lead through their actions and through their teaching, those who seek to engage imagination in envisioning new possibilities for their schools and school communities. It is for those who seek to understand and then enrich imagination within school communities so they can best identify what is possible in creating a more just and equitable world. This book is for those who believe that the human imagination can improve schooling for all learners. It is designed to be used in graduate and undergraduate programs, in courses in education and leadership, as well as for the professional development of experienced leaders. This book foregrounds research, stories of leaders' lived experiences, and practical strategies and implementable techniques to provide current and future leaders with an imaginative learning experience that invites curiosity and cultivates imagination.

BOOK STRUCTURE

Leadership scholars offer theoretical and practical examinations of imagination in the field of leadership. Chapters are organized into three themes: *Exploring Possibilities, Poetics of Memory*, and *Imagination's Role in Social Justice and Equity*. Together they support understanding what imagination is, its application in aesthetic and pragmatic domains, and its role in leadership for social justice. We encourage readers to envision the text like a field of wildflowers. Each chapter is rooted in the soil of imagination and explores a different aspect of imagination within the context of education. Just as the shapes and colors of petals among a cluster of wildflowers draw our attention in different directions, the chapters can be read in any order. Each is "complete" on its own. At the same time, each exists in relation to the others, such that the richness and color of one chapter may also be viewed in complement or contrast to others. Collectively, each chapter adds beauty to this wonder-full, diverse field of leadership scholarship.

This book is designed to engage and teach. In a recurring section planted throughout the book called *Cultivating Curiosity, Conversation, and Imagination*, we invited contributing authors to read one another's writing and to share their questions, musings, and responses. We include their questions and evocations at the end of each scholarly chapter in these *Cultivating Curiosity, Conversation, and Imagination* sections as a way to stimulate individual reflection and collaborative discussion. These curiosity-evoking, open-ended, evocative musings and questions may be used individually for personal growth or collectively within formal or informal learning communities to expand, deepen, and apply concepts.

The book is also designed to *grow* imagination and includes activities that employ *cognitive tools*, learning tools based on a theory of human development called Imaginative Education (IE; Egan, 1997, 2005). Applying these tools of imagination through the book serves to *ground* imagination, making it more tangible and accessible to all leaders. These are tools that put imagination into action.

Building upon the theoretical foundation of the book chapters, we compiled an online collection of stories from practicing educational leaders for readers to access.[1] These are stories of lived experience, of imagination in action. Together, the scholarly chapters and the online stories explore varied perspectives of imagination as a concept and a human capacity and indicate the myriad ways in which imagination contributes to leadership practices.

CULTIVATING LEADERSHIP IMAGINATION WITH COGNITIVE TOOLS

IE is an approach to education that connects a theoretically rich conception of human development with practical strategies that maximize the growth of imagination and support meaning-making for all learners (Egan, 1997, 2005). Specifically, IE theory outlines how *cognitive tools*[2] such as the story form, vivid mental images, emotionally charged tensions, or a sense of agency can be employed by all educators to engage and grow students' imaginations (see the appendix for an application of cognitive tools to deepen understanding and generate ideas, engage others, and support equity, diversity, and inclusion).

Kieran Egan (1997, 2005), the educational philosopher who developed IE theory and practice, posits that understanding intellectual development requires an understanding of the different intellectual tools that shape it. Egan's work shows that human beings pick up different features of language from their cultural contexts that shape their psychological development and understanding. These features of language are "cognitive tools." Cognitive tools, in Egan's formulation, bring together three components that tend to be addressed separately in educational theory: the epistemological, the psychological, and the emotional.

Therefore, not only are cognitive tools tied up with knowledge and central to our psychological development, they also engage our emotions and imaginations. By using a cognitive tool, we can acquire knowledge in a particular way, and we can engage our emotions in the process. Our bodies, intellects, and emotions work together. Egan indicates how these cognitive tools are not unique to schools but are in fact cultural tools we use as human beings to make meaning in our daily lives; they are features of our imaginations that help us learn.

This book takes these cognitive tools and applies them in the context of leadership, illustrating how they may be employed by educational leaders to develop their imaginations in the process of their daily practice to enact positive change. To support the practical development of imaginative capacities in this book, the book's sections on *Cultivating Curiosity, Conversation and Imagination* include examples of cognitive tools and prompts for use that can support leaders in deepening understanding of issues, ideas, and concepts; generating new ideas; engaging people in their school communities; and creating socially just and inclusive communities. For example, the following cognitive tools can be employed to deepen understanding of an issue or topic:

- Engage Your Inner Rebel (cognitive tool: *revolt and idealism*)

What limitations do you face when dealing with this issue/topic? Which would you, ideally, like to surpass? Which rules are "breakable"?

- Play: Practice "What If-ing" (cognitive tool: *sense of wonder/ playfulness*)

What do you wonder about? Use your sense of wonder to create a new ideational space. Set practicalities aside—engage in some *extreme* "what if-ing" about the topic/issue. Which of your questions might be explored in more detail?

As shown throughout this book, leaders are encouraged to employ these tools in the ongoing context of their practices and in their communities to engage and grow their imaginations.

Overall, the text explains and *opens up* the concept of imagination, encouraging leaders to engage with its nuance and complexity, to provide imaginative responses, to practice and employ imaginative tools in real life. With diverse perspectives, voices, and openings to foster individual and collective growth, this text can nurture open-ended, possibility-focused conversations among all educational stakeholders. Knowing that it is never too late to *cultivate* the imagination in leadership, experienced leaders will find fresh perspectives and ideas that fuel their work. We hope readers move through the chapters in this text in an imaginative way, returning to those that engage them affectively, and playfully connecting with the ideas. We hope that with time this book becomes dog-eared with use, ideas and insights filling the margins, and sticky notes marking favorite sections.

REFERENCES

Egan, K. (1997). *The educated mind: How cognitive tools shape our understanding.* University of Chicago Press.

Egan, K. (2005). *An imaginative approach to teaching.* Jossey-Bass.

Judson, G. (2020). Conceptualizing imagination in the context of school leadership. *International Journal of Leadership in Education.* https://doi.org/10.1080/13603124.2020.1818289

Introduction

Gillian Judson and Meaghan Dougherty

> The quality and durability of any creative act depends in great measure on the fertility and force of the imagination that feeds the act. This is where it all begins. We reap what we sow.
>
> (Liu & Noppe-Brandon, 2009, p. 21)

The shape of our future depends on our ability to imagine what is possible now. As Liu and Noppe-Brandon (2009) suggest, we first *imagine* a future that is different—just and equitable—before we create it. This is the great opportunity imagination affords human beings. It is imagination that grasps the *possible* and the *not yet*. It is imagination that educational leaders can cultivate and employ to flexibly adapt to change and to create engaging and equitable school communities.

This text is rooted in a desire to better understand the great potential of imagination for leadership, how leaders can employ imagination to envision what is possible, and then work, with hope and integrity, toward that future. This Introduction situates the research and stories on imagination and leadership that are sown in the pages that follow. To do so, we dig into two key concepts: imagination and leadership. Following an exploration of these concepts, we indicate how each of the chapters contributes to a multifaceted and dynamic story of how effective leadership for an equitable and just world is rooted in imagination.

CONCEPTUALIZING IMAGINATION

We understand imagination as *"the ability to envision the possible in all things; it is the generative feature of mind that enables understanding of the self, and others, and that fuels creativity and innovation"* (Judson, 2020, p. 8). Definitions, on their own, rarely move people to action. Images and metaphors—tools of the imagination—do. So we invite readers to think about imagination as like fertile *soil* out of which leadership practices grow (Judson, 2021). A leader's ability to connect with and engage others, to envision and affect change, to deconstruct accepted conventions, and to enact equity, *grows out of* the ability to conceive of the possible.

Our understanding of imagination is *grounded* and *ordinary* rather than surreal and extraordinary. Rather than solely being the realm of fantasy and make-believe, a grounded understanding returns imagination to the realm of *everyday* engagement and also to *everyone*; imagination is a capacity of all human beings (Liu & Noppe-Brandon, 2009). Imagination is an integral part of play and creative work, and of inspired leadership.

In this text, we conceptualize imagination as the fecund terrain of possibility from which we reap a range of leadership capacities and outcomes. Imagination supports understanding of self and other, envisioning and enacting what is possible, supporting meaning-making within schools, and cultivating equitable communities. It is the terrain of contextual, collective, ethical, and emergent leadership practices. These leadership practices have the potential to change our schools, our communities, and the wider world. We reap what we sow.

Imagination is the soil that supports us all individually and connects us collectively. Like soil, imagination is something that can be *cultivated*; it *grows in richness* with use (Asma 2017; Egan, 1997, 2005; Liu & Noppe-Brandon, 2009; Pendleton-Jullian & Brown, 2018). Thinking about imagination as soil can help differentiate words like "creativity" and "innovation" that are often, and incorrectly, used synonymously with imagination (Judson, 2020, 2021; Liu & Noppe-Brandon, 2009; Pendleton-Jullian & Brown, 2018; Robinson, 2017). All creative acts, all innovations are *rooted in imagination*.

Overall, there is limited scholarship on what imagination is and how it contributes to leadership (Judson, 2020). A premise of this book is that the neglect of imagination in the context of leadership studies reflects a lack of knowledge of its relevance and roles rather than a sign of its insignificance or unrelatedness.

As the chapters in this text will indicate, effective leadership requires imagination. We want to acknowledge that failing to understand imagination—including what it is, the multifaceted ways in which it works, and importantly, how it can be developed and applied in action—may undermine leaders' abilities to create and nurture cultures that support creativity in others. Knowledge of how leaders engage, grow, and employ imagination in their professional practices is needed to nurture imagination and, ultimately, creativity and innovation, in school contexts broadly. Imagination is essential for change. Neglecting imagination means leaders are supporting the status quo and (perhaps unintentionally) reproducing social inequities and injustice. Imagination allows leaders to do the challenging work of supporting equity and social justice in their schools, communities, and beyond. Without imagination, we cannot envision how things may be better and how we can contribute to making them better (Pendleton-Jullian & Brown, 2018).

CONCEPTUALIZING LEADERSHIP: A RELATIONAL PERSPECTIVE

So who is an educational leader? In our work with graduate students in educational leadership, we find that the terms *leader* and *principal* are often used interchangeably. Unfortunately, educational leadership is often viewed as synonymous with holding certain formalized positions (e.g., principal, superintendent, etc.) in a school or school district. It is assumed that those in positions of responsibility and power act as leaders in these environments. However, while some people may enact leadership in these roles, holding a formal administrative position is neither a necessary nor a sufficient condition of leadership. Some people in positions of power lead, in our sense of the term, while others in similar positions do not. Alternatively, people who do not formally hold leadership positions may enact leadership; this includes "those who take on decision making functions through distributive leadership" (Shapiro & Gross, 2013, p. 4) as well as those who develop into a leadership role more organically or informally. While certain roles or formalized positions may involve managing individuals and teams as part of the articulated job responsibilities, managing and leading can be examined as two distinct processes that only sometimes overlap.

Rather than emphasizing formalized roles, we see leadership as a relational process. Leadership occurs *between* people, *within* relationships. Uhl-Bien (2006) delineates relational leadership theory into what she terms *entity perspectives* and *relational perspectives*. To summarize, entity perspectives focus on the individual entities that form relationships and how interactions between individuals (i.e., leaders and followers) are perceived and experienced by those in the interactions. Individuals enter into leadership relationships with their own experiences, beliefs, skills, values, and perspectives, and the interaction with others' experiences, beliefs, skills, values, and perspectives influences the outcome of the relationship.

Rather than seeing leadership as the relating of individual entities, the relational perspective argues that leadership emerges with and in relation; roles and ideas of leadership come out of the collective. Elements of the collective are constituted in the form of leaders and followers in that interaction, and the boundaries and expectations of the collective are distinct to that leadership interaction. That is, in a relational perspective, one type of communication or one specific leadership skill (e.g., being genuine or trustworthy) is not valued above others; the types of interactions and the skills and traits necessary emerge in relation to the specific collective and context. Similarly, the relational perspective helps us understand the nuance of values and ethics-based leadership; where scholars argue for the importance of ethics-based leadership (Duignan, 2006; Shapiro & Gross, 2013), a relational view highlights that how values and ethics are expressed or enacted is always contextual to the specific collective being considered.

Although her work is contextualized within management discourse, Uhl-Bien's (2006) idea of leadership as a social process that emerges from relationship is helpful to our examination of imagination in educational leadership. The relational perspective highlights that leadership is not a prescriptive enactment of certain traits or skills but that leadership emerges in the relationship. Education is a relational field, and we, as educators, are aware of the importance of relationships with students, families, colleagues, and others.

Being a leader is a significant responsibility. We recognize that leading has real impacts on the lives of others. Like Duignan (2006), we advocate the need for ethical, authentic leadership. In their relationships with others, authentic leaders critically examine what is assumed to be true and demonstrate the courage to "challenge unethical and immoral policies and practices wherever they find them" (Duignan, 2006, p. 11). Critical ethical leaders place social justice and democracy at the heart of leadership, interrogating inequities and advocating and working for change through relational and educative processes (Smyth et al., 2014). As part of collectives, leaders use their power for good, serve others, work collaboratively, and connect their leadership practices to authentic teaching and learning experiences (Duignan, 2006). Imagination is the fertile ground out of which ethical and authentic leadership practices can emerge. Imagination also provides us, as leaders, with a hopeful idea of what could be when navigating the tensions involved in educational leadership.

THE IMPORTANCE OF UNDERSTANDING IMAGINATION IN LEADERSHIP

Leading in an ethical, authentic way that promotes equitable outcomes is increasingly challenging (Shapiro & Gross, 2013). Education operates within a globalized neoliberal landscape. Neoliberal ideology reduces social and human interests in education to market-based principles, like efficiency, standardization, and competition (Ball, 2012; Giroux, 2014). Given the focus on the financial bottom line, efficiency is vitally important; leaders must demonstrate their ability to do more with less, minimizing cost and maximizing output. Leaders must be able to flexibly envision what is possible. They must be able to improvise and adapt.

Leaders experience the tension of leading within this managerial environment while attending to the people comprising the school community (Duignan, 2006), including students, caregivers, teachers, support staff, administrators, and community stakeholders. The needs and interests of these school community members are often in conflict with pressures for efficiency, standardization, and market-based decision-making. Working within these tensions, educational leaders need to recognize how their decisions can reinforce the status quo, further entrenching social stratification (see Labaree, 1997) and promoting "a growing indifference to communitarian justice and equality" (Duignan, 2006, p. 7). Shoto et al. (2011) note that this is a foundational shift, as historically, the role of educational administrators was to protect the legitimacy of schooling and validate the education system, rather than providing critique or promoting more inclusive practices. Imagination is essential for leaders to be able to empathize with all members of their communities, to grasp relational dynamics, then to effectively juggle multiple needs and changing circumstances without losing sight of the moral purpose of being an educational leader: to improve conditions for students, families, and communities.

In addition to navigating these neoliberal tensions, educational leaders are attempting to lead our schools in a wider context of climate change, natural disasters, famine, war, economic collapse, and ever-increasing economic disparity and social divisiveness. The COVID-19 pandemic has added to the complexity of our shared global environment and has highlighted existing social and economic disparities based on race, gender, class, age, and ability. According to the Centers for Disease Control and Prevention (CDC, 2021), those who have died in large numbers as a result of the virus are elderly, people confined in inhospitable conditions, and disproportionately people of color who suffer from preexisting conditions due to poorer social determinants of health. Inequity and suffering are catalyzing a growing resistance and demand for transformation; this resistance is met by growing support for nationalism and protection of the status quo, resulting in increasing divisiveness and conflict.

Making ethical decisions in an educational context, in a wider world of injustice, suffering, and divisiveness, is increasingly complex (Shapiro & Gross, 2013). In the following chapters, we ask questions such as: *How can imagination serve in ethical and generative leadership? How can we lead in a way that promotes social justice rather than reproducing existing inequities?* Imagination allows leaders to critically examine the climate/current context, analyze challenges or areas for improvement, and create adaptive, innovative ways of doing things differently. We recognize the need to imagine new possibilities, to lead ethically with strength and courage, and to stand up to injustice.

In *Pragmatic Imagination: A New Terrain*, Pendleton-Jullian and Brown (2018) provide a theoretical and practical framework for "imagination put to purpose" (p. 7). Their Pragmatic Imagination framework reveals the myriad ways in which imagination contributes to all forms of cognitive activity and how imagination "is a critical vehicle for turning ideas into action" (p. 78). They argue that it is imagination tied to action that is required to navigate and thrive in a "broadly connected, rapidly changing, and radically contingent world" (p. 7).

Pendleton-Jullian and Brown (2018) challenge the belief that imagination applies solely to artistic endeavors, fantasy, or abstract, impractical ideas. Rather, they indicate how imagination contributes in substantial ways to a range of cognitive activities, including perception, reasoning, speculation, experimentation, and free play: "The Pragmatic Imagination is a framework that sees the imagination as a spectrum of coherent, synthetic image making that runs from dealing with the known to project the novel, and from prosaic sense making to *poïetic* sense breaking" (p. 75). Pendleton-Jullian and Brown also challenge the juxtaposition of imagination with reasoning and other higher-order thinking processes:

> [T]he imagination is not *separate from* reasoning or conceptual thinking—it is not an exotic *other* kind of mental activity that one calls upon when other methods are insufficient—but, instead, serves as fuel and/or driver for all of them, to different degrees. It is fuel for perception and reasoning, but fuel-*and*-driver for speculation, experimentation, and free play. (p. 79)

They reveal how imagination is both an integrative and generative force; it "resolves" gaps between what is known and what is new as we perceive the world and as we engage in different forms of reasoning. In this way, it supports sense-making by connecting and integrating seemingly disconnected ideas. It helps organize experience. But the real force of imagination lies, they argue, in how it also "widens" gaps between the known and the new to create space for possibility:

> [T]he speculative imagination, the experimental imagination, and the imagination of free play, are our most powerful allies for "anticipating the world meaningfully," and for "turning ideas into actions," in a world that requires radically new visions and actions. (pp. 79–80)

The *dis*organizing and sense-*breaking* features of speculation, experimentation, and free play allow us, as school leaders, to see the possible within the actual, to push boundaries and surpass constraints to create space for new interpretations.

At the heart of this work is a belief that imagination is an ongoing and important force in meaning-making; it is required in decision-making and problem-solving, and is "essential for working on complex, radically contingent problems, and for the kind of novelty that moves culture and society forward" (p. 75). While showing how imagination is inseparable from key cognitive processes, they also challenge the idea that the most open, free, and seemingly "untethered" imaginative activities are not or cannot also be *pragmatic*. The Pragmatic Imagination connects thought, context, and action in an ongoing and dynamic cycle.

For school leaders, this work shows how imagination fuels understanding *what is*—understanding our school communities, students, processes, and policies in light of our specific contexts. Imagination supports our sense-making as leaders. At the same time—and this is where we, as authors, in line with Pendleton-Jullian and Brown (2018), see imagination's power for leadership—it also supports our sense-*breaking*—an important requirement to move past the status quo to seek positive change. Leaders constantly negotiate between a vision for what is possible, and the constraints or even obstacles of context and the lived reality of schools. Imagination is necessary to work with this friction: "In this ongoing negotiation, the imagination is critical for moving over rough terrain, and for agile pivoting when one hits an impasse" (p. 79). Overall, the imagination is the fuel behind *both* convergent and divergent thought processes, allowing leaders to see possibility in current situations, act in those situations, and then make meaning of this new action in context.

This text takes up Pendleton-Jullian and Brown's (2018) call to "instrumentalize" imagination and illustrates how to set it in motion.

Following each scholarly chapter that looks at different theoretical and practical dimensions of imagination in leadership, readers will find an activity page entitled *Cultivating Curiosity, Conversation, and Imagination*. This page describes cognitive tools that leaders of all kinds can employ to engage imagination and to set it in motion, in practice, in actionable, context-specific ways. By interweaving imagination with knowledge and thinking, cognitive tools can support all leaders in making meaning and seeing possibility in their professional contexts (Egan, 1997; Egan & Judson, 2016). Whether it is understanding an emergent situation, engaging with a colleague, considering viable or seemingly unviable alternatives to a problem, or envisioning new realities for school, using a cognitive tool (such as story, vivid mental imagery, sense of wonder, identifying patterns, or identifying heroic qualities) is an imagination-driven way to approach any aspect of leadership.

Cognitive tools can support leaders in seeing seeds of possibility in actual contexts, in imagining "the actual in light of meaningful and purposeful possibilities" (Pendleton-Jullian & Brown, 2018, p. 77). The appendix offers a guide to using cognitive tools to deepen understanding of what is and generate new ideas, to engage others in meaning making, and to support equity, diversity, and inclusion.

Through the contributions of educational leaders and leadership scholars, this text provides diverse perspectives on what imagination's role in educational leadership is and what it offers to our students, schools, communities, and the wider world. It explores theoretical and practical dimensions of imagination in the context of school leadership and all that entails, from understanding oneself as a leader, to understanding the perspectives of those one leads; from deepening one's personal understanding of issues to engagingly expressing those ideas to others; from forming and guiding ethical and inclusive school communities, to creating and implementing policy. This text clearly shows the value of taking imagination seriously as an important component in improving the quality of leadership in education. As a result, the work brings needed clarity to the broad scope of imagination, helping to address misunderstanding and parochial thinking so that imagination can be acknowledged as part of and a generative source for the daily practices of educational leaders.

THE VALUE OF IMAGINATION FOR EFFECTIVE LEADERSHIP

Overall, this text unearths the multifaceted ways in which imagination does and can contribute to leadership. Part I of the book is about *possibility*. In Chapter 1, "Exploring the Possible in Leadership: Inviting

Stories of Imagination," authors Gillian Judson, Craig Mah, Rose Pillay, Courtney Robertson, and Jonathan Sclater describe their collaborative and imaginative quest to understand leaders' uses of imagination in practice. They identify relationships, engagement, and processes of change as firmly rooted in the soil of imagination. In Chapter 2, "Exploring Possibilities: How School Leaders Employ Imagination to Build Thriving School Communities," Tara Preston shares research on how leaders employ imagination to build strong school cultures and how imagination contributes to her sense of identity as a new leader. In Chapter 3, "A Leadership Journey Toward Innovation Through Wide-Awakeness, Curiosity, and Imagination," Karen Steffensen shares her story of being diagnosed with a rare form of cancer and how a doctor willing to explore *what might be* saved her life. Applied to educational leadership, she identifies imagination—that ability to explore *what might be*—as essential for moving past *what is*, for transforming the status quo.

Part II, "Poetics of Memory," contains three chapters that explicitly employ tools of imagination (including poetry, metaphor, imagery, play, and story) in the context of school leadership. In Chapter 4, "A Bridge Across Our Fears: Poetic Imagination as a Catalyst for School Change," Sarah Pazur discusses how poetry facilitates the growth of educational leadership capacities and enables leaders to "yield to the unreal" as they address leadership challenges and work to transform schools. In Chapter 5, "Education Policy: Imagination, Creation, and Innovation," Dan Laitsch and Gillian Judson explore policy in leadership by employing metaphors of imagination as soil, policymakers as gardeners, and the education policy cycle as creating a garden. In Chapter 6, "Embodying Imagination: Creative Leadership in Compassionate Action," Lynn Fels sheds light on the importance of creative play, performance, inquiry, and self-reflection for developing leadership and exploring leadership practices for social justice.

"Imagination's Role in Social Justice and Equity" is the focus of Part III. Beginning with Chapter 7, "Troubling Educational Leadership: Exploring Influences of Imaginative Practices on Equity and Social Justice," Zachary Thomas and James W. Koschoreck identify entry points for employing imagination in leadership to create a socially just world. Chapter 8, "Rewilding Imagination: Reorienting Eco-Leadership in Education," by Mark Fettes and Sean Blenkinsop, challenges school leaders to critically examine Western human-centric views of imagination and to explore the possibilities for decolonizing schools and school leadership if imagination is understood from an Indigenous perspective, as embedded in the natural world. Finally, in Chapter 9, "Disrupting Deficit Through Radical Reimaginings of Urban Student Subjectivities and Knowledges," Kathryn Strom, Kara Viesca, and Jessica Masterson apply a posthuman theoretical lens to leadership in schools and challenge deficit-focused narratives of students and schools.

This text contains three stories of leadership imagination in action. The QR code below offers readers access to a larger online collection of leaders' stories that complement what is discussed in this text. These are stories of leaders' experiences of imagination put to purpose (Pendleton-Jullian & Brown, 2018). Educational leaders' stories indicate the myriad ways in which imagination contributes to leadership practices. Together, the scholarly chapters and stories offer articulations of theory and practice that deepen and expand understanding of imagination in leadership. The chapters invite the reader to cultivate their imagination and engage in relational leadership that promotes positive change.

Inspired by Maxine Greene's (1995) description of imagination as *seeking openings*, we conclude the book with an *opening*. In the final chapter, "Postscript and Possibilities," author Laurie Anderson examines *opensure* as an alternative to closure. Rather than trying to wrap up and finalize learning from the contributing authors, Laurie identifies the need to be "curious, responsive, and agile" in continuing to develop our imaginations. In the spirit of envisioning the *not yet*, the text ends with an invitation to continue to explore the possible—to cultivate imagination and enact imagination in our relational educational encounters. This is a call to action to not only imagine what is possible, but to work, with diligence and integrity, toward making things better.

REFERENCES

Asma, S. T. (2017). *The evolution of imagination*. University of Chicago Press.

Ball, S. J. (2012). *Global education inc.: New policy networks and the neo-liberal imaginary*. Routledge.

Centers for Disease Control and Prevention. (2021, February 21). *What is health equity?* www.cdc.gov/coronavirus/2019-ncov/community/health-equity/race-ethnicity.html

Duignan, P. (2006). *Educational leadership: Key challenges and ethical tensions.* Cambridge University Press.

Egan, K. (1997). *The educated mind: How cognitive tools shape our understanding.* University of Chicago Press.

Egan, K. (2005). *An imaginative approach to teaching.* Jossey-Bass.

Egan, K., & Judson, G. (2016). *Imagination and the engaged learner: Cognitive tools for the classroom.* Teachers College Press.

Giroux, H. (2014). *Neoliberalism's war on higher education.* Haymarket Books.

Greene, M. (1995). *Releasing the imagination: Essays on education, the arts and social change.* Jossey-Bass.

Judson, G. (2020). Conceptualizing imagination in the context of school leadership. *International Journal of Leadership in Education.* https://doi.org/10.1080/13603124.2020.1818289

Judson, G. (2021). Cultivating leadership imagination with cognitive tools: An imagination focused approach to leadership education. *Journal of Research on Leadership Education.* https://doi.org/10.1177/19427751211022028

Labaree, D. F. (1997). Public goods, private goods: The American struggle over educational goals. *American Educational Research Journal, 34*(1), 39–81. https://doi.org/10.2307/1163342

Liu, E., & Noppe-Brandon, S. (2009). *Imagination first: Unlocking the power of possibility.* Jossey-Bass.

Pendleton-Jullian, A., & Brown, J. S. (2018). *Pragmatic imagination: A new terrain.* CreateSpace.

Robinson, K. (2017). *Out of our minds: The power of being creative* (3rd ed.). Capstone.

Shapiro, J. L., & Gross, S. J. (2013). *Ethical educational leadership in turbulent times: (Re)solving moral dilemmas* (2nd ed.). Routledge.

Shoto, A. R., Merchant, B. M., & Lugg, C. A. (2011). Social justice: Seeking a common language. In F. W. English (Ed.), *The Sage handbook of educational leadership* (2nd ed.) (pp. 35–55). SAGE Publications, Inc. http://dx.doi.org/10.4135/9781412980036.n4

Smyth, J., Down, B., & McInerney, P. (2014). *The socially just school: Making space for youth to speak back.* Springer.

Uhl-Bien, M. (2006). Relational leadership theory: Exploring the social processes of leadership and organizing. *The Leadership Quarterly, 17,* 654–676. https://doi.org/10.1016/j.leaqua.2006.10.007

Part I

EXPLORING POSSIBILITIES

Imagination in Action
A Leadership Story

What If? Walking Just Paths in Educational Leadership

Lori Driussi

Walking school hallways, my rubber soles catch on the linoleum in the way my "what ifs" catch on the constraints of a public system. There isn't quite enough friction to stop my progress or imaginative musings but just enough to trip me up, slow my pace, and have me long for a more comfortable, old shoe. As a school principal, I am accountable to many stakeholders, each with their own views about what schools ought to do, what schooling should look like, and what it means to be educated. Over the years, my students have shown me that the practicalities of living the policies and structures surrounding public education mean that it is not welcoming to everyone. This is where the rubber hits the road, as they say. Do I remain within the boundaries that seem to successfully guide the path of most, or do I imagine another way, a more socially just way, that opens the path for all?

The very idea of education is to keep moving and learning; to step into discomfort, the not-yet-known, and into what might be. Believing in the possibility of education and leadership potential means asking "what if" and pursuing the questions despite the obstacles. It is to imagine the horizon of the best of us and forge a path with others in its direction, no matter the challenges. There are two quotes guiding my steps just now:

> "It is precisely where the reach of the imagination meets the friction of materials . . . that human life is lived."
> —Timothy Ingold

"Wanderer, there is no road. The road is made by walking."
—Antonio Machado

The best way I know to exemplify the quotes above is to tell the story of Quinn[1] (pseudonym). Quinn gifted me with an opportunity to feel the friction, imagine the possible, and take some steps to forge a new road. They showed me what leadership for social justice might look like.

Quinn is in grade 5 and seemingly disengaged from school and life in general. Other than skateboarding, they claim to have no passions, nothing they wish to learn about, and no desire to attend school "except for seeing my friends." Quinn is participating in a Learning in Depth project about mushrooms (see Egan & SFU Faculty, 2010). Their teacher is feeling frustrated about their lack of project participation in the classroom and asked for help.

What if I take Quinn outside?

So, on a West Coast day, I don my rain boots and we take a walk together to collect mushrooms, with a shovel and terrarium in hand. Asking Quinn what they thought about mushrooms, they replied, "I don't like them. I mean to eat." Asking Quinn what they knew about mushrooms, they responded there was nothing really that interesting about them "except for they can be drugs that get you high." We continued walking, with me wondering about the best way to connect Quinn with their topic to which they seemed relatively indifferent. "Hey Ms. Driussi, look! Lots of them!" Quinn spotted a cluster of tiny mushrooms in the damp grass and bent down to get a closer look. They wondered aloud about what kind they were, if they were edible or poisonous, or the type that can get you high. They also wondered what eats them and what happened when the grass was mowed. Digging gently, Quinn unearthed a grouping to put in their terrarium. While a minute ago disinterest prevailed, Quinn was now asking questions and digging with care. Quinn's imaginings activated an emotional response in them and in me.

We continued to the small forest, where we discovered larger mushrooms and plants that Quinn collected to enhance the landscape in which they had replanted the found mushrooms. "I'm going to put in this grass because they are used to having it around. This rock too because it makes [the terrarium] look more real." As they dug into the earth they exclaimed, "I love the smell of nature. It clears my head."

Take a breath on that comment . . . what an insight.

This child, who struggles to function productively and respectfully in their classroom, who is insecure about their ability to learn, and whose brain feels "foggy" indoors, became a different person before my eyes. They shared information with confidence and enthusiasm; they designed a terrarium with intention, their shoulders relaxed and their expression softened. They took a breath and so did I. They presented themself, through words and gestures, as capable and engaged. On this walk, we found a new relationship with new understandings about each other. Neither of us wanted to return to school when the bell called us back. We walked slowly, talked quietly, and decided on the best possible locations for the mushroom terrarium.

As Quinn went upstairs to join the class and I reluctantly returned to the paper pile in my office, I wondered how many experiences in the forest it might take to bring the confidence and calm expressed outside, inside. I wondered about outside engagement and inside disengagement. I wondered why this learner was being deprived of being their best self most of the school day. Where is the justice in that? Many *what ifs* were sparked, such as:

- What if more of Quinn's school day could be outside?
- What if other children "loved nature" and had "clearer heads" outside?
- What if we built outdoor time into the schedule for *all* learners?
- What if outdoor learning could be a *choice* for anyone?

These kinds of questions are critical for educational leaders to consider. They invite us to imagine and evolve daily practices and more socially just systemic policies. We can walk toward real and perceived obstacles (e.g., curricular demands, teacher/administrator comfort, parent expectations, assessment, and safety concerns) knowing this is where *human lives are lived* and imagine a way through.

Time outside with the school principal is not a common practice, but clearly, it was the right thing to do. Quinn returned to the classroom engaged with learning and enthusiastically articulated to their teacher the decisions for what was included in the terrarium. Parents, teachers, and perhaps my supervisors may question our time outside. They may ask: What am I not doing in my office, what is Quinn missing in their classroom? This is *where the reach of the imagination meets the friction of materials*. We will encounter resistance on our quest, and this is when leaders resole their shoes and advocate! We gather our courage and imagine new spaces for learning, collaborate with our colleagues, navigate logistics like supervision and schedules, share with our stakeholders, and *make the road by walking*. We create and offer more equitable and just learning environments, not just for Quinn, but for all learners. We develop practices inspired by one that could eventually serve many.

As leaders, it is our responsibility to be imaginative, to live in the land of *what if*, to push against seemingly unalterable structures and policies, and to advocate for more equitable systems. Imagination and stories like Quinn's move us toward increasingly inclusive classrooms and schools. "The fact of possessing imagination means that everything can be redreamed" (Okri, n.d.), and social justice lives in such dreams.

Let's walk.[2]

REFERENCES

Driussi, L. (2013). Cultivating Canadian learners—outside! In S. Knight (Ed.), *International perspectives on forest school: Natural spaces to play and learn* (pp. 174–183). Sage. https://dx.doi.org/10.4135/9781446288665.n13

Egan, K., & SFU Faculty. (2010). *Learning in depth: A simple innovation that can transform schooling.* University of Chicago Press.

Ingold, T. (2013). *Making: Anthropology, archaeology, art and architecture.* Routledge.

Machado, A. (n.d.). *Antonio Machado quotes.* Goodreads. www.goodreads.com/author/quotes/34610.Antonio_Machado

Okri, B. (n.d.). *Ben Okri quotes about dreams.* Inspiring Quotes. www.inspiring-quotes.us/author/4115-ben-okri/about-dreams#

CHAPTER 1

Exploring the Possible in Leadership
Inviting Stories of Imagination

Gillian Judson, Craig Mah, Rose Pillay, Courtney Robertson, and Jonathan Sclater

According to relational researcher Hosking (2011), "Doing research with others means creating opportunities for dialogues" (p. 58). This chapter describes a collaborative inquiry project rooted in dialogue and in imagination. We, the co-authors, were co-learners in an exploration of educational leaders' stories of imagination in action. By *imagination* we mean "the ability to envision the possible in all things, the generative feature of mind that enables understanding of the self, and others, and that fuels all creativity and innovation" (Judson, 2020a, p. 8). We share an interest in increasing the prevalence of imagination in schools for all learners, and we seek to better understand how leaders can and do use imagination to create schools in which it can flourish.

As you read of our learnings about imagination's roles in educational leadership, we invite you to envision *imagination* as fertile soil in which all creativity and innovation is rooted (Judson, 2021). Though often unseen and overlooked in favor of the fruits that it produces (Liu & Noppe-Brandon, 2009), imagination may be understood as underlying and supporting our individual and collective actions as leaders (Judson 2020a, 2021). Our inquiry, as detailed in this chapter, was *about* imagination; it is also in the soil of imagination that this collaborative, community-based research project finds its roots.

Over the course of 1 year and 10 dialogic sessions, we wandered (and wondered) our way into and throughout inviting terrain: imagination's roles in educational leadership. At first, we did not know what we would find—*how do leaders talk of imagination in their practice?*—or how we would deepen our understanding—*how can we learn?* We experienced uncertainty, ambiguity, empowerment, playfulness, and pleasure. Dialogue formed the heart of our work together. It was through dialogue that we ultimately defined our research question: *What do educational leaders' stories reveal about the roles of imagination in leadership?* We began by each writing, sharing, and collaboratively analyzing a lived story of imagination in action in our own leadership. Then we invited educational leaders from our professional learning communities to share their stories of imagination in action in their leadership. And *inviting* stories is what we received. Through an ongoing process of reading our own and other leaders' stories, reflection, and collaborative discussion, we noticed *relationships, engagement,* and *change* bloom as three key ways that imagination contributes to leadership practice.

This chapter focuses on leaders' stories of imagination in action. We *aspire* to *inspire*: We hope our reflections as co-learners in this inquiry will be *inviting*, inspiring you to dig into an online collection of stories located on imaginED[1], a website dedicated to imaginative practices in pedagogy and leadership. We hope you are inspired to employ your own imagination in action to enact positive change, and to catalyze conversations within your own context, to, ultimately, bring imagination to a more central place in the field of leadership theory and practice.

OUR RESEARCH STORY

We (the co-learners and co-authors of this chapter) were connected through professional networks before this project began. In my then role as executive director of the Centre for Imagination in Research, Culture and Education (CIRCE), I, Gillian Judson, invited local community leaders, school administrators, educators, graduate students in Imaginative Education (IE) programs, and professors from Simon Fraser University (SFU) to join a cohort of graduate students in an educational leadership program in a collaborative project investigating the role of imagination in K–12 education in British Columbia. COVID-19 caused this Imaginative School Symposium Series (ISSS) to pause (Judson, 2020b). During this COVID-provoked pause, I asked participants who might be interested in sharing their perspectives on how imagination contributes to their leadership practices. Rose, Craig, Courtney, and Jonathan expressed interest in this exploration, and our inquiry group was born.

As I (Gillian Judson) embarked on this collaborative project, Potts and Brown's (2015) work on anti-oppressive research resonated strongly with me. Anti-oppressive researchers "do research that challenges dominant ideas about research processes as well as research outcomes" (p. 19). Anti-oppressive research entails, in part, foregrounding relationships, nurturing collaboration, challenging the researcher–participant boundary, resisting conventional research practices, and working toward equity in terms of roles in research. I was also inspired by Liu and Noppe-Brandon (2009), who succinctly state: "To be truly imaginative is to run to the right when everyone else is running to the left, to defy convention and reject the comfort of conformity" (p. 24).

This work involves us, as co-authors and co-researchers, *running in a different direction*, as we have resisted more traditional research relationships, processes, formats, and outcomes. We prioritized dialogue. Our process emerged as we did the work. At the first meeting, for example, we discussed how we wanted to proceed. *How could we best understand imagination's roles in leadership?* We decided that we should share and analyze our stories, our examples of how we have imagined the possible in our work. Later, after weeks of analyzing our stories, we decided to seek other leaders' stories, too. I invited leaders in the ISSS, and more broadly across my social media networks, to write and share a story of imagination in action in their leadership work for publication on imaginED. We remained open to the emergence of our topic as we learned more. After multiple meetings and discussions, we identified our inquiry question: *What do educational leaders' stories (ours and others') reveal about the roles of imagination in leadership?*

Scholars identify story as valuable for leadership practice and research (see Cheng et al., 2017; Cleverley-Thompson, 2018; Mahoney, 2017; McLean, 2015; Orr & Bennett, 2017; Rasmussen, 2019; Wilson, 2019). Leaders' stories are valuable for our inquiry, as they offer "an authentic expression of [their] lived experience" (McLean, 2015, p. 4). Stories represent "expressive aspects of leadership practice" (Orr & Bennett, 2017, p. 525). Stories reveal the emotional commitments of the teller; they reveal particular "truths" and perspectives. They are *stories* because the teller has shaped them to bring out their emotional force (Egan, 1997, 2005; Egan & Judson, 2015).

Stories are particularly valuable for a study of imagination. Through history, storytelling has been one of the main ways in which imagination has developed across cultures and individually (Asma, 2017; Egan, 1997). Human beings are storytelling animals; story is our currency (Asma, 2017; Egan, 1997, 2005; Egan & Judson, 2015). Story is imagination in action—one of the main ways in which imagination is manifest (Asma, 2017).

During our 10 meetings between May 2020 and March 2021, we studied a total of 12 leadership stories—all of which you can read for yourself in the online collection accessible through the QR code in the

Introduction. Our meetings involved ongoing collaborative discussion, reflection, and thematic coding. From the beginning, we have all been co-researchers and co-learners and have now co-authored this work. We have intentionally resisted creating a single voice or offering a *single story* and, therefore, have individually authored different sections, each with our own style. While unique in voice, the content in these sections reflects our shared understanding of the stories and the themes within them.

The next section shares the following overarching themes, or *storylines*: imagination's roles in generating relationships (authored by Courtney Robertson), engagement (authored by Craig Mah), and change (authored by Jonathan Sclater). Our professional learning experience in this research represents the fourth and final storyline (authored by Rose Pillay).

IMAGINATION AND RELATIONSHIPS

A Matter of Heart

Leadership isn't for the faint of heart. Some people may take this expression to primarily mean that leaders need to be courageous, strong, and firm. While I, Courtney Robertson, agree that effective leaders must demonstrate courage, strength, and fortitude in their practice, our study of imaginative leaders' stories reveals a different understanding of *heart* in leadership. For me, talking about relationships in leadership involves discussion of aspects of relationship-building that include emotion, care, empathy, and trust. I think the expression "leadership isn't for the faint of heart" refers to more than emotional strength or courage. It speaks to *heart* in the metaphorical sense of *caring* that originates in and is fueled by *empathy*. In the stories we studied, leaders speak of *heart* as they discuss relationships, empathy, trust, and risk-taking (e.g., Anderson; 2020; Charles, 2021; Robertson, 2020). I believe that leaders need this kind of *heart* to be successful.

Acknowledging that relationships matter for leadership is not new. Fullan (2002) suggests that successful leadership happens when one realizes that leadership is achieved through the building and fostering of connectedness. Fullan describes, further, how relationships motivate, support, and help people succeed in their work: "This is why emotional intelligence is equal to or more important than having the best ideas. In complex times, emotional intelligence is a must" (p. 7). Our excavation of leadership stories suggests that *heart* goes hand in hand with imagination. From my experience, this is a new dimension of relationship talk in leadership.

When invited to describe imagination at work in their practices during our inquiry, leaders' stories describe *connecting to others* in order to understand and provide support. For example, Anderson (2020) describes the important leadership practice of seeking to understand those we serve. This act of empathy requires imagination (Greene, 1995; Judson, 2016). It takes imagination to see another perspective, to empathize, and to connect to something we have yet to experience. Maxine Greene (1995) speaks to the important role of imagination in connection, stating:

> Imagination is what, above all, makes empathy possible. It is what enables us to cross the empty spaces between ourselves and those we ... have called "other" over the years.... of all our cognitive capacities, imagination is the one that permits us to give credence to alternative realities. It allows us to break with the taken for granted, to set aside familiar distinctions and definitions. (p. 3)

Charles (2021) highlights the relational needs of educators and leaders. In her view, educators are not only in the business of teaching; they must relate and connect to one another. In her story, Charles discusses how the pandemic has led her to recognize that the role of educators is far from "just" teaching. Rather, it is the job of an educator, especially during challenging times, to create connections, build community, and provide a safe place for all members of the community. *Leadership isn't for the faint of heart.*

Trust and *risk-taking* are two other themes that emerge from the leadership stories we explored. I see these as intimately connected to relationship and to imagination. My own story describes how I created a space for trust, and possibility, by sharing my story with a colleague and being open to hers. Through the act of storytelling, imagination can support relationship-building. So, rather than just a topic of conversation, *story* works to connect us through the sharing, and the telling itself. Connecting to others through story can create trust and encourage empathy.

Landy (2020) outlines a range of different ways that his imagination supports his educational leadership. In reference to relationship, Landy writes of how the trust he has built with staff supports people to take risks and try new ideas. Further to this, Landy also shares how he encourages his staff to "wonder" about different solutions to problems. Having people join him in taking leaps of faith and being curious stems from trust in relationship. Again, *leadership isn't for the faint of heart.*

Janzen (2020) describes her risk-taking in the midst of a pandemic, leading her support staff in the use of different teaching techniques to engage their learners. Pillay (2020) discusses the risk involved in creating a different type of professional development for educators. These stories suggest that if leaders have built relationships of trust and a culture in which risk-taking is encouraged, they may have more freedom to solve problems in unique, imaginative ways. At the same time, leaders must take *heart* to not damage relationships with colleagues and co-workers. Ideally, the strong foundation of the relationship will bear the weight of the risk. Again, *leadership isn't for the faint of heart*.

Our exploration of stories revealed how leaders connect imagination with *emotional* work, with *heart*. Imagination enables us to empathize and to build relationships that support cultures of trust. Those trusting relationships enable leaders and the communities they serve to take leaps of faith and to do things in new, novel ways. So, we see that *leadership isn't for the faint of heart*; it involves empathy, connectedness (relationship), trust, and risk-taking, all of which are rooted in imagination.

IMAGINATION AND ENGAGEMENT

On any given Friday at 5:30 p.m. you would find me, Craig Mah, in my office bouncing between ordering takeout food and proofreading *The Friday Frenzy*. Hitting the send button on this weekly email to the local parent community was my ticket to starting the weekend. The *Friday Frenzy* highlighted news, events, and other information items that the community needed to know. The contents were not the most exciting topics, but I took an imaginative approach to compel parents to read and, thus, increase engagement. Sometimes, I put in driving tips or unhinged weather reports. Sometimes, I peppered in *Star Trek* analogies in my messages. The final *Friday Frenzy* I authored before leaving my last school contained a short story called "The Ballad of the Peeing Bandit."

Engagement is a second theme we identified in the leadership stories. To be clear, our use of the term *engagement* refers to more than communicating information; for leaders, *being engaging* involves more than sending an email or a tweet, or hosting a meeting. Engagement involves effective communication, problem-solving, and emotional connection. The stories we studied show how leaders use imagination to elevate how they communicate with staff and community members beyond sharing information about hot-lunch days and upcoming professional days. Similarly, talking about staff and community members as *engaged* refers to more than just hearing or understanding information. An *engaged* person is emotionally connected, too; they are interested. We learned that imagination allows leaders to solve problems in unique ways; it offers new ways of being and doing. Imagination allows the structuring or packaging of ideas in ways that emotionally engage members of the community.

Beginning with solutions, the stories we read, as co-authors, pointed to how imagination enables leaders to come up with novel approaches to problems they face or to situations they seek to improve. For example, Pillay (2020) writes about the novel approach to *Ignite* professional development talks. (An *Ignite* presentation is composed of short, 5-minute presentations supported by 20 slides. Each slide is timed to 15 seconds. For more information, visit www.ignitetalks.io.) Pillay's story describes how her brother observed that locally organized professional development events may leave educators from other districts feeling excluded. He saw a better way to host professional development sessions that would be more inclusive of educators from other jurisdictions. He changed the typical professional development format (daytime and located in schools) into something radically different (evening event, hosted in the community, paired with fun themes and tasty food). The *EDvent* series was created (Pillay, 2020).

My own leadership story (shared in this volume) describes how I attempted to solve traffic issues at my school using humor and Twitter. Steeped in pop culture references, and with an attempt at humor, my tweets and messages tried to improve the parking situation while engaging the community to care about the subject. It worked. The reaction from the community was mostly positive, and there was noticeable improvement in the parking situation. I recently visited my former school, and after a 7-year absence, a parent asked me if I would be tweeting about the parking situation again. Overall, I tried to solve a problem by structuring and packaging ideas in unique ways.

Earlier I referenced the terms *structuring* and *packaging* of ideas. (Metaphors engage imagination!) We noticed leaders use imagination to put a unique spin on what and how they communicate. Employing imagination seems to increase the *memorability* and *meaning* of ideas and events. For example, Anderson's (2020) story evokes the dread and anticipation of facing an undesirable task. He humorously compares a challenging leadership task to "having a triple root canal without an anesthetic." As readers, we felt a sense of gloom, suspicion, and despair. He engaged our imaginations in describing the unpleasantness of the task he was asked to do. The imagery sets the tone but also provides insight into the gravity of the situation the community was experiencing.

In like manner, Boullosa (2021) elegantly writes about how imagination allows us to complete ourselves. Lacking imagination "can be fatal; it undermines happiness, love, and prosperity. How else could we put ourselves in the shoes of others?" With references to a range of remarkable human stories ranging from Galileo to Pascal, Boullosa evokes the need for imagination as leaders to address issues of injustice and poverty. These are topics that leaders face daily in their school settings. Similarly, Sclater's story (2020) uses metaphor to engage. He connects leadership to building a shelf. Froese (2020) shares memories of her childhood and how they shaped her career in education. The memories she shares in her story of imagination in her leadership caused us, as readers, to *lean in*, to emotionally connect with her message. The way these leaders structured and packaged their stories drew on our emotions as readers, promoting engagement.

In summary, while leaders are constantly communicating with their staff and parent communities, sending information does not necessarily result in or increase engagement. Leadership stories reveal that through storytelling, humor, metaphors, and other tools of imagination, leaders can emotionally connect with others and meaningfully convey messages. *Imaginative* packages for communication support the imaginative leader in engaging their audience. Consider the difference between reading a menu and reading a well-written review of someone's experience at the restaurant. The former is forgettable; the latter stays with you. When imagination is used by a leader, communication can become more meaningful and memorable for students, staff, and parents. As Mr. Spock might say, an imaginative leader can engage their communities in infinite diversity in infinite combinations. (Still wondering about "The Ballad of the Peeing Bandit"?) Up next: how imagination can support and promote change.

IMAGINATION AND CHANGE

Change is a third theme that floated to the surface in this research. Our exploration of leadership stories revealed how imagination helps leaders to (1) better *prepare* for change, (2) *respond* to change, and (3) have the courage to *cause* change when that is what is needed.

Preparing for Change

Through our analysis of leadership stories, we learned how imagination enables leaders to see what is possible beyond the current context, circumstances, and limits that exist (e.g., Boullosa, 2021; Froese, 2020; Reid & Iannuzzi, 2021; Sclater, 2020). Often leaders prepare for change by casting a vision (e.g., Judson, 2020b; Mah, 2020; Sclater, 2020). As a leader, I, Jonathan Sclater, think about this in terms of "steering the ship in the right direction." Imagination allows leaders to get out their binoculars to search wide on the horizon for new opportunities and use their reading glasses to focus on the finer details to navigate and map the many twists and turns along the journey safely.

The stories we reviewed reveal how imagination is used by leaders to help their teams, not by simply seeking problems, but by envisioning what is possible (e.g., Boullosa, 2021; Froese, 2020; Landy, 2020; Reid & Iannuzzi, 2021; Sclater, 2020). The development of the imagination is described by Froese (2020) as a habit to think wide and consider possibilities. This preparatory work of the imagination can start with something as simple as keeping our minds open to the *what ifs*, and this way of thinking can lead to reaching beyond the limits or barriers that exist (Landy, 2020). This imagination, used repeatedly in practice, will carry leaders through some turbulent waters and unknown challenges that lie ahead.

Developing a vision as a leader can be challenging, and gaining the support of people in your organization even more so. Leaders' stories also suggest that employing imagination in leadership is not about being the captain of a ship in isolation; it is about building a reliable crew. Leaders must communicate with the crow's nest and boiler room alike, as everyone makes an important and meaningful contribution to positive school culture. As co-researchers, our discussions revealed how we have all experienced the difficulties of evoking and moving toward change, and in inviting others along for the journey.

So, what is required to encourage others to prepare for change? The stories we read point to the role of authentic relationships. One leader, Anderson (2020), writes about his experience working with community members during a possible school closure: "The result was a generative, collaborative and ultimately transformative experience for everyone involved." Spending time getting to know people individually to hear their stories before any big decisions are made is crucial to developing trust and moving forward, especially when coming into a new setting and leadership role (Robertson, 2020; Sclater, 2020). Leaders use their imaginations to form supportive relationships that enable the whole organization to adapt, get unstuck, and move forward together in the winds of change.

Responding to Change

Leaders' stories reveal that when responding to change, they use imagination to envision multiple possibilities through planned designs, but are also open to in-the-moment improvisations (e.g., Anderson, 2020; Charles, 2021; Janzen, 2020; Judson, 2020b; Landy, 2020; Mah, 2020; Sclater, 2020). Leaders' stories have shown the importance of embracing the journey, remaining flexible and open, and responding to change with confidence.

Change can be difficult. Using imagination helps leaders to see change as opportunity and not as an obstacle. By being imaginative in their approach, leaders can disarm fears, disappointments, and uncertainty, and open up the possibilities for deeper and lasting shifts in how people perceive and act toward familiar and unfamiliar situations alike (e.g., Anderson, 2020; Janzen, 2020; Judson, 2020b; Mah, 2020; Pillay, 2020; Robertson, 2020; Sclater, 2020).

The ways in which leaders meet with people along the voyage are as varied as the shorelines they pass by. By being open and responding in real time, leaders can also use their imaginations to address issues of equity, access, and inclusion; they can reimagine and change how they support students and families, such as meeting through new virtual means (Janzen, 2020). Having imagination can enable leaders to respond to change by transforming typically confrontational encounters, like a potential school closure, into empowering experiences (Anderson, 2020). When leaders respond to change with imagination, the possibilities to connect meaningfully with others open wide, and they can chart a new course to calmer waters—unless, of course, the aim is to intentionally make waves; leaders can also instigate change, and imagination helps them do so.

Causing Change

Change also takes place *intentionally*, resulting in new routines that were previously unseen (Froese, 2020; Mah, 2020; Sclater, 2020). Imagination helps leaders to think about their contexts in new ways and shift away from how things are "to bring into reality what is not yet but should be" (Boullosa, 2021). Although change may cause discomfort, leaders know that by using imagination to cause change, they can bring life to a stagnant situation with the sights, sounds, and smells of a new destination. By imagining a change of context and through the use of imagery, metaphor, and story, leaders can create the conditions for change.

Change takes courage because leaders do not always know what lies ahead. "We do this, not by having all the answers, but [by] having the courage to set a plan into motion despite many unknowns" (Sclater, 2020). Bringing leaders together through the ISSS, for example, to explore a field of study where the outcomes are unknown . . . now, that is adventurous, daring, and full of imagination (Judson, 2020b).

In summary, change is not just a single event that leaders prepare for, respond to, or make happen. It is an ever-evolving process that requires imagination to see the possibilities and bring a vision into reality. With imagination, leaders are best equipped to navigate change through big plans and little movements; however, only when they let the sails fully out are they able to completely test the limits of their vessels and see what is over the horizon.

THE PARTICIPANT EXPERIENCE: LEARNING THROUGH STORY

For where am I to go? And by what shall I steer? What is to be my quest?
Bilbo went to find a treasure, there and back again.
But I go to lose one, and not return, as far as I can see.

—Frodo Baggins, *Lord of the Rings*

When I, Rose Pillay, reflect on my experience as a participant in this project, I feel like I have been on a quest. Not quite Jason and the Argonauts, we were Gillian and the administrators searching for the Golden Fleece of imagination-rich schools. We were recruited to write and read, reflect and risk. In disclosing our individual experiences with imagination, we lowered our shields and exposed our vulnerabilities. We exhaled authenticity and inhaled "aha's." But doing so made room for us to grow: "It has stretched me to think about how . . . I have used my experiences . . . in ways that reach others" (Mah et al., 2021, p. 3).

Some of us were reluctant heroes questioning whether we belonged: "I see myself as the outsider of the group" (Mah et al., 2021, p. 3). Others arrived in battle-tested armor forged by their station as school-based leaders. But we all went forward toward an unknown destination emboldened by the courage that comes from camaraderie and community: "How easy we have come to form this group. We all have different experiences and ideas, but we are definitely supportive and interested in each other's professional experiences" (p. 2).

Our expedition was more of *a book club without refreshments* than the Labors of Hercules. We encountered tales of perils (e.g., teaching and learning during the pandemic), problems (e.g., fighting school closures, resolving parking lot woes), and pursuits (e.g., establishing new communities). *How did imagination help us/them slay the dragons: the difficulties, dilemmas, and drama of leading others?* We summoned Imagination as we prodded, picked, and pulled at the words. "Show yourself!" We peered into the stories through a kaleidoscope of filters, including relationship, engagement, and change.

We had no map. Early on we discovered that *there is no direct path, and therefore we require imagination to navigate* (Mah et al., 2021, p. 2). Imagination gave us permission to trek ahead. The learning labyrinth revealed itself from one intense hourlong discussion to the next. Through revisiting stories, we found our vision had improved. It was as if we had received corneal transplants: we saw more, and more clearly with every candid conversation. Questioning and critiquing one another's stories gave us "a sounding board for (our) own experiences" (p. 3). Huddled around the glow of our individual screens, we listened intently to the voices rising from the narratives. But now I wonder if we were hearing our own echoes. "It's easy to cast our own experiences on others as we see the world through our lens" (p. 2). In studying, scrutinizing one another's stories, were we looking into a reflective pool? When did my story and their story become our story? Was this the treasure we were seeking?

Within the *sandbox* of Zoom-based meetings, we dug deep (and deeper) for nuggets of wisdom from the diverse narratives. What would we learn from an exploration of our experiences in "breaking the mold on how things have always been done" (Mah et al., 2021, p. 5), in being problem-solvers and possibility-shapers? For starters, we learned *that your imagination grows the more you invest in it.* "It has an exponential growth pattern, slow and hard to detect at first, but soon takes over and permeates all thinking" (p. 5). I learned that imaginative leaders see in Technicolor whether the black and white of the printed page or the world is before them. "We not only see the possibilities that exist, but we look for ways to get there!" *(p. 2).* They may not always be looking for a fight, but imaginative leaders are in some ways fearless. From our reading of these stories, we see that when they happen upon crises, concerns, and challenges, imaginative leaders choose to face things head-on over fleeing. Their default disposition is to pivot toward the positive; to seek solutions rather than remain stressed. There is an aura of calmness, peacefulness in how they resolve tensions, survive turmoil, and face trouble. Their imaginations allow them to be much more hopeful, assured when things seem impossible. They are in constant motion, always recalibrating toward their true north: "There is always a different if not better way" (p. 4).

But alas, we did not find the Holy Grail of imagination in leadership or the Fountain of Youth, although "as we have been meeting, we have also been creating a new image of imaginative leadership. We've been slowly working... to define something that isn't yet clearly or fully defined" (Mah et al., 2021, p. 4).

Sometimes it is what you lose rather than what you find that gives meaning to the search. Like the Mandalorian, whose odyssey ended when he had to let Baby Yoda go, we let go of what we knew. The following quotes illustrate how we, the participants, altered our understanding of imagination as leaders:

> *Before*, I thought that imagination was about Willy Wonka's Chocolate Factory. *Now*, I think that imagination is a strategic approach to leadership.
>
> *Before*, I thought that imagination was synonymous with creativity (or being creative). *Now*, I think that imagination is demonstrated through creativity.
>
> *Before*, I thought that imagination was necessary for play and frivolous flights of fancy. *Now*, I think that imagination is a transformative and generative power (capacity) of the human mind.
>
> *Before*, I thought that imagination was only possible in teaching where there is some autonomy. *Now*, I think that imagination is possible in everything—especially in leadership. It not only should be permitted, but it is also an essential requirement to endure the challenges of the job—whatever the leadership position might be!
>
> (Mah et. al, 2021, p. 4)

And so, we grew. Is our quest over? Are we there yet? I do not think so.

Along the way I learned that the word *leader* derives from the Old English *lædere*, "one who leads," the agent noun from *lædan*, "'to guide, bring forth'" (Kelly, 2014). A leader finds a way from *a* to *b*. But the imaginative leader finds a way to be better. Therefore, after months of journeying together, *we each ended up where we needed to be* (G. Judson, personal communication, December 14, 2020). Perhaps it is not how far we've come but who we've become. The transformation rather than the destination is indeed cause for celebration.

CONCLUSION

This collaborative inquiry project has been rooted in imagination. Our knowledge has grown from *inviting* stories: by inviting discussion of our own and other leaders' stories of imagination in practice, but also from the evocative *inviting* stories themselves. These stories ignited our emotions and caused us to *lean into* discussion and inquiry. The act of collaboratively exploring stories—imagination in action—has created a liminal space not only for understanding leadership, but for us to reveal the shape of our own imaginations as educational leaders.

In terms of future learning, we wonder: *How does imagination serve as fecund terrain for the cultivation of authentic, equitable, and empowering relationships in school communities? How can imagination's tools, such as storytelling, imagery, metaphor, and play, help leaders become more engaging and effective communicators? How can growing their own imaginations enable leaders to flexibly respond to complex challenges? How can imagination be effectively cultivated to create lasting and meaningful change?*

This process has been highly generative for our professional learning. It may be that the study of leadership stories is a professional learning practice worthy of exploration for other leaders seeking to understand leadership imagination. For now, we invite you, reader, to wander through the leadership stories in action in the online collection, to enjoy the evocative leadership stories of imagination it contains, and to consider what cultivating imagination in your leadership would mean for the communities you serve.

The next chapter builds on this exploration of imagination and leadership to explore the role of imaginative leadership in promoting thriving school communities.

CULTIVATING CURIOSITY, CONVERSATION, AND IMAGINATION

After reading this chapter, what evokes your sense of wonder? What are you curious about?

For Consideration and Conversation

In this chapter, Judson et al. explore stories in order to understand the ways in which imagination contributes to leadership. In your own leadership, how does story or the story form aid in connection and engagement? How does it support the creation of new ideas and possibilities? How does it support change?

This chapter offers its own story of an emergent inquiry process in which the path and destination were not confirmed from the start. How do you create space in your leadership for open-ended processes of discovery? How do you and your community engage in processes that support exploring new, as-yet-unexplored ideas and possibilities?

Cultivate Imagination With Cognitive Tools

Narrative Structure

The authors use a collaborative approach to offer a unique narrative structure. While each author contributes to the collective experience, their individual perspective (their own learning story) is maintained. How can leaders ensure that stories told in/of school culture support inclusion and collaboration without essentializing voices? How do we keep our narratives rich with ideas and diversity?

REFERENCES

Anderson, L. (2020, October 26). *From panic to possibility: The power of imagination to transform.* imaginED. www.educationthatinspires.ca/2020/10/26/from-panic-to-possibility-the-power-of-imagination-to-transform/

Asma, S. T. (2017). *The evolution of imagination.* University of Chicago Press.

Boullosa, P. (2021, January 19). *Completing ourselves.* imaginED. www.educationthatinspires.ca/2021/01/19/completing-ourselves/

Charles, A. (2021, January 12). *"You belong among the wildflowers...": A reimagined school community blooming into a new way of belonging.* imaginED. www.educationthatinspires.ca/2021/01/12/you-belong-among-the-wildflowers-a-reimagined-school-community-blooming-into-a-new-way-of-belonging/

Cheng, E., Wu, S., & Hu, J. (2017). Knowledge management implementation in the school context: Case studies on knowledge leadership, storytelling, and taxonomy. *Educational Research for Policy and Practice, 16*(2), 177–188. https://doi.org/10.1007/s10671-016-9200-0

Cleverley-Thompson, S. (2018). Teaching storytelling as a leadership practice. *Journal of Leadership Education, 17*(1), 132–140. https://doi.org/10.12806/V17/I1/A1

Egan, K. (1997). *The educated mind: How cognitive tools shape our understanding.* University of Chicago Press.

Egan, K. (2005). *An imaginative approach to teaching.* Jossey-Bass.

Egan, K., & Judson, G. (2015). *Imagination and the engaged learner: Cognitive tools for the classroom.* Teachers College Press.

Froese, C. (2020, November 7). *Imagination in leadership.* Inquire2Empower Consulting. https://inquire2empower.ca/2020/11/07/imagination-in-leadership/

Fullan, M. (2002). *Principals as leaders in a culture of change.* [PDF file]. https://michaelfullan.ca/wpcontent/uploads/2016/06/13396053050.pdf

Greene, M. (1995). *Releasing the imagination: Essays on education, the arts, and social change.* Jossey-Bass.

Hosking, D. (2011). Telling tales of relations: Appreciating relational constructionism. *Organization Studies, 32*(1), 47–65. https://doi.org/10.1177/0170840610394296

Janzen, G. (2020, December 11). *Imagination for inclusion in a pandemic.* imaginED. www.educationthatinspires.ca/2020/12/11/imagination-for-inclusion-in-a-pandemic/

Judson, G. (2016). *Empathy requires imagination.* imaginED. www.educationthatinspires.ca/2016/11/28/empathy-requires-imagination/

Judson, G. (2020a). Conceptualizing imagination in the context of school leadership. *International Journal of Leadership in Education,* 1–13. https://doi.org/10.1080/13603124.2020.1818289

Judson, G. (2020b). *Imaginative schools, imaginative leadership, Imaginative Education*. imaginED. www.educationthatinspires.ca/2019/10/22/imaginative-schools-imaginative-leadership-imaginative-education/

Judson, G. (2021). Cultivating leadership imagination with cognitive tools: An imagination-focused approach to leadership education. *Journal of Research on Leadership Education*. http://doi.org/10.1177/19427751211022028

Kelly, R. (2014). The root of leadership. *Leadership Issues*. www.leadershipissues.org/the-root-of-leadership/

Landy, I. (2020, October 7). *Day 22 (of 190) . . . How has engaging your imagination . . . #illg Thank you @perfinker*. Technolandy: Site of Ian Landy. https://technolandy.wordpress.com/2020/10/07/day-22-of-190-how-has-engaging-your-imagination-illg-thank-you-perfinker/

Liu, E., & Noppe-Brandon, S. (2009). *Imagination first: Unlocking the power of possibility*. John Wiley & Sons.

Mah, C. (2020, September 3). *Parking: The imaginable (or unimaginable) final frontier*. imaginED. www.educationthatinspires.ca/2020/09/03/parking-the-imaginable-or-unimaginable-final-frontier/

Mah, C., Pillay, R., Sclater, J., & Robertson, C. (2021). *Reflecting on our process & learning leadership story project*. Unpublished document.

Mahoney, A. D. (2017). Being at the heart of the matter: Culturally relevant leadership learning, emotions, and storytelling. *Journal of Leadership, 11*(3), 55–60.

McLean, D. (2015). *Exploring constructs of relational leadership through story*. Sage Publications.

Orr, K., & Bennett, M. (2017). Relational leadership, storytelling, and narratives: Practices of local government chief executives. *Public Administration Review, 77*(4), 515–527. https://doi.org/10.1111/puar.12680

Pillay, R. (2020, August 5). *EDvent: An event for educators*. imaginED. www.educationthatinspires.ca/2020/08/05/edvent-an-event-for-educators/

Potts, K. & Brown, L. (2015). Becoming an anti-oppressive researcher. In S. Strega & L. Brown (Eds.), *Research as resistance: Revisiting critical, indigenous, and anti-oppressive approaches* (pp. 17–42). Canadian Scholars' Press.

Rasmussen, J. (2019). Storytelling as a guiding leadership principle: A framework for cocreating narratives with leaders. In J. Chlopczyk & C. Erlach (Eds.), *Transforming organizations* (pp. 137–154). Springer International Publishing. https://doi.org/10.1007/978-3-030-17851-2_10

Reid, L., & Iannuzzi, R. (2021, January 25). *The power of imagination: From possibility to reality*. imaginED: education that inspires. Retrieved from: http://www.educationthatinspires.ca/2021/01/25/the-power-of-imagination-from-possibility-to-reality/

Robertson, C. (2020, July 30). *Building relationships in leadership: Empathy and imagination*. imaginED. www.educationthatinspires.ca/2020/07/30/building-relationships-in-leadership-empathy-and-imagination/

Sclater, J. (2020, December 4). *Imaginative leadership: Building shelves.* imaginED. www.educationthatinspires.ca/2020/12/04/imaginative-leadership-building-shelves/

Wilson, A. (2019). The role of storytelling in navigating through the storm of change. *Journal of Organizational Change Management, 32*(3), 385–395. https://doi.org/10.1108/JOCM-12-2018-0343

CHAPTER 2

Exploring Possibilities
How School Leaders Employ Imagination to Build Thriving School Communities

Tara Preston

> It was the last day of school, at the end of what may go down in history as one of the hardest teaching years, and I felt a sense of gratitude and warmth in my heart. We made it. We survived teaching during a global pandemic. As we gathered to say our goodbyes, I noticed it was not just me tearing up. As staff members spoke kind words to colleagues, I observed emotion in their voices and a genuine sadness. We had supported one another, grown closer, and dreamed together ways to make our school community stronger despite COVID-19 restrictions. The school year had been hard, but we had come together as a staff that year like never before.

Being involved in a thriving school community where both students and staff feel connected and supported has always been a desire of mine. During 2020, in my teaching position, I had the privilege of experiencing a strong, thriving school community. Despite the challenges of teaching and leading in a global pandemic, I experienced our team growing more supportive, cohesive, collaborative, and willing to imagine new possibilities. We learned to trust and rely on one another, take risks, and be flexible and compassionate in our responses to constantly changing demands and stressors.

In my experience as an educator, principals play an integral role in building a strong school community. It seems like common sense that principals help steer their schools in a positive direction, creating a climate where people feel connected and have a desire to contribute (Hauserman & Stick, 2013). They can make an impact on schools by cultivating vibrant learning communities where there is trust among individuals, a love for learning, and a sense of belonging (Brown, 2015;

Tschannen-Moran & Gareis, 2015). Principals influence school culture or climate, what MacNeil et al. (2009) describes as essentially the heart and soul of the school—the way people are drawn together to love the school and have a desire to be involved in it. Principals build positive school cultures or thriving school communities by taking the time to build positive working relationships, communicating effectively, and casting vision. There is a significant amount of literature on the importance of these aspects in leadership generally, and educational leadership specifically. My research interest was different; I was interested in the role of imagination in relation to these, and other, leadership practices.

I am particularly curious about the role of imagination in leadership that builds strong school culture. As a current teacher and future leader—I hope to work as a vice principal or principal—I wanted to explore how current leaders understand imagination and the role it plays in their leadership, and how they build strong school communities. In this chapter, I employ Egan and Judson's (2016) definition of imagination as "the capacity to think of things as possibly being . . . the source of invention, novelty, and generativity" (p. 4). To support my learning in these areas, I engaged in a graduate program focusing on imaginative educational leadership in K–12 settings. As part of this program, I conducted a qualitative study exploring the role of imagination in leadership. I wonder: What is made possible by leading with imagination? How do leaders conceptualize imagination, and what role does it play in their leadership? How do leaders engage imagination in their practice? How does imagination catalyze thriving schools?

In this chapter, I offer the thoughts and experiences of the leaders I interviewed as a way to begin to explore the possibilities for building thriving communities offered through imaginative leadership. First, I examine the existing literature on effective leadership practices. Then I put the interviews with imaginative leaders to work to explore the role of imagination in these practices. Last, I reflect on how this exploration shapes my understanding of imaginative educational leadership moving forward as an emerging leader.

THRIVING COMMUNITIES: RELATIONSHIPS, COMMUNICATION, AND VISION

Educational leadership research indicates that thriving communities require leaders who build strong relationships, communicate effectively, and envision new possibilities for the future. One of the simple yet incredibly meaningful things that effective principals do is take time to build relationships; stopping in the hallways to chat with teachers, popping into classrooms to see students and teachers, and showing genuine interest can lead to trust within the school community (Barnett & McCormick, 2004; Hollingworth et al., 2018). Staff reported enjoying working with school leaders who took time to get to know them (Leithwood & Steinbach, 1993) and who supported them (Hauserman & Stick, 2013; Kelley et al., 2005).

To build these positive relationships, school leaders need to be able to communicate effectively (Hollingworth et al., 2018). Effective communication can involve sharing important and timely information with staff and listening to their concerns (Kelley et al., 2005). These leaders set standards of hard work required in teaching (Barnett & McCormick, 2004), while valuing dialogue, and offer suggestions to teachers (Blase & Blase, 2000). These leaders do not shrink back from uncomfortable conversations that need to take place with their staff (Leithwood & Steinbach, 1993). Effective communication also involves giving encouragement (Hollingworth et al., 2018) and praise (Blase & Blase, 2000), collaborating (Blase & Blase, 2000; Hauserman & Stick, 2013), and involving others in decision-making (Leithwood & Steinbach, 1993).

Having a strong vision for schools and communicating that vision helps to support positive school environments (MacNeil et al., 2009). School leaders set the tone for their schools (Williams et al., 2008), identify new opportunities for their communities (Barnett & McCormick, 2004), and involve others in working toward the shared vision (Barnett & McCormick, 2004).

As an educator and future leader, I believe imagination has an integral role in relationship-building, communication, and creating visions for the future. In the following section, I explore the topic of imagination in leadership with current educational leaders with an academic background in Imaginative Education (see Egan & Judson, 2016).

RESEARCH ON IMAGINATION FOR LEADERS

Exploring the use of imagination for leaders in educational settings is an area with limited research (Judson, 2020, 2021). Some scholars have studied transformational leadership and have found imaginative thinking is critical in transformational leadership (Curtis & Cerni, 2015; Curtis et al., 2017). Imagination is described as "an ally in leadership, enabling leaders to generate new ideas, meaning and relationship in their daily practices" (Judson, 2020, p. 9). Hopkins (2019) argues that we need leaders in all spheres to use their "collective imaginations to solve our greatest challenges" (p. 141), to cast new visions, and to reimagine our societies, including the educational system. I wanted to explore how imagination helps educational leaders as they envisage new possibilities for a thriving school community.

To find out, I interviewed three leaders who completed a Master's of Education (MEd) Degree in Imaginative Education (IE) and who now hold administrative leadership roles as principals or vice principals in the K–12 system in the Greater Vancouver area. I chose to interview these leaders because they explored the facets of the imagination in their graduate coursework and could offer breadth and depth to the discussion of the role of imagination in educational leadership. I wanted to learn what educational leaders glean from the theory of Imaginative Education and how they apply this theory to their leadership roles to engage imagination in their practice. Ultimately, I was interested in the role of imagination in relationship-building and collaboration among colleagues and in cultivating a thriving school community.

I know that leadership, and more specifically leadership within schools, is not an easy pathway to navigate. If imagination is the ability to think of the possible (Egan, 2005), then I want that in the forefront of my mind as an emerging leader. I wanted to explore whether there are ways in which I can use my imagination in educational leadership settings that could positively affect the school communities that I work in. I believe imagination is critical in supporting my lifelong journey of inquiry. When thinking about my research, I approached this work with questions about how imagination might be one facet in educational leadership to build thriving school communities where wonder and deep learning are at the forefront for all. In the following section, I share the participants' ideas about what it means to be an imaginative leader—how, in their practice, imagination is integral to problem-solving, risk-taking, relationships, and perspective-taking. These are interconnected aspects of imaginative leadership, and recognizing the connection between these practices is essential in understanding imagination in a thriving school environment.

Embodying Imaginative Leadership

During the inquiry, leaders discussed what it means to be an imaginative leader; they shared what they see their role to be and how they put imagination to work in their leadership role. One leader, Clara, explained that overall, imaginative leadership "is just looking at different possibilities, and giving space and freedom to staff to also look at different possibilities." She explained that her understanding of imagination has changed over time:

Exploring Possibilities

When I first started my MEd, I thought imagination just equaled creativity, but now I understand it to be more about problem-solving, flexible thinking, and critical thinking. So, imagination, you know, if you do like a quick Google image search with imagination, there's often a rainbow. (laughs) Yeah, and pretty clouds and maybe a unicorn will also be in your search, but I think it's far more than that.

Clara used humor to articulate that her understanding of imagination has grown more nuanced, in seeing imagination as an integral part of problem-solving, flexibility, and critical thinking. She believes imagination is much more than rainbows and unicorns and being creative. She later explained that when a leader recognizes the importance of imagination in leadership, they operate in that imaginative "philosophic framework all of the time."

Moreover, Laila explained that being an imaginative leader:

is looking at all sides of the story, just being open, sharing your own lived experiences, making yourself vulnerable, or, you know, showing up . . . show up to the arena, just be there, get messy. Be a listening leader, of course.

Laila's explanation highlights the importance of how leaders engage relationally—with vulnerability, a willingness to get messy, and ready to listen.

Greg also emphasized the importance of relationships in teaching and leadership:

So, to me, our job is never number one to deliver content. It's always about developing relationships with others, and it's always about finding an interesting way to do that. To me that's where having an imaginative mindset comes in. But not everyone is on that same page, so I have to figure out as a leader, little bits to give them, little seeds to plant, to grow that [relationship] over time.

Greg sees imagination as fundamental in building relationships with others; imagination allows him to figure out, as a leader, how to grow relationships with each team member over time. He went on to explain:

That's how we got onto that track for our school. The way we got there to me is that it was tapping into people's stories and experiences. Rather than saying, what is the data we need to collect? It started with the people . . .

because to me anytime we're talking about imagination we're talking about relationships, emotions, people's engagement with each other.

Here Greg recognizes the importance of relationship and engagement in addressing problems in the school community. He explained that to make positive changes to his school community, he needed to start with people's stories and their experiences. Imagination acts as an integral element in building relationships, and these relationships form a foundation for exploring problems differently.

Imagination and Problem-Solving

Greg, Laila, and Clara all discussed the role of imagination in how they view and respond to problems. As educational leaders, they expressed similar ideas about moving beyond a problem being solved by a right or wrong solution. Instead, they focused on ideas, possibilities, and the willingness to be vulnerable and admit you do not have all the answers. Laila explained that to her, "problems" are problematic. She talked about how she moves beyond the problem to think of the possibility:

> ... that's something that's kind of become like a honed-in skill of mine now so you're always aware of the possibilities, and you're always tuning into, is this imagination at play? ... And I always give the benefit of the doubt, to a teacher, or a student, or a parent, or a colleague of mine, and I try not to think about the problem but I think, is this an imaginative solution? It kind of gets me out of the right and wrong. Is this person doing the right thing? Is this person doing the wrong thing? It gets me out of that ... and just, looking for the possibilities. Is this a new possibility? Is this an existing possibility? And I try not to just fixate on *is this a problem*? ... Like I just try to think outside of that box, because I find problems problematic.

Clara had a similar approach:

> So, what's *the* solution? What is *a* solution? Do we have ideas? So, allowing people the time, and also the sense of agency to come up with a solution is very powerful ... So, what are the solutions? ... And so always know that there's an open door when it comes to new ideas, because I don't have all the answers. And it's a very vulnerable thing to say, too. It's a really scary thing to be vulnerable in front of people. ... So you're really going out on a limb by saying help me. But you can't have all the answers as a principal.

Greg also focused on not knowing all the answers and instead, looking at possibilities. He describes:

> I'm coming to realize more that having imagination doesn't mean we've seen into the future and know all the answers. It means to me, that I'm developing the capacity to get involved in a situation, even if it's challenging or messy and I know that I will have many possible ways, or outcomes, out of that. And I can be okay in that moment with many possibilities. See, if you come from a mindset that is kind of fixed and that there's one way to do things and you're used to teaching and having a certain outcome and it's a very direct kind of experience. Challenges are very problematic because you wanna have a solution. Before we even talk to people, people want to have it all figured out. To me, having imagination means I'm just there to listen . . . And I'm also willing to risk failing in that, by attempting a few things to see if it makes a difference . . . it's a suspended kind of knowing of what will happen.

In their discussions of how imagination catalyzes their approach to problem-solving, these leaders highlight the importance of vulnerability, not knowing, and risk-taking.

Imagination and Risk-Taking

Throughout their discussions of imagination and leadership, the leaders discussed the impact of the pandemic on their leadership. The global context precipitated the need to be imaginative and flexible and take new risks. Laila explained:

> I think during these COVID times [imagination] became a bit of a life raft for me, thrown into this type of mix as a new administrator. It's kind of shown me other ways of thinking and knowing and thinking outside of the box and taking those risks.

There is an inherent risk in doing things differently from how they have been done in the past, in pushing outside of the comfort zone. Having positive and productive relationships encourages trust and the willingness to take those risks.

Imagination and Relationships

Greg, Laila, and Clara all emphasized the importance of relationships. They discussed the need to spend time together, build trust, truly listen, and create meaningful moments together. Greg explained the importance of working collaboratively with a team:

> I can't accomplish anything on my own—I have to have a team. I have to be able to share a vision that I have and have other people become part of that vision. So, if the vision is about me, it's not going to work so it has to be through relationship, it has to involve other people.

Building this productive team environment takes imagination. Laila explained that it is important for her to feel connected to her team, as well as to build their connections to her. Building on previous themes of being humble, curious, and willing to be vulnerable, Clara, Laila, and Greg emphasized the importance of being real with their teams: they highlighted the need to lead by example, to try new things, to not be afraid to fail, and to truly listen to others. A key aspect of building relationships is reflecting on one's own position and being open to the positions of others. Laila explained:

> I think it's really important to lean into your own biases and to really be reflective and think about those. Oftentimes before you do approach a difficult conversation with a colleague, or, you know, approach a challenge in your school, or think about imaginative solutions, I think it's really important to look at your own biases of a situation . . . I think that's a really important tool that I've learned is to just take a step back and think about myself first before approaching a really difficult conversation. I'm only human and I can make [mistakes], I speak and say things but I need to be aware of my own biases and just really own them.

Greg also articulated the need to bring people together in meaningful ways:

> I always feel that—this is a value of mine at least—that school should be fun. There should be an element of play, discovery. There should be an element of being willing to take some risk and try new things. As a leader, my job as I see it is to have a vision that extends into the future, but then think back to what is the first step to be there and usually it's around shaping a story together. So one of the values is trying to bring people together in a team. So teamwork and relationships take time. You know building trust . . . but I guess like a core value for me is that we should enjoy what we are doing, otherwise we should be doing something different.

Exploring Possibilities

He went on to provide a specific example of using the staff meeting time as an opportunity to connect and build a story together:

> When I get into staff meetings, it's not just about agenda items. I'm trying to think about a *moment* within a staff meeting because that's really the time I get with teachers ... that thread of building our story together. I think about a moment we can have there to talk about where we're going, who we are. I think good leaders might do that anyways, but having the imaginative piece allows me to play in that area instead of feeling like I just have a bunch of tasks that I have to get done.

Building meaningful, collaborative relationships takes time and imagination. Through imagination, leaders can build empathy and understand the perspectives of others; this ability to see other perspectives allows leaders to engage their staff and envision a story together.

Imagination and Perspective-Taking

As previously noted in Laila's example, building a trusting, working relationship requires reflection on one's own position and bias. In addition to attending to multiple perspectives, the leaders shared, in different ways, the importance of helping others take varied perspectives. The leaders engage the imaginations of others—staff, teachers, students—so they can look at a situation or problem from a different perspective. For example, Greg discussed how he has been working with teachers to reframe their understanding of play and learning:

> Sometimes [teachers] want to show me something about how kids are having fun in an activity, and I'll use that moment to say ... yeah, through their drama and play, *this* is their learning. And sort of having that conversation around, this isn't just like a fun little side thing, this can be it. You don't have to teach a bunch and then let them play, this play is an aspect of what they're doing. Even today when we had our door decorating, kids were having, using all kinds of core competencies, measuring things, talking together about how they'll plan it, how they'll do it. And I said this is it, this is your math today, this is your evidence of their communication.

He went on to explain:

> To me, that's how actually having the imaginative mindset really blends well with the new curriculum and competencies, because it can happen through just a fun activity that we thought was a side thing, and sometimes

teachers might see it as, well, we'll do this, but then we've got to get back to our work. I'm like no, *this* is it. This is the richness. And I know I can see it, because of my ability to access all the [cognitive] tools [of imagination] and see how those are actually connecting kids in their learning and developing those skills.

Perspective-taking and imagining the experience of others can have significant implications for leadership and for teaching and learning. Leaders can promote perspective-taking in teachers so that they have a better understanding of the experiences of their students. As Greg explained:

Right now I've been trying to describe it more [to teachers] as seeing the experience through the eyes of their learners instead of how they see it, and what does it feel like to be them? And I have more and more teachers accepting the fact that there are a number of kids that need breaks to reset and come back, and they're finally okay with that. They're letting go of their own perspective of what the kids should do. And now they're connecting more with what that child actually needs at that moment so that they are able to do something. I have more teachers taking their classes outside and feeling free to do that, and going on walks and to the ravine, because I'm describing to them that your lesson can happen in that space, you can create and plan ahead to think about science or different aspects of math or anything that can happen there and I have more teachers doing that now. All those things have been layered in.

The leaders with an educational background in Imaginative Education emphasize the role of imagination in building productive working relationships, problem-solving, risk-taking, and perspective-taking. In their discussions, these various aspects of leadership are intertwined and connected. They recognize that an imaginative approach to leadership is not something one puts on and takes off, but a mindset or an approach that influences how they view their role, their teams, and their priorities. Imagination is part of who they are, as leaders. Their imaginative approach takes humility in knowing they do not have all the answers and need the engagement and collaboration of their team. Their approach also takes vulnerability in their willingness to take risks and to fail in front of their teams.

The ideas espoused by the participants contribute to more nuanced understanding of the existing educational leadership literature. While existing literature highlights the importance of relationships, communication, and casting vision, it does not speak explicitly to the role of imagination in enacting these practices. This exploration with imaginative leaders demonstrates the importance of imagination in building relationships—in being genuine, demonstrating empathy, and taking multiple perspectives—and investing time and energy into those relationships.

Imagination also plays a significant role in communication; in creating a story of who the school team is, where they have been, and where they want to go together. Imagination aids communication in leaders' ability to be reflective and self-aware, and to envision different ways to frame their communication. School leaders need to imagine and dream about what is possible for their schools and work together with teachers and other staff members to bring dreams into reality for their learning community. Envisioning what is possible requires imagination. Imagination enables leaders, with their teams, to determine new directions for their school and work collaboratively toward that end. Within a trusting and collaborative team environment, imaginative leaders can deconstruct what has always been and be willing to explore what is possible. This collaborative revisioning and action are at the heart of thriving school communities.

CONCLUSION

What's next for me as a leader? Ultimately, I wanted to know if imagination could help leaders to build thriving school communities. In exploring the potential of imagination, I learned more about the kind of leader I want to be. I was challenged by the leadership stories the participants shared and left with a desire to push outside of my comfort zone. I want to ask questions, to take risks, and be open to not having all the answers. I want to approach my work in schools from a place of curiosity.

I recognize that modeling risk-taking, curiosity, and vulnerability allows others to engage differently—this can shift the school culture. For far too long, I have heard leaders state that "this is the way we need to do this" or "this is the way things have always been done." The imaginative leaders highlighted the need to push beyond the usual and imagine things differently. Their stories affirmed the power in deconstructing the way things are always done and exploring what is possible, collaboratively with their teams. I understand now that leadership involves opening my heart up to listen to others and creating space for multiple perspectives to help shape the story that we can create together. Imagination is my friend on this leadership path as I recognize how I can envision and enact change within myself and my team to build a thriving school community.

The next chapter continues this exploration of the possible, considering how imagination allows leaders to push past the status quo to enact positive change.

CULTIVATING CURIOSITY, CONVERSATION, AND IMAGINATION

After reading this chapter, what evokes your sense of wonder? What are you curious about?

For Consideration and Conversation

How do we cultivate an imaginative mindset in ourselves and others? What does an imaginative mindset look, sound, and feel like in your practice?

As leaders, how can we explore our own vulnerabilities—for example, taking risks, making mistakes, and not knowing—in a generative way? What is the role of imagination in doing so?

Cultivate Imagination With Cognitive Tools

Transcendent Human Qualities

In this chapter, Preston considers how imagination supports thriving school communities. Think about the ways in which your school *thrives*. What is *heroic* about your school? What qualities currently define your school community (e.g., belonging, trust, motivation, respect, curiosity)? What qualities do you want to see enacted in action? Engage your school community members (teachers, staff, students, parents) in discussion: What is heroic about the learners in our school? What practical actions can enrich our learners and support their journey to greatness? What is heroic about our teachers and staff? What practices can enable our teachers and staff to thrive?

REFERENCES

Barnett, K., & McCormick, J. (2004). Leadership and individual principal-teacher relationships in schools. *Educational Administration Quarterly, 40*(3), 406–434. http://doi.org/10.1177/0013161X03261742

Blase, J., & Blase, J. (2000). Effective instructional leadership: Teachers' perspectives on how principals promote teaching and learning in schools. *Journal of Educational Administration, 38*(2), 130–141. http://doi.org/10.1108/09578230010320082

Brown, G. (2015). Strong one lasting one: An elementary school principal's ability to establish a positive culture by building trust. *Journal of Cases in Educational Leadership, 18*(4), 309–316. http://doi.org/10.1177/1555458915606768

Curtis, G. J., & Cerni, T. (2015). For leaders to be transformational, they must think imaginatively. *Journal of Leadership Studies, 9*(3), 45–47. https://doi.org/10.1002/jls.21401

Curtis, G. J., King, G., & Russ, A. (2017). Reexamining the relationship between thinking styles and transformational leadership: What is the contribution of imagination and emotionality? *Journal of Leadership Studies, 11*(2), 8–21. https://doi.org/10.1002/jls.21508

Egan, K. (2005). *An imaginative approach to teaching.* Jossey-Bass.

Egan, K., & Judson, G. (2016). *Imagination and the engaged learner: Cognitive tools for the classroom.* Teachers College Press.

Hauserman, C. P., & Stick, S. L. (2013). The leadership teachers want from principals: Transformational. *Canadian Journal of Education, 36*(3), 184–203.

Hollingworth, L., Olsen, D., Asikin-Garmager, A., & Winn, K. M. (2018). Initiating conversations and opening doors: How principals establish a positive building culture to sustain school improvement efforts. *Educational Management Administration & Leadership, 46*(6), 1014–1034. https://doi.org/10.1177/1741143217720461

Hopkins, R. (2019). *From what is to what if: Unleashing the power of imagination to create the future we want.* Chelsea Green Publishing.

Judson, G. (2020). Conceptualizing imagination in the context of school leadership. *International Journal of Leadership in Education.* https://doi.org/10.1080/13603124.2020.1818289

Judson, G. (2021). Cultivating leadership imagination with cognitive tools: An imagination-focused approach to leadership education. *Journal of Research on Leadership Education.* https://doi.org/10.1177/19427751211022028

Kelley, R. C., Thornton, B., & Daugherty, R. (2005). Relationships between measures of leadership and school climate. *Education, 126*(1), 17–25.

Leithwood, K., & Steinbach, R. (1993). Total quality leadership: Expert thinking plus transformational practice. *Journal of Personnel Evaluation in Education, 7*(4), 311–337. https://doi.org/10.1007/BF00972508

MacNeil, A. J., Prater, D. L., & Busch, S. (2009). The effects of school culture and climate on student achievement. *International Journal of Leadership in Education, 12*(1), 73–84. https://doi.org/10.1080/13603120701576241

Tschannen-Moran, M., & Gareis, C. (2015). Principals, trust, and cultivating vibrant schools. *Societies, 5*(2), 256–276. https://doi.org/10.3390/soc5020256

Williams, E., Persaud, G., & Turner, T. (2008). Planning for principal evaluation: Effects on school climate and achievement. *Educational Planning, 17*(3), 1–11.

CHAPTER 3

A Leadership Journey Toward Innovation Through Wide-Awakeness, Curiosity, and Imagination

Karen Steffensen

It was 3 days following my cancer surgery. I laid in the hospital bed reflecting on my journey with this frightening disease. This rare form of bone cancer, chondrosarcoma, resulted in the necessary removal of a large portion of my hard palate. The typical course of treatment following the surgery would have involved insertion of an obturator (a prosthesis used to close the opening left as a result of the removal of bone and tissue), but fortunately for me, my course of treatment was not typical. I was under the care of an innovative and talented surgeon who has transformed the level of patient care, particularly for this form of oral cancer. As I lay there, I heard a familiar voice. I looked up and at the open door of my room stood Dr. Gilbert.

Dr. Gilbert was dressed in shorts and smiling. This was completely unexpected, since it was a holiday (August 1, 2008) and I had been informed that no doctors would be making rounds today. As he entered the room he asked, "How is my patient doing today?" I was thrilled to see him and so impressed at the degree of caring he showed, taking time during this holiday (his day off) to make an unscheduled visit. We talked about the next steps involved in my recovery and then, during our discussion, something quite magical happened. Like a lightbulb going off in my head, I could see the connection between this surgeon's unyielding commitment to patient care, his innovative practice, and how these beliefs, actions, and way of thinking needed to somehow be captured and transcended into educational reform. What I realized at that very moment was that I needed to understand why this physician desired to revolutionize patient care and understand what pushed him past the resistance of the status quo. I wanted to find a way to connect my understanding of how this surgeon's thinking, passion, commitment, and drive could lead to a framework for how we can make a difference in our schools, organizations, and educational institutions.

My personal experience with a rare form of cancer has afforded me insights into how imagination underpins organizational change and transformation in education and how it enlivens the mindset of a leader embarking upon a journey of change. Throughout this chapter, I share a small part of my personal story with a cancer diagnosis and an innovative surgeon who was able to envision the possible and save my life (Steffensen, 2012). My 35-year career in education—serving as a classroom educator and a school-based and system-based leader within a pan-Canadian context—has exposed me to diverse circumstances and opportunities that required me, as an educator and leader, to see beyond a current reality. I have learned to see *what might be* rather than *what is*. I have learned that moving past the status quo—or *beyond the diagnosis*—is a necessary skill for transformational leadership and innovation to emerge. To move from a current state toward an improved future or desired state, leaders must face and address the existing challenges of a situation with curiosity and imagination.

So, how do we lead ourselves forward beyond a diagnosis? Uncovering the answer to this question in the final stages of my journey with cancer, I learned what I call *artful-mindedness*—a leadership mindset fueled by a desire to innovate, and shaped by curiosity, imagination, caring, and wide-awakeness (Steffensen, 2012). At the heart is the power of the imagination, a force that enables significant transformation in our own lives and within the lives of others. Imagination involves forming a mental image of something that is not present (Asma, 2017). As mentioned throughout this book, imagination enables enduring, impactful ways forward, unlocking our collective ability to see the possible within the impossible (Judson, 2020). Imagination in action is exploring possibilities (that which could be, rather than holding onto what is). To imagine or *re*imagine involves conceiving things in new ways, innovating (Laruccia, 2009), and fueling transformation.

In 2012, I concluded a narrative inquiry into the paradoxes of innovation and the factors that promote or limit innovation in a system, organization, or institution (Steffensen, 2012). In that research I explored factors that affect an individual's desire or ability to create or innovate and how individuals might better negotiate and navigate the constraints within organizations, thinking "anew and acting anew, rising with the occasion, overcoming the dogmas of the past" (Lincoln,

1989, pp. 414–415). I learned that to lead for innovation, a leader must embrace uncertainties by approaching them with alertness, or wide-awakeness, curiosity, empathy/caring (for those at the center of the current reality), creativity, and imagination.

Leveraging curiosity and imagination in crucial leadership moments is needed in order to successfully shift a course of action, to adapt, or to greet a new reality. Moving beyond *what is* involves a leader approaching challenge, uncertainty, disruption, or a critical problem at hand with an open-to-learning stance (curiosity). The leader garners critical insights by pausing in the moment to wonder "why," seeking to understand "what's really going on versus what's happening" (wide-awakeness). The leader uncovers their internal will and the will of others to adapt to the circumstance at hand and to move forward differently. This transformative process for innovation is fueled by imagination.

In this chapter, I focus on the role of imagination in transformative leadership, resulting in impactful innovation. Specifically, I conceptualize imagination and indicate how it is required to move beyond the status quo—the dominant ways of knowing and doing that can prevent change. I connect my story of Dr. Gilbert's medical innovation with Maxine Greene's and Paolo Freire's scholarship to highlight key features of imagination's vital role in leadership for transformation and innovation.

UNDERSTANDING IMAGINATION'S ROLE IN LEADERSHIP: INSIGHTS FROM MAXINE GREENE AND PAULO FREIRE

> In our dialogue, it became apparent that Dr. Gilbert's first priority was enhancing the quality of a patient's life. He was empowered by the belief that the status quo was not good enough. He believed that if one really cares about a patient's quality of life, a better solution needs to be pursued and found. His quest for a better solution, to imagine a new possibility, unfolded over a period of 8 years and within the context of over 2,000 surgeries. I asked him how he came to develop this radical method of bone and tissue graft (which utilizes the shoulder blade and muscle) as a new standard of reconstructive surgery for this particular form of maxillofacial cancer. He explained that the previous method of treatment involving prosthesis (which was widely accepted and practiced by most doctors around the world as the standard form of care) did not provide the patient with adequate quality of life. In this standard approach, the patient is left with facial abnormalities that are never fully rectified, since without a replacement of the removed bone, the face literally drops when

the obturator or prosthesis is removed. Having been in the position of facing this as my possible reality, I recall the emotion that completely overwhelmed me at the thought of the permanent disfigurement that I would have endured if this standard approach had been utilized.

Maxine Greene's (1978, 1979, 1994, 1995, 2001, 2007, 2010) scholarship provides a lens through which I understand both imagination's role in leadership and the evolution of my leadership practice. Greene contends that imagination can transform current educational systems, institutions, and organizations. I believe that Greene's views on the imagination are deeply connected to critical elements of Paulo Freire's theories, as expressed in *Pedagogy of the Oppressed* (1970). Freire's work indicates the pivotal point at which understanding and problematizing *what is* is necessary for leveraging meaningful system transformation. Below, I explore what Greene and Freire can offer understanding imaginative leadership.

For Greene (1995), "imagination breathes life into experience" (p. 22). As discussed in the Introduction, imagination leads to creation, knowledge, and understanding. She states that "the role of imagination is not to resolve, not to point the way, not to improve. It is to awaken, to disclose the ordinarily unseen, unheard, and unexpected" (p. 28). Greene (2001) argues that the idea of the possible (distinguishable from the predictable) is central to creative and appreciative experiences. The imagination opens to each of us a vision of *what might be* which, if paired with action, can change reality. In *Carpe Diem: The Arts and School Restructuring* (1994), Greene explores how imagination allows for understanding of what *is not yet*:

> Imagination, as is well known, is the capacity that enables us to move through the barriers of the taken-for granted and summon up alternative possibilities for living, for being in the world. It permits us to set aside (at least for a while) the stiflingly familiar and the banal. It opens up to visions of the possible rather than the predictable; it permits us, if we choose to give our imaginations free play, to look at things as if they could be otherwise. (p. 1)

Imagination also allows human beings to empathize and understand the "other":

> Imagination is what, above all, makes empathy possible. It is what enables us to cross the empty spaces between ourselves and those we have called "other" over the years. If those others are willing to give us clues, we can

look in some manner through strangers' eyes and hear through their ears. That is because, of all our cognitive capacities, imagination is the one that permits us to give credence to alternative realities. It allows us to break with the taken for granted, to set aside familiar distinctions and definitions. (p. 3)

So, Greene's body of work identifies imagination as a vital element for leaders to employ to enter into realms of new possibility. Imagination, as a driver for empathy and possibility, inspires leaders to move into new ways of being in institutions, schools, systems, and organizations. Leaders may transform the places and spaces which currently exist, by thinking and "act[ing] anew, rising with occasion, and overcoming the dogmas of the past" (Lincoln, 1989, pp. 414–415).

Freire's (1970) work points to the growth that is possible when we challenge the problematic spaces and perspectives present. Freire proposes that one must problematize one's own life in order to realize that a different status is required and can be achieved. He proposes two stages of transformation: The first stage involves becoming conscious of the reality that the individual lives as an oppressed being, subject to the decisions that the oppressors impose. The second stage refers to the initiative of the oppressed to fight and emancipate themselves from the oppressors. Freire (1970) suggests that "limit-situations" block change or development; the oppressing class uses these obstacles, or limits, to protect their status. Oppressors naively think that the oppressed should adapt to existing, limiting conditions rather than construct new and appropriate conditions required for critical thought—the kind of thought that builds spaces and opportunities for liberation and for overturning oppression through conscious action. Thus, for school leaders, moving beyond "limit-situations" is where the possibility exists.

The next section indicates how Greene's and Freire's scholarship informs my experience working with Dr. Gilbert to move *beyond the diagnosis*. Understanding why imagination is necessary and how overcoming the status quo can launch us, as leaders, into action, offers crucial, complementary perspectives that frame my journey in education as a school and system leader seeking the imaginative spaces of possibility and innovation. Greene's work indicates that imagination ignites the passion and desire to leverage change; it enables leaders to conceptualize clarity of vision and direction previously hidden from view, enabling the ability to transform organizations. Freire's work suggests that emerging action arises from a place of challenge, conscious action that leads to liberation from a current, oppressed reality. Beginning by understanding one's position, leaders may move to a place of new possibilities by imagining, generating, and creating a different reality that was otherwise invisible.

IMAGINATION MOVES BEYOND THE DIAGNOSIS

Dr. Gilbert went on to explain that in order to develop a bone and tissue graft to replace the removed portion of the jaw and palate, he would need to use a bone that had a blood supply so that it would continue to be integral to the body and would survive radiation, should this be required as a follow-up treatment. He carefully reexamined the human anatomy, searching with relentless curiosity and wide-awakeness, imagining which bones with blood supply could potentially be used for grafting purposes. In his quest for the ideal bone, he noticed that the shoulder blade's shape closely resembles the shape of the bone in the jaw. Dr. Gilbert wondered if there might be an answer in this discovery. To be sure, he created an overlay of the two areas, and remarkably, as the two images were superimposed on each other, he discovered they were virtually a perfect fit. The challenge now became how to harvest this bone and tissue and develop surgical procedures and techniques to ensure success.

Many colleagues were wary and skeptical of this new treatment option, warning him that it was too radical and extremely risky. But, convinced that it could be done, he persevered and innovated treatment protocols and developed groundbreaking procedures that are now world-renowned. Even today, as Dr. Gilbert presents this technique in medical conferences worldwide, he is occasionally greeted with skepticism and doubt. However, his record of over 2,000 surgeries with a 99% success rate speaks for itself. Dr. Gilbert's use of imagination, his imaginative frame for thinking, and his creative mindset provide great potential and inspiration as a model for innovation—the power of imagination as a driver of change, to enact the possible in the face of the impossible.

This story offers a lesson to us all that is "morally resonant and contributes to our knowing" (Witherell & Noddings, 1991, p. 1). When considered through Freire's (1970) and Greene's (1994, 2001) conceptions of imagination and education, this story of Dr. Gilbert's imagination in action can act as a frame of reference and inspiration, if not a catalyst, for system change and innovation in education.

Dr. Gilbert problematized the issue of quality of life for me, his patient, and in doing so, he realized that a different state was required and could be imagined and realized. The oppressor, in this narrative, is represented by the dominant traditional body of knowledge in the medical profession and the status quo approaches and prescriptive standardized way of dealing with maxillofacial cancers. The doctors who embraced the traditional way, informed by their current body of knowledge, acted as the oppressors in their attempt to block Dr. Gilbert's imaginative creativity to initiate and develop an innovative approach to overcoming a rare form of cancer.

The doctors within the existing medical community embraced what they considered to be safe—an established, traditional approach as the preferred standard of practice. The dominant narrative reinforced that the patients (the oppressed) should adapt to existing conditions, accept *what is*, and embrace the status quo (by enduring the prosthesis) rather than experience a newly imagined and liberating possibility (the bone graft innovation imagined, inspired, and created by Dr. Gilbert) that would ultimately enhance patient quality of life.

Dr. Gilbert's medical innovation, fueled by his imagination, resulted from an unyielding and deep care for his patients and his desire to create a better possible future for patients. The result of his imaginative, transformative leadership was an innovation that influenced the future direction of the treatment of maxillofacial cancers around the world. Overall, Dr. Gilbert's imaginative, innovative, and comprehensive approach treating this form of maxillofacial cancer illustrates the mindset necessary to navigate differently and reach beyond existing practices within the medical community.

Dr. Gilbert's imagination was supported; he worked in a culture that valued innovation in service of an improved patient outcome. The University Health Network (UHN), of which Dr. Gilbert is part, describes itself as a "caring, creative and accountable academic hospital" dedicated to "transforming health care for our patients, our community and the world" (University Health Network, 2008, p. 2). The 2008 UHN statement of purpose lays a foundation for the underlying conditions ideal for innovation to flourish. One of the conditions for innovation is a collective energy, a disposition and mindset of individuals within the organization who are empowered by imagination to seek out new possibilities, not constrained or bound by current beliefs, perspectives, or realities. Innovation requires leaders to be open to seeing things in new ways, seeing the potential first rather than only noticing the drawbacks or risks—to use imagination as a driver toward success. I believe that the degree to which innovation can occur in an organization ultimately depends on the imaginative mindsets and desires of empowered individuals within organizations. When individuals are supported by clarity of purpose, focused on improving the human condition, and fueled by curiosity and imagination, then great achievements are possible. Dr. Gilbert's story offers important lessons for leadership.

IMAGINATION FOR INNOVATION IN EDUCATIONAL LEADERSHIP

In *Metaphors We Live By*, Lakoff and Johnson (1980) share that "our concepts structure what we perceive, how we get around in the world and how we relate to other people" (p. 3). If we, as school leaders, are limited by our concepts of *what is* in education, we cannot be responsive to the students and communities we work with; we remain unable to see and understand their challenges and needs, bound by the systemic structures that create barriers to success. By adopting a limited view of the world, we ignore the uniqueness of the needs of others and supplant them with a "my way is the right way" frame of mind. My journey through cancer left me deeply contemplating the significance and impact of leaders embracing wide-awakeness, lingering in curiosity, and leveraging imagination in order to not "drift or act on impulses of expediency" (Greene, 1978, p. 43).

I have learned that navigating educational transformation requires a leadership mindset grounded in imagination. When talking to Dr. Gilbert about how often he gets the opportunity to see things differently and wonder what else might be possible, I asked him, "How can your insights about imagining forward differently be applied to transforming education?" He responded with clarity regarding the mindset necessary for successful actions to improve the student experience. He articulated his belief about seeing things not as they are but as what they can be, being curious about what might be possible, and being open to innovation, as well as not being fearful of being an agent of change.

The ability to be an agent of change is a result of one's own personality—a personality driven largely by a mindset of never being satisfied with *what is*—that is to say, something can always be made better or improved in the realm of patient care or student learning (Steffensen, 2012). This highlights for me the important concept of the individual and the social. The two (the individual and social) are inextricably linked to each other. Dr. Gilbert is continuously driven to do something better by his individual persona or drive. Because patient care is always in need of improvement (a social dilemma), Dr. Gilbert remains open and welcoming of the possible. He imagines what might be possible and does something better (his individual response to the social situation). Dr. Gilbert improves patient care because he imagines, creates, and enacts the new possible, doing something better, being innovative with this knowledge.

If we embrace imagination as the fundamental leadership mindset necessary within our schools, organizations, and educational systems, the challenges we face might be changed into inspirations. Perhaps we can transform, as Carl Jung said, "what has happened to us" into "what we choose to become" (Strobel, 2020, p. 44). Greene (2007) suggests that to

> activate the imagination is to discover not only possibility, but to find the gaps, the empty spaces that require filling as we move from the *is* to the *might be*, to the *should be*. To release the imagination, too, is to release the power of empathy, to become more present to those around, perhaps to care. (p. 4; italics added)

The social imagination, for Greene (1995), is "the capacity to invent visions of what should be and what might be in our deficient society, on the streets where we live, in our schools" (p. 5). Guyotte (2018) highlights the possibilities offered by a social imagination that surpasses limitations and constraints:

> To begin with, the social imagination is to acknowledge the shortcomings, the dead ends, the limitations in both the educational system and the societal structures that organize our daily lives. These limitations are not intended to cause paralysis by critique; however, they operate to help individuals envision what might become and why such a becoming is desirable, even necessary. In seeing the social world as a space of possibility for movement, rather than as a static entity, the social imagination is always already at work. (p. 64)

The social imagination unites the social and the individual in order to create new possibilities for overcoming current reality, to navigate past the status quo and become an agent of change.

CONCLUSION

As I look back on my entire journey with cancer, I see that each stage of the journey brought a new level of awareness to my beliefs about the power of imagination in leadership. What I initially perceived as an unfortunate event in fact has turned out to be extremely pivotal. I now see this experience as a catalyst and inspirational event in my life. It has reinforced my perspective that a leader's lack of wide-awakeness and lack of desire to determine "what is really going on" (Bolman & Deal, 2017) can become a roadblock to moving beyond a current reality to an improved future state of being. One might describe this state of mind as having a lack of curiosity, being closed to seeking or seeing other possibilities, having the incapacity "to look at things as if they could be otherwise" (Greene, 1995, p. 19) or to lack the belief and desire to leverage the power of imagination.

With imagination we can move *beyond the diagnosis*. As I continue to work in the spaces of education that seek continuous quality improvement, I wonder and cling to the hope and unyielding belief that when curiosity and imagination are at the heart of who we are as learners and leaders, and when imagination is front and center in how we lead and leverage change, we can transcend the most challenging realities in our educational systems and institutions. The imagination lying at the heart of empowered improvement and innovation is the ultimate answer to transforming the places we call school into powerful places of possibility in which our communities truly flourish.

The chapters in the following section discuss the poetic dimensions of imagination and how aesthetic engagement can support leadership for social justice.

CULTIVATING CURIOSITY, CONVERSATION, AND IMAGINATION

After reading this chapter, what evokes your sense of wonder? What are you curious about?

For Consideration and Conversation

What role does imagination play in challenging oppression? Share an example of when you have felt pressured to adapt to the status quo rather than to challenge systems or practices in your community.

This chapter reveals the courage required to challenge the status quo. How can leaders keep fear from impeding their imaginations? What conditions are necessary for imaginative leadership practices to develop? What supports would make you feel more comfortable employing imagination in your leadership?

Cultivating Imagination with Cognitive Tools

Practice "What if-ing" (Sense of Wonder)

What diagnosis or diagnoses is your school community currently facing? Choose one challenging diagnosis to explore with imagination. Begin by evoking your sense of wonder to better understand the challenge. What is unique about the challenge? What is unique about your context and, thus, the challenge itself? Now, consider what could uniquely serve as a resolution. Setting practicalities aside, begin by engaging in some extreme "what if-ing" about ways to differently, even radically, address this challenge. To engage your imagination, you can *what if* from different perspectives. Approach the topic in role as teachers, support staff, learners, parents, members of minoritized communities, learners with special needs, and so forth. As a group, identify which of your options you can explore in more detail and how you might move this idea to action.

REFERENCES

Asma, S. T. (2017). *The evolution of imagination*. University of Chicago Press.

Bolman, L. G., & Deal, T. E. (2017). *Reframing organizations: Artistry, choice, and leadership*. Jossey-Bass.

Freire, P. (1970). *Pedagogy of the oppressed*. Continuum Publishing.

Greene, M. (1978). *Landscapes of learning*. Teachers College Press.

Greene, M. (1979). *Teacher as stranger: Educational philosophy for the modern age*. Wadsworth Publishing Company.

Greene, M. (1994). Carpe diem: The arts and school restructuring. *Teachers College Record, 95*(4), 494–507.

Greene, M. (1995). *Releasing the imagination: Essays on education, the arts, and social change*. Jossey-Bass.

Greene, M. (2001). *Variations on a blue guitar: The Lincoln Center Institute Lectures on aesthetic education*. Teachers College Press.

Greene, M. (2007). *Imagination and the healing arts*. https://maxinegreene.org/uploads/library/imagination_ha.pdf

Greene, M. (2010). Wide-awakeness. In *Encyclopedia of curriculum studies*. Sage Publications.

Guyotte, K. (2018). Aesthetic movements of a social imagination: Refusing stasis and educating relationally/critically/responsibly. *Critical Questions in Education, 9*(1), 62–73. https://files.eric.ed.gov/fulltext/EJ1172312.pdf

Judson, G. (2020). Conceptualizing imagination in the context of school leadership. *International Journal of Leadership in Education*. http://doi.org/10.1080/13603124.2020.1818289

Lakoff, G., & Johnson, M. (1980). *Metaphors we live by*. University of Chicago Press.

Laruccia, M. (2009). From creativity to innovation in organizations. *Inter Science Place, 2*(9). https://mpra.ub.uni-muenchen.de/17918/1/MPRA_paper_17918.pdf

Lincoln, A. (1989). *Abraham Lincoln speeches and writings, 2 1859–1865 (LOA #46)*. Penguin Random House.

Steffensen, K. (2012). *Optimizing innovation in praxis: Imagined possibilities and new realities: Exploring narratives of educational transformation*. (Unpublished Master's Thesis). York University, Toronto. www.researchgate.net/publication/320934154_optimizing_innovation_in_praxis_imagined_possibilities_and_new_realities-exploring_narratives_of_educational_transformation

Strobel, B. (2020). *Pursuing excellence: A values-based, systems approach to help companies*. Productivity Press.

University Health Network. (2008). *Annual report 2007/08*. www.uhn.ca/corporate/AboutUHN/Documents/UHN_AR_2008.pdf#search=2008%20Mission%20Vision%20Purpose

Witherell, C. & Noddings, N. (1991). *Stories lives tell: Narrative and dialogue in education*. Teachers College Press.

Part II

POETICS OF MEMORY

Imagination in Action
A Leadership Story

Parking: The Imaginable (or Unimaginable) Final Frontier

Craig Mah

Do you see your dentist patrolling the parking lot at their office? How about your banker standing outside directing traffic? Leadership programs and district procedures do not address all the situations a principal will encounter at their school. How could they?

A few years ago, parking was an issue at my school. The school has a pick-up/drop-off zone, just like the airport, with "No Parking. Pick Up and Drop Off Only" signs. Parking is scarce and many parents choose to drive to school. Drivers learned that they could arrive 45 minutes early and park in the pick-up zone for their convenience. As time crept closer to 3:00 p.m., other vehicles would arrive but could not enter the pick-up zone. Traffic on the street would begin to back up. Vehicles would be double-parked in the pick-up zone and on the street. Children would run between cars to get to their parents. My school became a dangerous game of Frogger.

Principals should be present at the end of each day to say farewell to their students. Yet I had to shift my supervision from students to cars, putting on my safety vest and directing traffic. Responses from talking with drivers included: "How about one more minute?" or "I didn't know I couldn't park here. Nobody told me." I sent home several very nice, professionally worded emails outlining the expectations for parking. However, the problem continued.

One afternoon, I watched the cars pile into the pick-up zone. The sun glinted off the windshields of the highly polished cars. It looked like the shimmering, iridescent hull of the Starship *Enterprise*.

I thought, "What would Captain Kirk from *Star Trek* do?"

If the parking lot was the Neutral Zone, the invading cars were Klingon battle cruisers, and a peaceful, diplomatic solution was needed (no phasers, please), what would Captain Kirk do?

He would set up a blockade and he would tell the Klingons—he would open a hailing frequency and tell everyone he was setting up a blockade.

But if he did not have subspace communications, he would use email and Twitter.

I sent home an email to parents. The message went something like this:

> The parking situation continues and, unfortunately, I need to restrict access to the pick-up zone beginning Monday. Our "Neutral Zone" is being occupied by Klingons who are not following the rules. Parents arriving early should find legal parking and walk to school. Don't be a Klingon. I will be live tweeting. Tune in if you want to see the action. Over and out.

On Monday afternoon, at 2:00 p.m., I brought out large traffic cones and blocked the entrance to the pick-up zone. I tweeted a photo of the empty pick-up/drop-off zone with the caption, "All clear. The Neutral Zone will open at 2:55 p.m." Parents who lived in the neighborhood walked to school to watch. It had the feeling of a spectator sport. Cars arrived early and circled the street like vultures. At 2:55 p.m., I removed the cones, and traffic flowed in and out. There was no traffic jam.

I kept up this routine for several weeks. I tweeted pictures of vehicles illegally parked. In one picture, a silver Mercedes was parked in front of a fire hydrant. I tweeted a photo of the car with the caption: "The fire hydrant does not have a cloaking device. Please do not park here." A driver did not use their turn signal when trying to turn into the parking lot. My tweet read: "Turn signals are now standard features on cars. Instructions must be in Romulan, not Klingon."

Each day I would tweet a picture of the parking situation. I was careful not to tweet photos of the driver or their license plate. However, photos of their cars were fair game. The tweets and email messages shaped a narrative that began to have an impact. Parents commented on how they found it amusing but also better understood the problem.

The behavior of the drivers began to change, so I eased the blockade. The early bird drivers were following the rules. They, too, laughed at the absurdity of the situation. Within a month, I no longer needed to put out the traffic cones. When an errant driver did park illegally, they were reminded of parking expectations from other parents. By creating a narrative using social media, I could engage the community about this problem without having to fire a single phaser.

CHAPTER 4

A Bridge Across Our Fears
Poetic Imagination as a Catalyst for School Change

Sarah Pazur

When I was a high school principal, I often turned to poetry to soothe and inspire me. During my most difficult days in leadership, when the system felt unimaginative and hopeless, I listened to Mary Oliver (1986) read her poem "Wild Geese." The poem permitted me to accept imperfection—*You do not have to be good*—and shunt despair—*Whoever you are, no matter how lonely / the world offers itself to your imagination.* When the poem ended, I felt activated, empowered.

Leadership relies on language to protest, imagine, and accomplish change. Many leadership models address the importance of creative language, like storytelling, to evoke emotions and move stakeholders to action (Chapman, 2006; Conrad, 2016; Deal & Peterson, 2013). An example of this can be seen through the use of poetry, which shares, with myth and fable, the "strategy of building story around human experience, as a means of explaining that experience, or attempting to, and as a means of (sometimes) offering instruction regarding that experience" (Phillips, 2004, p. 11). Poetic language helped me process and move past my own fears and insecurities as a leader. Poems also unlocked my imagination so I could see other possibilities. On those days when I faced existential crises and questioned my effectiveness, Mary Oliver's poetry would remind me of my purpose. Leaders who adopt a poetic practice can leverage the power of poetic imagination in order to subvert the dominant discourse and accomplish real transformation in their organizations.

This chapter will explore the role of poetic imagination in educational leadership; specifically, I will outline the ways in which poetic imagination and poetics (the theory of techniques in language) can challenge the boundaries of new institutionalism. I will place poetry in conversation with institutional theory to see how school leaders may institute a poetic practice to accomplish lasting—and legitimate—change.

WHY POETRY NOW?

Language is a critical force in educational discourse because while it can be used to inspire, it is also used to manufacture fictive crises or exploit actual crises to stifle imagination and stall innovation. These crisis narratives instill institutional fear, forcing leaders to employ familiar, "safe" responses that have been deemed legitimate, evidence-based solutions. This infinite crisis-intervention response becomes an ouroboros, an endless cycle that few school leaders can escape.

While on the surface, crises such as the COVID-19 pandemic have presented school leaders with an opportunity to exercise imagination, the traditions of new institutionalism press down and close in, leaving leaders thinking that there is no other way but to resort to the status quo. New institutionalism, discussed in more detail later in the chapter, is the notion that organizations must "bend to values and other cultural expectations in order to achieve legitimacy" (Marion & Gonzales, 2014, p. 321). Put plainly, crisis narratives reinforce the need for "trusted" interventions instead of imaginative solutions. The empowered principal needs poetry to resist the rhetoric of fear and guilt driving such narratives.

In her essay "Poetry Is Not a Luxury," Audre Lorde (1977/2020) says, "Poetry is not only dream and vision; it is the skeleton architecture of our lives. It lays the foundations for a future of change, a bridge across our fears of what has never been done before" (p. 5). Lorde's words resonate at this particular moment in history. Post-COVID, K–12 leaders will face pressure to "re-legitimize" schools using familiar norms and structures. They will be called to preserve enduring mythologies about the institution of school. It feels especially urgent, then, for leaders to summon the power of poetry to imagine educational reform.

AN IMAGINATION PRIMER

> If the painter presents us with a field or a vase of flowers, his paintings are windows which are open on the whole world. We follow the red path which is buried among the wheat much farther than van Gogh has painted it, among other wheat fields, under the clouds, to the river which empties into

the sea, and we extend to infinity, to the other end of the world, the deep finality which supports the existence of the field and the earth.

—Jean-Paul Sartre (1948), *Literature and Existentialism*

In her seminal work, *Releasing the Imagination: Essays on Education, the Arts and Social Change,* Maxine Greene (1995) argues that "of all our cognitive capacities, imagination is the one that permits us to give credence to alternative realities" (p. 3). Imagination makes it possible for educators to break free from prescribed, often taken-for-granted systems and boundaries. As mentioned earlier in this book, Greene argues that social imagination, specifically, is the capacity to invent visions of what *should* be in our society; social imagination helps us respond to the cultural or institutional deficits we encounter.

However, imagination is complex. It is often mentioned alongside creativity, yet these concepts are not the same; imagination *fuels* creativity (Asma, 2017; Judson, 2020; Liu & Noppe-Brandon, 2009). The fact that we all have imaginations does not automatically mean we feel compelled or encouraged to exercise them in new or novel ways. Educational leaders, especially, feel pressure to imitate "successful" schools, to employ what they are led to believe are tried-and-true methods. Therefore, while imagination plays a role in conceiving change, it does not always revolutionize our actions.

Imagination's elusiveness also makes it difficult to cultivate and put into practice. Many artists, philosophers, psychologists, and scholars have attempted to define imagination, and there is a long lineage of literature about it. Imagination has been defined in the Introduction to this text, but there are several entry points into the conversation. For example, Mary Warnock's (1978) book, *Imagination,* supplies educators with a deep understanding of imagination's origins, its relationship to education, and finally a critical launch point for thinking about poetic imagination, which I discuss in the next section.

Warnock traces her concept of imagination to philosopher David Hume's *Treatise of Human Nature,* though she emphasizes that he was not necessarily the "inventor" of imagination. For Hume, everything we perceive in our mind's eye, our knowledge of the world, is derived from impressions. These acts of perception allow us to think about things in their absence. Warnock describes Hume's concept of imagination as empirical imagination, meaning it relies on prior knowledge, sensory experiences, and images of things to help us conceptualize something when it is not in front of us. As we perceive or experience things, we also associate them with feelings and make copies of these experiences in our psyches and, according to Hume, use imagination to draw upon them in order to process future encounters.

Philosopher Immanuel Kant built on Hume's theory of imagination, but ultimately departed from Hume's notion that our minds passively receive impressions. Warnock says Kant describes the imagination as a "mysterious faculty which enables us to go beyond the immediate object of sense, and recognize it as a member of objects . . . which we can form for ourselves in our minds" (Warnock, 1978, p. 33). In this way, we have some agency in making meaning of the phenomena in front of us as more than just replicas of what is, but also visions of what could be, blueprints for something else.

Both Hume and Kant mostly shared the opinion that imagination is analogical, that whether passive or active, we perceive and construct images based on schemata we have built over time. However, these philosophers also acknowledged that the imagination perceives the absent past, the absent future, *and* the absent-as-nonexistent. Warnock turned to Jean-Paul Sartre to explain the "absent-as-nonexistent."

In order to imagine something that is absent and nonexistent, we must be able to "detach ourselves from our actual situation, and envisage situations which are non-actual" (Warnock, 1978, p. 197). For example, if we look at a painting, we may conceive of it as a portrait, but in reality, it is an assemblage of canvas and paint. We suspend the literal interpretation of what we see (the canvas, oil paint) and imagine that it is an image of a person. Warnock (1978) believed we all have this ability to construct something new despite the reality we see:

> There is in all human beings a capacity to go beyond what is immediately in front of their noses. Indeed, there is an absolute necessity for them to do so. That they are able to use language is sufficient proof of this, since to speak in truisms, that we describe things and classify them entails that we look beyond the immediately present, by relating the present to the past and future, to what we have experienced before and expect to experience again. (p. 201)

Language playing a critical role in imagination means that even in everyday speech we use imaginative functions to relay information to others to form images that help us communicate what we picture in our minds. Imagination's reliance on image and language makes poetry a prescient device to foresee the "absent-as-nonexistent" in the future of education. The absent-as-nonexistent encompasses the things that public school reformers may have dreamed about but have not been able to adopt due to institutional barriers. Absent-as-nonexistent interventions could include eradicating high-stakes testing, decentralizing the school campus, disrupting prescriptive age and grade-level progressions, and eliminating sorting and ranking mechanisms. Or they could be improvisations educators have yet to imagine.

Warnock (1978) elaborated on how our imaginations work, showing the way they function to form and communicate perceptions about our reality and what might be missing from reality:

> There is a power in the human mind, which is at work in our everyday perception of the world, and is also at work in our thoughts about what is absent; which enables us to see the world, whether present or absent, as significant, and also to present this vision to others for them to share or reject. (p. 196)

Warnock reminds us that our imaginations are at work every day; they point out what is lacking, and therefore, what is possible. We live in our minds and therefore our imaginations, so it can be easy to take imagination for granted. For this reason, school leaders must be mindful of the inner workings of imagination and how they can maximize its faculties. Understanding the evolution of the concept of imagination serves as a basis to explore poetic imagination.

POETIC IMAGINATION AND POETICS

Reading or writing poetry creates a special type of imaginative thinking that "reflects the competence to inextricably intertwine all types and forms of images with the philosophical, phenomenological, psychological, and artistic threads of the imagination" (Zalipour, 2011, p. 491). Poetry's ability to generate this type of complex and highly synthesized mode of imaginative thinking warrants a deeper look.

Poetic imagination relates to the creative dimension of imagination. It does not rely on the senses or manipulable objects in the same way that other forms of imagination do; rather, it deviates from reality in ordinary language and vision, and moves toward a renewed reality (Zalipour, 2011). Put differently, when we read or listen to a poem, we are interpreting an unconventional arrangement of words and images that stimulate a specific type of imaginative reading, leading us toward new ways of thinking about everyday experiences and challenges. When we speak of image in conjunction with poetry, we are not merely referring to pictures conveyed with words, but the poems themselves concoct an image on the page that is transposed in the reader's mind.

When reading poetry, educational leaders both literally and figuratively become visionaries. They must consider the shape of the language on the page in concert with the denotations and connotations of that language. The shape of the poem itself becomes a vision, the reader of the poem, a visionary. Consequently, poetic imagination has exciting practical implications for educational leadership, which I explore later in a section on praxis.

Poetic imagination draws on the fullness of language to seek a changed vision of personal and political reality or historical understanding. It is "an effort of hope" (Chapman, 2007, p. 15). We know that transformational leaders have to think imaginatively in order to create these visions (Curtis & Cerni, 2015). Poetry uses language and typographical shape to stimulate the type of imaginative thinking that can lead to new ideas and understandings, to organizational transformation. The challenge for leaders, then, is to be willing to engage with poetry, to pursue this "effort of hope," that can seem intimidating, mysterious, and even frivolous.

In his collection of essays *The Necessary Angel*, Wallace Stevens (1942) said, "We do not hesitate in poetry to yield ourselves to the unreal, when it is possible to yield ourselves" (p. 4). Sometimes our minds put up barriers that keep us from taking a risk or imagining a different solution. Institutionalism, which I explore in detail later in the chapter, makes it difficult for educational leaders to imagine different solutions. However, if leaders accept that poetry can help them yield to the unreal, and they engage in reading poetry, they are a step closer to enacting imaginative solutions.

We may also reject reading poetry as a means to enacting imaginative solutions because we are taught it is romantic and impractical. It often is dismissed as a trivial endeavor, perhaps enjoyable, but not necessary. The paradox of poetry is that (like the arts in general) society appreciates it but disinvests in it, mainly because its impact is difficult to quantify. Poetry's perceived ethereal nature invites skeptics, which makes poetry difficult to use in professions that want a "self-contained set of mathematical axioms" (Liu & Noppe-Brandon, 2009, p. 200). Consequently, poetry has not been able to penetrate educational leadership's data-obsessed landscape.

Society also manufactures the illusion that literature is subversive, that it should be feared or censored. Nussbaum (1995) argued that our culture's attempts to suppress and ban literature prove that literature possesses tremendous influence. As Stevens (1942) said, "No politician can command the imagination, directing it to do this or that" (p. 28). Imagination's uncontrollable nature is inspiring for some and fear-provoking for others. Perhaps society has cultivated poetry's romantic reputation to undermine its strength, to stave off the possibility that poetry could change the world.

In poetry, the tools and techniques of the imagination can be thought of as *poetics*. In her book *The Language of Inquiry*, Lyn Hejinian (2000) argues that poetics is both a theory of techniques in language *and* an attentiveness to the political and ethical dimensions of language. In other words, poetics assumes involvement in public life, public discourse. Education is a part of public discourse and, therefore, generates its own poetics, as the next section describes.

In "Understanding Leadership Through Poetics of Leadership: Searching for Personal Meaning and Authentic Understanding," Jenlink (2015) discusses the way poetics "illuminate the experiences of learning to lead within the social and political contexts of education" (p. 3). Jenlink argues that leaders who engage with poetry cultivate a poetics of leadership that helps them develop imaginative, ethical, and moral frameworks for leading. As explored in the next section, the social and political contexts of leadership are what perpetuate institutionalism; poetics, then, becomes important for its subversive and luminary effects. Poetics as a technique of the imagination can reveal what is "absent and present" in school systems, as Warnock says.

INSTITUTIONALISM AND SCHOOLS

The poem must, on whatever scale, dislodge assumption, not by simply opposing it, but by dismantling the systemic proof in which its inevitably is grounded. In other words: not "C is wrong" but "who says A has to lead to B?"

—Louise Glück (1994), *The Best American Poetry 1993*

To understand poetry's potential, it is critical to understand the institutional obstacles it faces in education. The enduring mythologies about school can prevent leaders from exercising the kind of imaginative thinking that could change their organizational ecosystem. Institutional theory describes how these mythologies influence leadership decisions. Institutional theory is the notion that fads and cultural assumptions drive organizational decisions more than the organization's goals. Philip Selznick, a seminal institutional theorist, defines institutionalism as the emergence of orderly, stable, socially integrating patterns out of unstable, loosely organized, or narrowly technical activities (Broom &

Selznick, 1955; Selznick, 1996). Selznick is attributed with developing "old institutionalism," which is the idea that organizations are defined by the tensions between their stated goals and nonrational constituents. For instance, while schools are organizations whose purpose is to educate students, they regularly contend with outside, sometimes competing, pressures that undermine their purpose.

Nonrational pressures reflect the values and ideologies of outside constituents, which may not directly serve the school's ultimate goal(s). Schools have to reconcile these expectations. For example, high schools in the United States experience a great deal of pressure to have robust Class A sports programs. According to institutionalism, the demand for athletic programs (even though these programs may be noble and aligned with cultural values) wrestles for attention and resources and can erode the purpose of schooling. Old institutionalism argues that organizations adapt their operations in relationship to these pressures.

"New Institutionalism" builds on this theory and emphasizes that organizations do not simply make a choice whether or not to adapt to cultural values, but that cultural values carry the enormous weight of legitimacy, making them nearly impossible to ignore. These nonrational constituents are the hallmarks that "accredit" schools or legitimize them in the eyes of stakeholders. Schools subscribe to them to achieve acclaim and prestige, or they will perish. In the example of sports, districts that choose not to implement sports programs risk lower student enrollment, which in turn leads to fewer resources to accomplish academic goals.

In other words, certain programmatic components have become so ingrained into school culture that they are difficult to disentangle from the school itself. In their groundbreaking paper, "Institutionalized Organizations: Formal Structure as Myth and Ceremony," John Meyer and Brian Rowan (1977) explain further:

> Many of the positions, policies, programs, and procedures of modern organizations are enforced by public opinion, by the views of important constituents, by knowledge legitimated through the educational system, by social prestige, by the laws, and by the definitions of negligence and prudence used by the courts. Such elements of formal structure are manifestations of powerful institutional rules, which function as highly rationalized myths that are binding on particular organizations. (p. 343)

These myths impose themselves on school leaders both consciously and unconsciously and act as barriers or obstacles, making it difficult for leaders to imagine and execute different responses. Public services like education, whose purposes are cultural rather than economic, are especially susceptible to these pressures.

The crisis narratives in K–12 education are also a response to institutionalism's cultural scripts and largely accepted myths that have persisted over time. These scripts define appropriate and legitimate behaviors in the field. Educational crises do not have to be devastating events; crises are also those low-level, omnipresent deficiencies that simmer below the surface. "School improvement" is one of these institutional markers embedded into the fabric of American schools, so entrenched that school leaders hardly question its existence in guiding their every move. By default, districts must complete a yearly school improvement plan. School improvement plans situate schools within a perpetual state of remediation. When schools struggle to meet the expectations of these plans (scripts), they turn to "evidence-based" strategies to solve their so-called shortcomings. These strategies reflect the institutionalism from which they were born. They are tautologous, only "measurable" because in the past they have been measured. Therefore, crisis-intervention responses inevitably lead to isomorphism—schools looking, acting, sounding, and responding the same.

School leaders who manipulate the system within institutionalism's rules can only make minor changes to educational outcomes. Fundamental change requires the design of new systems (Ogawa, 2015). Of course, designing new systems is easier said than done. It requires both seeing what is in front of our eyes but also what is absent and nonexistent. Imagine a world where the nonrational pressures included expectations that every child travel and study abroad, participate in arts and poetry programming, or design and execute global and community service projects. How different would school look and feel then? Poetry is one way educational leaders can unfetter themselves from institutional thinking and "create the imaginative space wherein democratic possibilities become reality when reality is transformed by the liberation of the mind" (Jenlink, 2015, p. 24). A poetic practice can help leaders disrupt nonrational thinking routines and amend routines that have failed to serve our students and educators.

THE POSSIBILITIES OF A POETIC PRACTICE

In our schools, we are told that our education is pragmatic, that the body of knowledge is divided into various "subjects," that all of these subjects on which we pour our youth are valuable and useful to us later in life. We are told that our civilization depends on further and new uses for everything it has, the development and exploitation of these. We may go ahead and specialize in any of these usable fields. Except for one. There is one kind of knowledge that will be given us all through school and high school which we are told is precious, it defies time, it strikes deep into memory, it must go on being taught . . . This is here to be passed on. But not to be used . . . This is what we learn about poetry.

—Muriel Rukeyser (1949), *The Life of Poetry*

So what exactly does a poetic practice for educational leaders look like? Reading and interpreting poetry demands a particular way of thinking that is beneficial in addressing economic, social, and political complexities (Morgan et al., 2010). I once heard someone describe a theoretical framework as being "good to think with," and I consider poetry to be similar, although I might add that it is good to feel with, too. When you read a poem, you engage in life's deepest questions about what it means to be human; you consider specific moral or ethical dilemmas; you gain empathy for others. However, the exhilarating (frustrating?) thing about poetry is that it does not provide answers to these mysteries. Instead, poems rouse your imagination and emotions—so much so that you can physically feel them. A shiver down your spine. A lump in your throat. A sinking sensation in your stomach.

Poetry, and other art forms, uniquely generate intellectual and physical experiences. The sensations we feel when a particular poem or piece of art resonates deeply within us are profound. However, poetry can transcend its characterization as awe-provoking and move into territories of action, change, and social justice (Vaquer, 2016). Leaders who frequently engage in the visceral experience of reading poetry to help them look to possibilities, who imagine from within that heightened emotional or physical state, are inhabiting a different conceptual space than the typical isomorphic, "data-driven" or "evidence-based" space from which most education leaders are expected to problem-solve.

Morgan et al. (2010) argue that these conceptual spaces are different because they "are associative rather than causal, imaginative rather than deductive, offer new ways of assessing relations between things, and encourage a radical skepticism of the nature of fact" (p. 23). Collectively, these characteristics have profound implications for educational leaders who have been pressured to think of leadership decisions as choosing from a menu of preordained interventions or responses to student learning and achievement or teaching practice. When leaders engage their poetic imaginations and are encouraged to question "facts" (i.e., institutional scripts), a host of possibilities reveal themselves. Leaders who succumb to these spaces can begin to ask, *why not?*

Curtis et al. (2017) found that imagination is positively correlated with transformational leadership, but they argue that imagination has to be nurtured and developed. A poetic practice creates the conditions for leaders to examine personal and professional experiences in a creative way, leading to imaginative moments "through which they could move beyond the realities of a world as it was or had been experienced" (Jenlink, 2015, p. 24). Reading, writing, and reciting poetry can foster and improve imaginative thinking. As discussed in the next section, adopting a consistent poetic practice can nurture and develop imagination over time and inoculate leaders against institutionalism's isomorphic traps.

POETRY AS LEADERSHIP PRAXIS

> When power leads men towards arrogance, poetry reminds him of his limitations. When power narrows the areas of man's concern, poetry reminds him of the richness and diversity of his experience. When power corrupts, poetry cleanses. For art establishes the basic human truth which must serve as the touchstone of our judgment.
>
> —John F. Kennedy (1963)

Poetic practice in leadership is not a five-step program, a prescriptive formula, or a catchy acronym. It is both limitless and meticulous. It is open-minded, but equally demanding in that the ideas must yield improvements. Hejinian (2000) says it best: "To be simultaneously permissive and rigorous is the challenging task that a highly functional community must attempt. A community that can manage it will be an improvement to the world that is always with us" (p. 35). Educational leaders must approach their poetic practice as Hejinian suggests: unrestricted, yet doggedly attentive to poetry's imaginative gifts. In this way, leaders can begin to dissolve some of the organizational structures that perpetuate institutional myths and scripts.

Like Hejinian, Greene (1995) perceived the arts as something rigorous. She warned against the tendency to consider poetry frivolous and romantic, something to balance out learning that is more "serious." Herein lies the challenge with prescribing poetry as a leadership development tool: It is as equally serious and rigorous a practice as it is amorphous and open-ended. It is scalable in that anyone can access and read poetry, but it is a highly personalized experience that, by its very nature, cannot be measured or described using institutional language or tools. Therefore, it can easily be discounted.

However, as argued in this chapter, when an educational leader with systemic influence experiences the intellectual and physical nature of poetry, they accept the invitation to imagine something beyond reality (i.e., the absent and nonexistent), and *act* upon it, thus attempting to bring new possibilities into reality; that is how they break through institutional barriers. Praxis, then, is part poetry and part courage.

Obviously, solutions that are absent and nonexistent are difficult to ground in praxis because they have yet to be imagined. So, in many ways, a poetic practice for school leaders is simple: read poems and surrender to the experience. But do not be fooled—this seemingly "simple" practice can culminate in transformational experience. As Liu and Noppe-Brandon (2009) point out about imagination, "routinizing imagination is not only the work of heroes—the geniuses, the luminaries, the elect. The work belongs to every one of us. Nor can this work only come in crisis. It must come every day" (p. 10). In an interview at the State University of New York College at Brockport, poet Li-Young Lee shared the same sentiment. He meditated on the way poetry was part of everyday life growing up, how his parents made it part of everyday conversations:

> Now listen to this, and [my mother] would speak a very moving poem—that to me was very important. I could see that poetry wasn't something we talked loftily about, but something you spoke while cutting vegetables with your child. And of course my father being a minister I had the King James Bible read to me and I read it myself; and I *heard* it read from the pulpit. When I witnessed that, I felt it was a great feeling of power. For me, poetry is both of those things: that power and yet some mundane—in the best sense—some mundane thing we do. (as cited in Heyen & Rubin, 1987/2006, pp. 18–19)

Lee's characterization of poetic practice, that it can be powerful and mystical yet wholly integrated into the mundaneness of our lives, is a useful description of poetics in educational leadership. To achieve this balance, leaders will have to be intentional about creating space for poetry so it can become, in the best sense, "some mundane thing we do." In the following section, I offer ideas for making time for poetic practice. These practices include seeking out poetry, sharing poetry with people in school communities, and keeping a poetry journal.

Seek Out Poetry

Leaders should return to poems that have moved them over the years. What poems have caused those hair-raising moments? Which ones have caused that audible reflex people have after they hear an especially moving poem, that deep guttural sigh, "uhhhhh," as if they had been holding their breath the whole time the poet read? Find *those* poems. Keep them close in a notebook, on a computer desktop, framed on a desk. Read them in the morning before school, before a staff meeting, before a difficult staff conversation, or after an especially difficult day.

Leaders should also listen to the poet read the poem in their own voice. Many poets have cultivated a theatrical reading voice. Hearing authors read their poems this way can be meditative and increase the intensity of the imaginative experience. I often search YouTube videos of my favorite poets and listen to poems before I go to sleep at night to help me process the day and bring perspective to the leadership challenges I am having.

Educational leaders should also explore the work of new and contemporary poets, not just the classics. An easy way to discover new work is to attend local poetry readings. These local poets are documenting the experiences of that leader's specific community, which can be helpful for understanding the needs and experiences of students who live in that community, too. Place-based poems can allow school leaders to understand on a deeper level the communities where their students live and learn. School and community are reconfigured, then, as not just shared geographical spaces but also as intimate (re)imagined spaces.

I once had the pleasure of hearing local poet Jamaal May (2016) read his work. At the time, I was a teacher in Detroit. His poem "There Are Birds Here," dedicated to the city, challenges the racist narrative that Detroit is a dangerous and unpleasant place, *And no / his neighborhood is not like a war zone*. May's poem was a tribute to the misunderstood, misrepresented place he grew up in. He calls out the way outsiders characterize Detroit, the way the children there may be pitied, feared, or cast off and the damage that this narrative can do to students' feelings of self-worth.

> *but they won't stop saying*
> *how lovely the ruins,*
> *how ruined the lovely*
> *children must be in that birdless city.*

So often school leaders reside outside of the communities in which they work. A poem like "There Are Birds Here" contains tremendous force for someone who, like me, is not subject to the racism inflicted on Black children from Detroit. May's poem leveraged poetic imagination to unlock social awareness and empathy. He challenged the harmful stories that others repeat as fact. This poem possesses incredible strength, the rebuttal for "You teach *there?*" Yes, and there are birds.

Introduce Poetry to Students, Staff, and Stakeholders

Leaders who tap into the collective, poetic imagination have an opportunity to spark different human interactions within their organizations. Martha Nussbaum (1995) describes the literary imagination as a public imagination, "an imagination that will steer judges in their judging, legislators in their legislating, [and] policy makers in measuring the quality of life of people near and far" (p. 3). Nussbaum riffs on Shelley, who famously said poets are the unacknowledged legislators of the world.

Leaders can trigger their colleagues' and students' imaginations by reading and discussing poems together at the beginning of meetings or assemblies; this can prompt new ideas and solutions that may have otherwise remained unexplored. They may choose to frame discussions about the school's vision, mission, and values through a particular poem that embodies these aspirations.

Imagine if a school leader in Detroit required their staff members to read "There Are Birds Here." What assumptions could the poem challenge? What changes might happen as a result? Leaders need to create a discourse community for discussing and interpreting poems in order to nurture the ideas and inspiration that spring up from poetry. Just as learning is a social act, so is reading and interpreting poetry.

Part of leading and working within an organization inevitably means resolving conflicts. Leaders may even choose to use poetry with students who are experiencing a conflict with one another. Having two students read a poem together and discuss it could bring down their defenses to more easily resolve the dispute and empathize with each other. The idea of using poetry for conflict resolution is a promising research topic with links to restorative practices, and it deserves further exploration.

Keep a Poetry Journal

Finally, leaders should maintain a physical record of their poetic inspirations and wonderings. Greene (1995) reminds us that aesthetic experiences such as reading poetry require our conscious participation in order for them to have an impact on our thoughts and actions. Much like forming a discourse community with whom leaders discuss poetry, leaders should consider keeping a written journal. As leaders engage in poetic practice, they can record reactions, meditations, and ideas that emerge from reading, listening to, or discussing poetry. A poetry journal could be a simple world processing document that the leader types in when inspiration strikes. The journal could become a running record of ideas that they can return to for brainstorming solutions or new programs.

CONCLUSION

In this chapter, I have presented the argument that poetry activates a specific type of imagination—poetic imagination—that has the potential to interrupt institutional thinking in education. Though it is well documented that poetry brings tremendous value to our lives, and that it can be a force for change, more research must be done to understand the impact of poetry on educational leadership. For now, school leaders can draw incentive from the emerging research.

In Jenlink's (2015) study, participants noted that poetics provided them a space for examining theory and practice and making connections that "heretofore had not existed" (p. 24). In her conceptual scholarship, Chapman (2006) makes the case that poetics is a key ingredient in servant leadership. She argues that servant leaders "often rely on the poet's figurative language ability to project a sense of vision and moral imagination, to speak and write in depth of a fresh approach, or to propose an altered path" (Chapman, 2006, p. 381). Finally, educational leaders can turn to Morgan (2010) for insight on how reading and discussing poetry together helped business leaders find meaning and inspiration in ambiguity, increase interpersonal understanding and empathy, and exercise analytical thinking.

Though influential, poetry remains mysterious. Poet and critic T. S. Eliot (1943) described poetry's reverberations across society in this way: "The influence of poetry, at the furthest periphery, is of course very diffused, very indirect, and very difficult to prove . . . it does, in proportion to its excellence and vigor, affect the speech and the sensibility of the whole nation" (p. 12). Eliot reminds us that despite its potency and reach, poetry is incredibly elusive and difficult to measure. Limited empirical evidence makes adopting a poetic practice a radical proposition for educational reform. The institutional traditions in education lead us (and sometimes force us) to believe that there is a prescribed set of responses and interventions we must employ to legitimately achieve quantifiable results. Liu and Noppe-Brandon (2009) describe these institutional arrangements as self-reinforcing; they are not necessarily failures of will, but rather they reflect an absence of imagination.

Lorde (1977/2020) highlights for us what is at risk if we dismiss poetry and poetic imagination as a luxury instead of lifeblood:

> In the forefront of our move toward change, there is only poetry to hint at possibility made real. Our poems formulate the implications of ourselves, what we feel within and dare make real (or bring action into accordance with), our fears, our hopes, our most cherished terrors. (p. 6)

Lorde encapsulates in equal proportion what educational leaders who stand at the precipice of change can gain from poetry: insight, inspiration, and resolve. Poetry, then, can be the acclivity we travel to reach more imaginative solutions for education's shortcomings and isomorphism. And when it is time to leap, poetry can be the bridge across our fears.

CULTIVATING CURIOSITY, CONVERSATION, AND IMAGINATION

After reading this chapter, what evokes your sense of wonder? What are you curious about?

For Consideration and Conversation

What is an example of a "crisis narrative" in your professional community? How could poetic imagination be employed to reframe this narrative? Once reframed, how can poetic imagination support actual change in your community?

How has language inspired, enhanced, and catalyzed your ability and desire to lead through school and system changes? How has language allowed you to garner greater success for all within the community? How might poetic language express what you imagine, dream, or wish could be unleashed in learning and education?

Cultivate Imagination With Cognitive Tools

Affective Mental Imagery

In this chapter, Pazur's use of poetry is an example of affective mental imagery: the words evoke images in our minds and somatic responses in our bodies. What affective mental image captures the emotional significance of a "crisis narrative" in your organization? How can you use words to create an alternative image for a different narrative? (Hint: Consider Pazur's use of the poem "There Are Birds Here" by Jamaal May.)

REFERENCES

Asma, S. T. (2017). *The evolution of imagination.* University of Chicago Press.

Broom, L., & Selznick, P. (1955). *Sociology: A text with adapted readings.* Row, Peterson and Co.

Chapman, N. (2006). A poetics of servant-leadership. *The International Journal of Servant-Leadership, 2*(1), 377–398.

Chapman, N. (2007). Vision and poetry. *The International Journal of Servant-Leadership, 3*(1), 15–16.

Conrad, D. (2016). Inspire innovation by telling stories. *Journal of Leadership Studies, 10*(1), 44–45. https://doi.org/10.1002/jls.21440

Curtis, G., & Cerni, T. (2015). For leaders to be transformational, they must think imaginatively. *Journal of Leadership Studies, 9*(3), 45–47. https://doi.org/10.1002/jls.21401

Curtis, G., King, G., & Russ, A. (2017). Reexamining the relationship between thinking styles and transformational leadership: What is the contribution of imagination and emotionality? *Journal of Leadership Studies, 11*(2), 8–21. https://doi.org/10.1002/jls.21508

Deal, T., & Peterson, K. (2013). Eight roles of symbolic leaders. In M. Grogan (Ed.), *The Jossey-Bass reader on educational leadership* (pp. 274–286) Jossey-Bass.

Eliot, T. S. (1943). *On poetry and poets.* Farrar, Straus and Giroux.

Glück, L. (1994). Introduction. *The best American poetry 1993.* The Ecco Press.

Greene, M. (1995). *Releasing the imagination: Essays on education, the arts, and social change.* Jossey-Bass.

Hejinian, L. (2000). *The language of inquiry.* University of California Press.

Heyen, W., & Rubin, S. (1987/2006). Seeing the power of poetry. In E. Ingersol (Ed.), *Breaking the alabaster jar: Conversations with Li-Young Lee.* BOA Editions, Ltd.

Jenlink, P. (2015). Understanding leadership through poetics of leadership: Searching for personal meaning and authentic understanding. *Education Leadership Review of Doctoral Research, 2*(2), 1–34.

Judson, G. (2020). Conceptualizing imagination in the context of school leadership. *International Journal of Leadership in Education,* 1–13. https://doi.org/10.1080/13603124.2020.1818289

Kennedy, J. (1963, October 26). *President John F. Kennedy: Remarks at Amherst College.* https://www.jfklibrary.org/asset-viewer/archives/JFKWHA/1963/JFKWHA-234-003/JFKWHA-234-003

Liu, E., & Noppe-Brandon, S. (2009). *Imagination first: Unlocking the power of possibility.* Jossey-Bass.

Lorde, A. (1977/2020). Poetry is not a luxury. In R. Gay (Ed.), *The selected works of Audre Lorde* (pp. 3–7). W. W. Norton & Company.

Marion, R., & Gonzales, L. (2014). *Leadership in education: Organizational theory for the practitioner.* Waveland Press, Inc.

May, J. (2016). There are birds here. *The big book of exit strategies*. Alice James Books.

Meyer, J., & Rowan, B. (1977). Institutionalized organizations: Formal structure as myth and ceremony. *The American Journal of Sociology, 83*(2), 340–363. https://doi.org/10.1086/226550

Morgan, C., Lange, K., & Buswick, T. (2010). *What poetry brings to business*. University of Michigan Press.

Nussbaum, M. (1995). *Poetic justice: The literary imagination and public life*. Beacon Press.

Ogawa, R. (2015). Change of mind. *Journal of Educational Administration, 53*(6), 794–804. https://doi.org/10.1108/JEA-06-2014-0064

Oliver, M. (1986). Wild geese. *Dream work*. Atlantic Monthly Press.

Phillips, C. (2004). Myth and fable: Their place in poetry. *Coin of the realm*. Graywolf Press.

Rukeyser, M. (1949). *The life of poetry*. Morrow Paperback Editions.

Sartre, J. (1948). *Literature and existentialism*. Citadel Press.

Selznick, P. (1996). Institutionalism "old" and "new." *Administrative Science Quarterly, 41*(2), 270–277. https://doi.org/10.2307/2393719

Stevens, W. (1942). *The necessary angel: Essays on reality and the imagination*. Vintage Books.

Vaquer, M. (2016). *Poetics of curriculum, poetics of life: An exploration of poetry in the context of selves, schools, and society*. Brill.

Warnock, M. (1978). *Imagination*. University of California Press.

Zalipour, A. (2011). From poetic imagination to imaging: Contemporary notions of poetic imagination in poetry. *Rupkatha Journal on Interdisciplinary Studies in Humanities, 3*(4), 481–494.

CHAPTER 5

Education Policy
Imagination, Creation, and Innovation

Dan Laitsch and Gillian Judson

In "Cultivating Leadership Imagination With Cognitive Tools: An Imagination-Focused Approach to Leadership Education," Judson (2021) uses metaphor and vivid imagery to conceptualize imagination as the soil from which educational leadership grows and thrives. This chapter uses the same strategy to explore the role of imagination in educational policy. Cognitive tools, like metaphor and vivid mental imagery, are used within Imaginative Education (Egan, 1997, 2005) to stimulate learning. We use those cognitive tools in this chapter to help us better understand key aspects of the education policy cycle: context/initiation, formulation, adoption, implementation, and evaluation (McKenzie & Wharf, 2016). We also add a sixth stage, continuation, which looks at responding to the results of the evaluation stage. By understanding the cycle, educational leaders can better engage with the policies that interact with their practice and seek to improve the teaching and learning experience.

A CRISIS OF IMAGINATION IN EDUCATION POLICY

Education plays a powerful role in the lives of people globally. It is the system that brings together national cultures, creates the framework for our values and beliefs, and provides the foundation for our understanding of how the world around us functions. It offers us access to a healthy life and personal well-being. It has been sold as a tool of social mobility and personal empowerment, as well as cultural change and societal improvement (McDonnell et al., 2000; View et al., 2013). In short, there is a lot resting on high-quality education systems—at the individual level (How will I grow as a person?), at the communal level (How will we function as a community/society?), and at the national level (What does it mean to be a good citizen?). As a result, education has taken on a political importance; understanding of policy in general, and education policy specifically, is crucial as educational leaders seek to maintain control of their practice.

Policymakers have a long and fraught history with policy in education (Daviter, 2015; Elmore & Camilli, 2008; Weiss et al., 2008). Over many years, they have tried to address the challenges they see schools facing, and yet much of that work has resulted in only minimal change in schools (Weiss et al., 2008). Every teacher has their own story regarding the reform of the day and its ultimate failure. From the reading wars to the math wars (and everything in between), policymakers and teachers have seen reforms come and go. This perceived lack of progress has frustrated policymakers, who increasingly want to know "what works" before investing in it. And this demand for certainty has led to calls for rigorous research-based recommendations for policy (Slavin, 2008). Research, in this view, holds the promise to tell us "what is," and as a result, if we base our reforms in education on "gold standard," experimental, empirical research that tells us "what is," we should finally be able to realize all of the potential identified in our educational aspirations. Except we will not—and indeed, we should not.

The drive for certainty and causation presents a very narrow view of research and a controlling view of policy—one that is focused on a belief in fidelity of implementation and that lacks the flexibility to adjust to local environments (Gorur & Koyama, 2013). This positivist view of policy change assumes consistency across settings, largely ignores contextual variations, and places substantial limits on professional autonomy and expertise. It is this drive for certainty and control that is creating a crisis of imagination in educational policy work.

Imagination always includes some amount of ambiguity because it involves the possible, not the actual (Asma, 2017; Egan, 1997, 2005). That is also the value of imagination in policy—because we must have the ability to envision the possible, otherwise we will just end up reproducing the status quo. The flexibility imagination affords can allow policymakers to react when our understanding of the system changes. Imagination is required to move from an understanding of what is, to *what if* and *what may be* and *what is possible*, to substantively advance positive change. By engaging the imagination, policy activists can use their creativity to push back on the view of research as constraining and controlling rather than flexible and empowering.

Imagination is needed to shift people away from a deficit-specific-problem focus in education policy to envisioning and building systems that *may be*. Judson (2021) makes a strong case for imagination in leadership. Here we make the case that imagination must also become a key part of educational policy and policymaking. Imagination, and the tools of Imaginative Education that support its growth, must move out of the classroom and into the power structures that support, and control, that classroom.

ENGAGING IMAGINATION TO UNDERSTAND POLICY

Judson (2021) uses the metaphor of soil to help readers think about imagination in the context of leadership. Soil (imagination) provides the nutrients and holds the roots of all that might sprout from it. Imagination, like soil, is bound by the resources within it, "just as sunlight, water, and nitrates feed healthy soil, knowledge, emotion and experience feed the imagination" (p. 4). Imagination, like soil, can (and must) be cultivated and developed to support richer growth. Judson describes how imagination can be cultivated to increase its fecundity by using cognitive tools, including stories and metaphor, but also activities like visioning, exploring affective opposites, changing perspective, engaging in what-iffing, investigating revolution, understanding agency, and finding the heroic (Judson, 2021). These activities are *good to think with*; they are *cognitive tools* that support learning by connecting emotion, imagination, and knowledge (Egan, 1997, 2005; Egan & Judson 2015).

In this chapter, we expand the soil-as-imagination metaphor to consider the broader place of imagination in the garden of the policymaking cycle. Policy is generally defined as a principle of action identified by a government or organization and intended to guide behavior to accomplish specific outcomes. Policy can be either *constraining*, in that it limits or incentivizes behavior in particular directions, or it can be *empowering*, in that it gives autonomy to individuals to act towards desired outcomes (McKenzie & Wharf, 2016). Policymaking, then, is generally concerned with the creation of principles of action to guide human ecosystems to achieve a particular vision.

Organizations, like gardens, require care, understanding, and planning to develop. Just as we might plan the plants, water features, and landscape of our gardens, we use policies to guide the growth and development of our organizations. Like an untended garden, policies left to go to seed can leave an organization cluttered, overgrown, and unproductive. Policy environments that are not carefully nurtured and maintained can become confused, with plants intertwined and competing for limited resources to function. Ultimately, it is easier to maintain and support the growth of healthy policies than it is to recover an overgrown garden.

THE POLICY CYCLE AS A GARDENING CYCLE

Healthy gardens do not rise intact from the ground, nor do organizations. Understanding of the local ecology—informed by careful study and research—is critical, as is the ability to imagine what that ecology could look like if properly managed. Careful formulation of a plan is needed, as is finalizing and implementing that plan. As the garden grows, careful evaluation—again informed by study and research—of its status is needed to ensure that it flourishes. Ultimately, the growing seasons move on, and gardeners need to decide what to do with the garden when spring next rolls around, and the cycle begins anew. The same can be said of policy. In fact, each phase of the policy cycle—context and initiation, formulation, adoption, implementation, evaluation, and continuation—parallels a stage in creating a garden. In what follows, we speak to you, the readers, as gardeners—as policy activists—and walk through the phases of gardening and policymaking. We are changing the context and inviting you to experience the policy cycle with your own imagination.

Context and Initiation: Selecting a Site and Exploring Planting Possibilities

One of the first things you will need to do to establish your garden is to find your green space and learn all you can about it, asking questions such as: What is the climate like where you will be growing? What is the soil like, and how is the ground situated? How did your plot get to the current state it is in, and what could it become? Do you have access to the land? Are there approval processes you will need to plant the garden (are there nearby gardens, farms, or wilderness areas to contend with)? What resources are available to invest in the garden? Is there a water source nearby, and if so, do you have access to it? Are there other gardeners working in the area who might work with you (or compete with you) in nurturing your garden? Before you plant your garden, you are getting to know the context of the environment where it is located, the resources available to support it, and potential difficulties that may need to be addressed.

Understanding what is (site selection and exploration) stems from using imagination and is very much about finding the story of the land—this is imagination in action (Judson, 2021). While your knowledge of the local environment will never be complete, the more you know going in, the more likely your imagined garden will begin to thrive. You will also need to be prepared to evolve your understanding of the garden as your knowledge of local environment changes. Having a plan to monitor what is happening in the garden can help you adjust your plans as you go, but also be used at the end of the season to help explore the overall project as you think about and plan for the next growing season.

Similarly, policy activists need to be sensitive to the context of the system in which they are working (or gardening). They need to understand the environment in which they are operating and how that environment was established. Systems, programs, organizations, and people are who and what they are today because of a long history of actions and experiences that form the narrative of the ground in which your policies will take root. The stories being told about policy help shape meaning and lay the foundation for growth and change (Judson, 2021). Without careful attention to this ground and how it was developed, new policies may end up conflicting with old policies, violating institutional norms, or creating conflict between stakeholders. In this initial phase of the cycle, learning about the system is important as policy activists keep track of available resources and stakeholders, and how they might support (or thwart) change. In particular, policy activists need a clear understanding of the policy approval processes in place and the stakeholders involved. In understanding what is and how it came to be, as well as what resources are available, the careful policy analyst can begin to imagine what might be. And, as with understanding of natural ecologies, understanding of human ecologies will never be complete. As a result, ongoing research, monitoring, and flexible design will be important as we tend our policy garden.

Once you have a good sense of your local ecology—the composition of the soil and the limits of the environment—you can begin to determine the right time to start your garden. This is the initiation stage in the cycle. Your ground may lay fallow for some time before you are ready to initiate action. You might look at the plot to determine its readiness and organize your resources to clear the land for planting. You might ask yourself if a garden really is needed and, if so, what type you desire: a flower garden, vegetable garden, meditation garden, or something else. You will want to think about how complex it will be to establish (the diversity of plants each garden type might require) and who is available to help. During this time, imagination will allow you to envision the possibilities of what your garden can become. You will identify and seek to understand the problems you are likely to face (insects, molds, fungi, rain, drought) and how they can be addressed. By understanding your needs for the garden, the problems you will have to address, and the resources available to address them, you will be setting up the framework for a healthy, vibrant green space.

With good knowledge of what is, policy activists can begin to look at the need for change and the complexity of issues to be faced. Who is available to help, and what resources can be brought to bear to make change? As with reflecting on the garden you want, policy activists will be assessing problems to solve, needs of constituents, and resources that can be leveraged to address issues and needs. This is where imagination and the use of cognitive tools to interrogate the context can be uniquely valuable.

One of the strongest critiques of traditional policy change is that it tends to be deficit-based (Davis & Museus, 2019; Dinishak, 2016; Green & Haines, 2012). That is, rather than using policy to create our best imagined futures, policy activists tend to focus on identifying and solving very specific problems. This often results in piecemeal and incremental policy changes—which while easier to implement, may have much less value for stakeholders. These targeted changes may also focus too narrowly on one plant, missing the impact on the rest of the garden. Leveraging cognitive tools to help activists imagine a powerfully different future could have real value in policy change efforts.

Here are some cognitive tools we, as leaders and policymakers, can employ to help cultivate understanding of *what is*:

- Envision (vivid mental imagery): What vivid mental images express what you know and feel about an existing school policy or a new school policy?
- Excavate (binary oppositions): What tensions do you feel in the organization? What biases, perspectives, and/or values does your understanding reflect? What is missing from your understanding of the context?
- Identify patterns/rhythms/processes (identifying patterns): What patterns contribute to the meaning of the experience for different stakeholders in the community? How does everything work together? What or who is left out?
  (Adapted from Judson, 2021)

Formulation: Planning the Garden

Now that we have done the work to understand our plot of land, determined the type of garden we need, and identified the problems we are likely to face, as well as the resources we can bring to bear in getting the work done, it is time to plan! This is both the fun part and the hard part as we decide practically what we need to do to get the garden we imagined. We must question: what plants to put in our garden and where; when to plant them and how; what long-term maintenance will be required; what fertilizing, watering, and nurturing will be needed; whether to use pesticides and herbicides; when we will harvest; and what we will do when the growing season ends. We might map out a number of different gardens to choose from before we decide to move forward and set priorities. This might include cost for plants, time, and effort needed for planting and maintenance, complexity, and return (in the form of vegetables and produce, or less tangibly, beauty and peace).

We will likely consult with the folks who will be helping us, and perhaps even with our neighbors, to make sure the garden meets their needs as well (particularly if we hope to sell our product at the local farmers' market!). Whereas before we were imagining our best possible garden, now we are looking at creatively applying our understanding of the land, environment, biology of our selected plants and their needs, and our resources to bring the imagined to life.

In policymaking, here, too, we are formulating policy alternatives that we might apply to addressing the problems we identified in the initiation stage, or if we were bold, the imagined future we want to achieve. While we have been working with stakeholders all along, we might engage in broader consultations here to ensure that there is support for the policy changes we have imagined and to make sure there are not underlying issues we have missed. By understanding the likely reaction to the potential changes, we can adjust our options to reflect those broader values and maximize the likelihood of successful change. Here, too, we move from the imagined to the practical in trying to creatively balance interests and create viable options for positive change.

Listed below are some cognitive tools we can employ to help cultivate understanding of what *could be*:

- Seek the story (the story form): What is the typical narrative or "story" about the organization (garden)? What other (possibly unusual but effective) narratives might bring to life your imagined garden? *What happens if* we change key parts of the story?
- Make meaningful metaphors (metaphor): What metaphors will help engage emotions and reveal the meaning of the vision for your garden/organization? What do you/we want the culture to resemble? What has never been done? Complete the phrase: Our garden is ____. We want it to be ____.
- Play: Practice "what if-ing" (sense of wonder/playfulness): What do you wonder about the garden/organization? What

do you *wonder if* for it? Use your sense of wonder to create a new ideational space. Set practicalities aside—engage in some *extreme* "what if-ing" about other ways to grow your garden/ organization. What does success look like (are the multiple paths to success)? What questions can you explore in more detail?
- Engage your inner rebel (revolt and idealism): What limitations do you face when dealing with *X* process/policy/issue? Which rules are "breakable"? How does "breaking the rules" support your vision? How can the "rules" be reimagined?

(Adapted from Judson, 2021)

Adoption: Understanding Established Relationships

Now comes the big moment—we have the land, we have done the research, and we have imagined alternatives. We have created a solid plan for moving our garden from vision to reality, and it is time to make a decision—or otherwise known as the adoption phase in the cycle. In this case, it is likely an easy process to complete, as we have been thinking about the garden from a largely individualistic perspective; however, the adoption process might be more complex. If our garden is on strata land, we might need our strata council to approve it. If we are moving into a communal garden space, there may be a committee that approves garden designs. Even if we are just putting it into our backyard, there may be bylaws regulating the types of plants we can have in our yard, and we may want our neighbors' support depending on the plants and spaces we plan to utilize. We still need to be prepared to creatively make the case for our garden to ensure buy-in. If our community balks, we may have to start the process again.

The same is true in the policy realm. When we plan to make policy change, we must address the problems and needs, and the resources available are critical. But even from the beginning we should understand the approval processes needed, whether we are operating inside the system (say as a manager in an organization or as a legislator) or from outside the system (as a policy analyst in a think tank, an employee, or a member of the public). If we are working from within and at the request of the system, adoption will likely be easier, but there can still be bumps in the process. We need to be ready to bring forth our policy options, highlight our recommended preference (based on an analysis of needs, resources, and outcomes), and make a clear case for the specific option we are advancing. As with our plans for the garden, if our stakeholders are not convinced of the need for change, the value of the changes we propose, or the beauty of the garden we have imagined, we may need to step back and start again.

Implementation: Seeding and Growth

The hard work to this point has been learning as much as we can about the ecology of our garden, identifying what we want to plant and how each piece of the garden relates to the other pieces, clearly understanding our goals, and planning how to realize that goal. Now we shift to actually planting our garden and letting it grow. While before much of our work was based in imagination, here we begin to shift to creativity in applying that vision. When we run into problems—and we always will since our knowledge can never be perfect (we may dig into an unexpected layer of clay, find an infestation of grubs beneath the surface, or discover a nearby colony of hungry rabbits)—we have to be prepared to creatively respond to the problem before our garden is badly damaged. As we plant and nurture our garden, we may find that we need to ask for help or add new plants like marigolds to drive away aphids, or shade cloth and irrigation to address an unexpected heat wave and drought. Here, we do not need to envision a different present; rather, we need to understand what is currently happening and respond accordingly.

The same is true as we implement our policy. To this point, we have been trying to envision how the policy will function once in place and help us move toward our vision for the organization. As with the complexity of a garden ecology, we can never achieve perfect knowledge of our human ecologies. We may have missed key stakeholders in our consultations, interpreted existing policy incorrectly, or inadequately trained practitioners in implementation procedures. Our policy communication may be imperfect, allowing for unintended interpretation of terms, or frontline implementers helping us maintain the garden may be overwatering or otherwise adjusting the plan to better meet the goals they perceive as important. A clear understanding of what is happening on the ground is critical to ensure our policy is implemented in a manner that best allows it to achieve the intended purposes (see Table 5.1 for a synoptic description of these policy stages and the tools of imagination that support them).

Here are some cognitive tools we can employ to help cultivate understanding of what *is happening*:

- Humanize the work (humanization of meaning): What stories guide the work of our community, from the front line to the boardroom? What decisions and actions support the

development of the garden/organization? Do the members of our community feel recognized, valued, and empowered or restrained, controlled, and oppressed?
- Find the hero within (transcendent qualities): What transcendent qualities currently define our community? What qualities do you want to see enacted in everyday action (e.g., community, respect, curiosity)? What is heroic about the stakeholders in our garden/organization? How does this vision interact with our efforts to move the garden/organization in a particular direction?
- Agency (sense of agency): How does implementing this policy interact with each stakeholder's life every day? What does it feel like to be empowered? How is each and every person not only an ally, but also an accomplice in the fight for change? That is, how can all stakeholders in your school move beyond the low- (or no-) risk stance of standing in support to becoming accomplices?

(Modified from Judson, 2021)

Evaluation: Harvesting the Garden

Once we have established our garden and creatively responded to address the expected and unexpected challenges we faced, we can begin to both enjoy our garden and reap our benefits, be they the experience of a peaceful retreat in nature or an abundance of fresh produce. At the same time, we will want to use the tools of imagination to help us examine our experience as we evolve to the end of our current growing season and the potential for replanting in the spring. Ideally, we have been collecting information about the garden throughout our project so that we have, as much as possible, a full recounting of our experience. We might raise questions to reflect and evaluate, such as: Did we get what we wanted from our garden? Do we want to do it again, and if so, can we do it better? Did our garden have impacts beyond our local community (did it reduce the availability of water for gardens downstream, or did it serve as a refuge for kids from a nearby school)? Is it time to mulch the remaining plants into the soil and start over again? Are there other people we should consult in the process—those who helped us or those who enjoyed the garden produce? Ultimately, did we bring to fruition the garden we imagined? Was our imagined garden the one our community actually needed? Going through this evaluation of the experience can help us, and our community, do it better next time.

Similarly, the same holds for our policy work. How did the process play out (*formative evaluation*), and did we accomplish what we set out to do (*summative evaluation*)? Can we reach out to stakeholders in our community to understand how they experienced the policy changes through a *participatory evaluation*? As with our garden, ideally, we have been collecting data (ongoing assessment) throughout the process so that we can reflect on both the past experience and what it means for our future work. Since policies in one area can have add-on effects throughout our system, can we look more broadly at outcomes from other areas of our community? And ultimately, how does what we learn from this examination help us understand the organization better, as well as plan for the future?

Here are some cognitive tools we can employ to help cultivate understanding of *what happened*:

- Story-shape issues/topics with cognitive tools (the story form): What was the significance of X policy/process/problem? How can you describe said policy/process/problem in a way that evokes emotion? (Think like a reporter—What's the headline? What's the story on X?)
- Everyone loves some drama: What dramatic tension offered initial access or understanding to the meaning of the policy/process/problem (e.g., help/hinder, timid/bold, fair/unfair)? How can you discuss the policy/process/problem with your community in a way that helps them feel an emotional tension within it?
- Find the hero(ic) within: What transcendent quality lies within the policy/process/problem (e.g., stewardship, discernment, organization)? What emotional dimension can community members relate to on an emotional level?
- The denouement: What is the climax of the story? Is there a resolution to the tensions or drama in the story? How has the policy/process/problem played out?

(Modified from Judson, 2021)

Continuation: Post-Harvest

At this point, the novice policy gardener may consider their job done. It can be tempting to move on to new tasks. However, left to its own devices, our imagined garden will change as growth continues unchecked, new plants and weeds are brought in by visiting animals, and old plants are forced out by the competition for resources. Like a garden gone to seed, policies left on the books without regular care and attention can end up evolving from their original purposes. Our once-imagined future becomes our staid present, and a policy once intended to empower positive change can become a mechanism of constraint.

Through this gardening process, we have imagined our best possible ecologies. We have gathered data to help understand the experience and used that understanding to build something valuable to ourselves and our community (or to identify where things went wrong). Now that we have evaluated that experience, we should have an even better understanding to work from. Rather than moving on to other tasks, it is time to use our new knowledge to fertilize the imagination. We till that knowledge back into the soil and begin to imagine a new cycle of growth and change. The cycle of policy change driven by our imagination, creativity, and innovation should be continuous (see Figure 5.1) as we reimagine our best future, work creatively to move toward that future in new and innovative ways, and then, after evaluating our progress, begin again. The life cycle of our policy garden needs to be continuous as imagination leads us toward a better future.

CONCLUSION

This stroll through the imagining and creation of our policy garden was intended to accomplish two purposes: (a) to introduce the concepts of the policy process through the presentation of an accessible narrative,

Figure 5.1 Policy Cycle

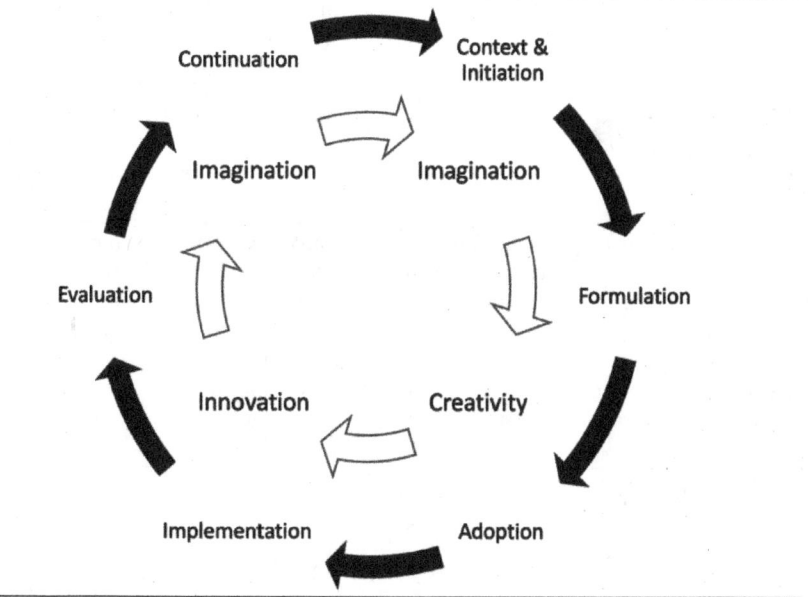

Table 5.1. The Policy Cycle as a Gardening Cycle: The Metaphor Unearthed

Garden Metaphor*	Cognitive tools**	In Practice	Policy Cycle***
Selecting a Site: Determining the location of your garden and the current ecosystem: the air, soil, rain, sun, temperature, flora, fauna, microorganisms	*Imagination:* Understanding what is	Understanding the context of the organization and system to which you are applying the policy	*Context:* Framing the issue, including understanding the problems, needs, and resources available
Exploring Planting Possibilities: Learning how to understand the local ecosystem and imagining the possibilities	Exploring what could be	Determining the current state and issues; envisioning where we are going and how we might get there; exploring the possible to guide and develop interventions	*Initiation:* Identifying the problem and converging interests, and framing the issue
Planning the Garden: Aligning the possible with the practical, exploring options Preparing the site: size, plant choice, timing, cost, labor, commitment	*Creativity:* Designing the imagined	Preparing the context and designing the policy; developing a plan for reaching our imagined future	*Formulation:* Developing and analyzing policy alternatives; consulting with stakeholders
Understanding Relationships in Place: Finalizing garden plan		Finalizing the plan of action	*Adoption:* Adopting the formal policy
Seeding and Growth: Planting, seeding, transplanting; caring and nurturing; fertilizing; watering; weeding; employing herbicides/pesticides	*Innovation:* Actualizing the imagined	*Implementing the policy:* Putting the policy into practice, adjusting practice, and responding to challenges as needed	*Implementation:* Putting the policy into practice

Garden Metaphor*	Cognitive tools**	In Practice	Policy Cycle***
Harvesting the Garden: Ripening, picking, storing, enjoying, using, processing	*Imagination:* Examining what is happening Understanding what happened	*Researching and evaluating the outcomes:* Deconstructing and reconstructing understanding of the policy problem	*Evaluation:* Using data and information to improve the process
Post-Harvest: Seasonal planning, mulching, composting, re/planting	Understanding what is now and what can be again	Comparing outcomes with desired outcomes; deciding to continue, revise, or end the policy	*(Dis)Continuation:* Applying evaluation data to revise policy
Resume cycle		Resume cycle	Resume cycle

Adapted from *Texas A&M AgriLife Extension (n.d.); **Judson, 2021; ***McKenzie & Wharf, 2016

and (b) to demonstrate how metaphor, storytelling, and imagery can be used as teaching tools for presenting complex topics. It would have been much easier to outline the policy process and describe each step individually; however, that approach likely would have been much less memorable and, in fact, would have offered a sterile and simplified vision of policy change. One of the disservices we do in discussing policy change is to make it seem clean, systematic, and easy. In truth, it is as messy and chaotic as a garden, and like gardeners, policy activists are likely to be confronted with myriad challenges and interruptions in the process of bringing change to life. That said, Table 5.1 offers a more succinct summary of the metaphor used; the continuum of imagination, creativity and innovation; and the policy cycle.

Policymaking is very much an act of creation and growth. It involves understanding where you are and knowing where you want to be, then mapping out a process for getting to that place. Without imagination, the best we can do is re-create and reinforce the status quo. Imagination in policymaking is the fuel for novel creation and, when applied, provides the stimulus for innovation in practice. It is an opportunity to realize a future state that is different, and better, than our present.

CULTIVATING CURIOSITY, CONVERSATION, AND IMAGINATION

After reading this chapter, what evokes your sense of wonder? What are you curious about?

For Consideration and Conversation

Metaphor is a generative tool of imagination and learning. What do you learn from the metaphors of imagination as soil, policymakers as gardeners, and the policy cycle as a process of cultivating a garden?

What is the role of imagination in responding appropriately and flexibly to changing educational systems in particular contexts? How do educational leaders enact imagination in advocating for and implementing policy change?

Cultivate Imagination With Cognitive Tools

Rhyme, Rhythm, and Pattern

Laitsch and Judson's gardening metaphor illuminates the importance of tending to the local context in the policy cycle. Think about your educational environment. What is the *dominant story* about learning there? Identify patterns of thinking, ways of being or talking about this story. How do the patterns you identify compare with your colleagues? How does policy support that dominant story? Now think about disrupting or changing these patterns. What policy changes are required to allow all members of your community to flourish? What new stories would support positive change, and what specific policies need to change to make this happen?

REFERENCES

Asma, S. (2017). *The evolution of imagination*. University of Chicago Press.

Davis, L. P., & Museus, S. D. (2019). What is deficit thinking? An analysis of conceptualizations of deficit thinking and implications for scholarly research. *Currents 1*(1), 119–129. http://dx.doi.org/10.3998/currents.17387731.0001.110

Daviter, F. (2015). The political use of knowledge in the policy process. *Policy Sciences, 48*(4), 491–505.

Dinishak, J. (2016). The deficit view and its critics. *Disability Studies Quarterly, 36*(4). https://doi.org/10.18061/dsq.v36i4.5236

Egan, K. (1997). *The educated mind: How cognitive tools shape our understanding*. University of Chicago Press.

Egan, K. (2005). *An imaginative approach to teaching*. Jossey-Bass.

Egan, K., & Judson, G. (2015). *Imagination and the engaged learner: Cognitive tools for the classroom*. Teachers College Press.

Elmore, P. B., & Camilli, G. (Eds.) (2008). Perspectives on evidence-based research in education. *Educational Researcher 37*(1), 5–50.

Gorur, R., & Koyama, J. P. (2013). The struggle to technicise in education policy. *Australian Educational Researcher, 40*(5), 633–648. https://doi.org/10.1007/s13384-013-0125-9

Green, G. P., & Haines, A. (2012). *Asset building and community development*. Sage.

Judson, G. (2021). Tools: An imagination-focused approach to leadership education. *Journal of Research on Leadership Education*. https://doi.org/10.1177/19427751211022028

McDonnell, L. M., Timpane, P. M., & Benjamin, R. (2000). *Rediscovering the democratic purposes of education: Studies in government and public policy*. University Press of Kansas.

McKenzie, B., & Wharf, B. (2016). *Connecting policy to practice in the human services*. Oxford University Press Canada.

Slavin, R. E. (2008). Perspectives on evidence-based research in education—What works? Issues in synthesizing educational program evaluations. *Educational Researcher, 37*(1), 5–14. https://doi.org/10.3102/0013189X08314117

Texas A&M AgriLife Extension (n.d.). *Gardening*. Texas A&M. https://agrilifeextension.tamu.edu/library/gardening

View, J., Laitsch, D., & Earley, P. (Eds.). (2013). *Why public schools? Voices from the United States and Canada*. Information Age Publishing.

Weiss, C. H., Murphy-Graham, E., Petrosino, A., & Gandhi, A. G. (2008). The fairy godmother—and her warts. *The American Journal of Evaluation, 29*(1), 29–47. https://doi.org/10.1177/1098214007313742

CHAPTER 6

Embodying Imagination
Creative Leadership in Compassionate Action

Lynn Fels

> We cannot go lightly into leadership . . .
> tread gently, oh, so gently.[1]

I wonder, as educational leaders, how we might invite fellow educators, students, and future leaders to reimagine the worlds we co-create and the roles that we, and they, play *here and now,* in the present, and in our imagining, who we may become in the future?

In Chapter 7 (this volume), Thomas and Koschoreck offer that by "cultivating imagination in leaders, teachers, and students, we can take learning beyond what we already know . . . Imagination among leadership creates openings and space that promote the possibilities for change." And, as Enlow and Popa (2008) propose, "imagination in a leadership context is a cognitive [embodied] orientation to the world that emphasizes engaging alternative perspectives and creating new possibilities for action" (p. 24). Varela (1987) reminds us, "What we do is what we know, and ours is but one of many possible worlds. It is not a mirroring of the world, but the laying down of a world . . ." (p. 62). Thus, embodied imagination—creative action—invites a playful interruption and re/visioning of what is known in order to create new possible ways of being in relationship. Imaginations embodied through creative play, pedagogy, and educational leadership intersect in performative spaces of inquiry.

The ability to listen to, be present with, and to respond in meaningful, imaginative, and compassionate ways is the task of a leader in these troubled and challenging times. Through creative play, or what I call embodied imagination, playful encounters create imaginary worlds of possibility: *what if, what matters, so what, who cares*? Within the context and nexus of education, cultural democracy, and social and environmental justice, I seek with my students to create communal spaces of invitation and permission to practice leadership, communication, compassion, reflection, and play. The focus and concern of this chapter is to offer pedagogical ways to enliven, nurture, and cultivate creative leadership in compassionate action through embodied imagination.

PERFORMATIVE INQUIRY AND PEDAGOGY: MEETING WHO WE ARE IN ROLE

> Recognizing, here and now, what is so wonderfully embodied in imaginative play.

As a performing arts educator, I seek to interrupt familial, communal, and institutional scripts that perform us, in the classroom, and in our lives. My students and I engage in role drama, tableau, scene creation, improvisation, and group storytelling; each activity is followed by reflection on what happened, how we encountered each other in play and in relationship with one another. We share what we learned; identify times when our habits of engagement led us to overlook other possible choices of action; we ask, did we lose someone in play; if so, how and why? To lose someone in play is to overlook, fail to listen, silence, presume a position, ignore.

Leadership in creative action arrives in the midst of collaboration—relational, compassionate, caring—through offering constructive insights, pedagogical enthusiasm, listening, encouraging, and organizational deftness: *"Yikes, we only have 10 more minutes before we have to perform!"* Our classroom is an experiential lab where we engage in role drama, theater activities, and creative playmaking, and through reflective dialogue and writing practices, we learn with and from one another. A Freirean practice of horizontality and hospitality creates a communal space for inquiry and creative play. Together, issues and relationships, and communal and individual actions and reactions, are realized, recognized, and documented as we create journey landscapes to explore through performative inquiry.[2]

The questions that inform my research and teaching practice are: *What if? What matters? What happens? So what? Who cares?*[3] Form, content, theory, environment, and practice inform one another.

"Whose scripts are you performing?" I ask my students. "Pay attention to the language that enacts you. What stories do you want to tell? What ones will remain unspoken? Attend to who is present in the room, and who is absent, and why. How you choose to be present, here and now, matters."

Notably, each one of us arrives from diverse and varied lived experience. Our circumstances—economic, social, communal, cultural, gender, historical—inform and perform our ways of being in action and relationship. In our creative work together, we focus on practices of listening, holding the space, taking care of one another, and documenting our learning in dialogue and writing. And, at times, I stumble in the interstices of lived experience and play, and thus, I encounter learning, as illustrated in the following activity a group of my students facilitated.

> A student places a disorganized pile of newspaper balls in the middle of our circle. Another hands out slips of paper, each with one of the following instructions: create a circle; create a square; create a pile. "Ready? Set? Go!" I read, *Create a circle of balls*. I commandeer newspaper balls, steal from others; I forget the rule, "don't speak," and, shamefully, I use my professorial position. A student shrieks as I broach their defense. Sounds of ripping newspaper are peripheral to my intention. Time is called. I stand alone, center stage, a solitary ball in hand. I tear the paper into small bits and lay down my circle. Our discussion following explored identification of who shared a similar goal; who cooperated, who didn't, and why?; the hoarding of resources; the generosity of those who collaborated, who shared; the abundance of possibility. Listening, I am appalled. *Who am I?* I wonder, *I teach leadership and collaboration, and yet play to win?* I didn't think to find my team or realize newspaper balls were available on request, or that I could problem-solve with others. The game becomes a teaching.

The game is designed to investigate teamwork and shared problem-solving. I ruefully reflect on the *absence* of *my* leadership as enacted in *my* disorganized scramble to achieve my self-interested goal. Whose ambitions am I performing and why? What values underpin my actions as an educational leader? In the heat of the moment, in work, in play, in role, who arrives?

ENCOUNTERING MAYOR FELS: PERFORMING LEADERSHIP

Sunnyvale is a role drama in which students encounter one another in role as entrepreneur, residential developer, reporter, art council member, environmentalist, or neighbor (Fels & Belliveau, 2008). An envelope marked "confidential" is visible in Mayor Fels's yellow jacket as she welcomes Sunnyvale citizens to the town hall meeting. Mayor Fels announces that a plot of land, Site 39, has been "donated" to Sunnyvale (in lieu of taxes). How shall we develop the land?

Throughout our role-play together, leadership emerges in various forms of engagement, as students in role actively lead community consultation in small groups, navigate conflicting agendas, negotiate consensus. A culminating broadcast reveals intentions, agendas, conflicting goals.

Six months later (we are an hour into our role drama), Mayor Fels announces a pharmaceutical company as the winning proposal, introducing the CEO, accountant, and scientist (three students now in new roles). Disinformation. Manipulation. A done deal. Who challenges a professor in role as Mayor Fels? Who dares to question? In role, students critically discern what the pharmaceutical company's proposal will mean for the town. Creative leadership and communal resistance are embodied in the challenging and perceptive questions posed.

Role drama is a collective inquiry during which students address a given problem, interact together, and make decisions, based on their role's responsibilities (Tarlington & Verriour, 1991). Role drama makes visible the scripts and language that perform us and creates openings for individual and collective reflection and critical awareness of the *how and why* of what we choose in creative play, and the metaphorical connections to our lives. Through dialogue and written reflection, we share our experiences; identify moments of resistance, moments that trouble or delight; and consider how else we might have chosen to engage in relationship.

Students enact pedagogical leadership as they initiate communal brainstorming, ask insightful questions, navigate dissent, offer creative possibilities, and negotiate consensus. Creative leadership in compassionate action arrives in multiple forms and contexts of engagement in and out of role.

I have witnessed how a restless jury, controlled by an overbearing judge enforcing his rules, disrupt into disobedience (Fels, 2004). And witnessed how interrupting the expected script of an educational leadership course invited first consternation and then facilitated learning (Nilson et al., 2016). And through a role drama on residential schools, I awakened to an understanding of resistance as agency (Fels & McGovern, 2002). As a tinker in role, I have stepped forward to protect the true leader of our fledgling democracy movement. Student teachers leading the role drama wondered why they, in role, had failed to similarly question the king's authority. "Will we be able to challenge authority in our lives if we failed to do so in role?" (Fels, 2002).

Role drama makes visible all the possible choices that one has or does not have, and invites us to wonder: "Why did I choose to do what

I did? How else might I have imagined myself in leadership?" The invitation of embodying creative leadership in compassionate action is to realize, recognize, and interrogate the institutional scripts that perform those who serve in leadership, and to ask ourselves, as educational leaders, how else might leadership within community be imagined?

Role drama creates an embodied imaginary world of inquiry where improvisation in role may make visible bias, presumption, and privilege embodied in creative action. The language and scripts that perform us in our everyday lives are revealed, often to our surprise, in playful encounter. "I was one of the senior citizens in role, and nobody came to talk with us. It was as if nobody cared about us." Sharing our experiences in role calls us to attention, *why did I, we, respond this way?* and to collectively reflect, *what else is possible?*

FILL THE SPACE: INTERRUPTING THE EXPECTED

I am frustrated as I lead my students through one of Augusto Boal's (2003) games for actors and nonactors. Participants are invited to engage physically in the game, and then to make metaphorical connections between their experience in play with their lived experience.

> "Fill the space!" I yell. "Now link arms with someone else. And now add a third person. Don't just walk around in one direction. Change directions!"
>
> But they ignore my directions and suddenly all are linked together, laughing, a twisting chain of interconnected bodies.
>
> "What are you doing?" I cry. "Let's begin again."
>
> *Let's do this right.* And then I debrief.
>
> "Who was leading? Did you decide where to go together or were you just dragged along? Was it easier to fill the space in groups of two or six? If linking arms and moving to find your empty space is a metaphor for educational leadership, how do you relate?"
>
> They respond to my questions, yes, but their enthusiasm, and the learning that might have been, is truncated. I had failed to recognize their spontaneous linking of arms as joyful resistance, an opening to a new possible inquiry. I apologize.

Embodying Imagination

"It's amazing," I say. "It's the first time I ever had a class spontaneously join together."

What if a Boal game[4] is taken outside and enacted beyond the classroom walls? Will they stay linked and interrupt the spaces they encounter? How will they be received?

"I have an idea. What if you all divide into two groups, 15 students each? Get your coats, and for 10 minutes, go outside and arm in arm, explore the campus."
Let's see what happens..

Fifteen minutes later a chain of linked students returns, all shouting, "We've brought someone with us!" They tell me that they traveled together to Starbucks, and linked arm in arm, three of them bought drinks.

"How was it?" I ask.
"It was weird."
"Everyone was looking at us!"
"They were afraid we would all order a drink!"
A chorus of voices. They laugh.

And then, they explain that on their return to our theater, the person at the end of their linked line started calling out, *join us, join us!* And all the students they approached turned away, except for this one young man, now standing in front of me with a bewildered happy smile.

"Welcome," I say. "Why did you join them?"
"I was tired of looking at my computer screen all day," he replies. "I wanted human contact."
"Where are you from?"
"Russia."

Disrupting the expected creates new possible worlds of encounter. How do I welcome this child-man who arrives in our midst?[5]
In play, I fall into habits of conventional leadership that I embody and perform so well. In moments of resistance, I am called by my students to notice the strands of the spider's web I have broken and must now repair. I must be willing to risk, to apologize when I trespass, to reach out a willing hand, humbly, to those who arrive to teach what I have yet to learn.

As educational leaders, we may ask: Is educational leadership an embrace of imagination in companionship, integrity, play, and respect? With what *intent* is educational leadership performed as an action site of collective imagination, creativity, and renewal? Just as Hannah Arendt (1958) asks educators if they love children enough so as to invite them into the world's renewal, so I ask educators, do we love our students *and* each other enough so as to invite each other into our world's renewal, through creative action, with compassion, and with shared vulnerability?

Amy Thomasson (2017) imagines vulnerability not as a solitary individual gesture but as a *liminal dynamic space* of shared vulnerability in action. Metaphorically, she describes two individuals who meet, fist positioned against fist. To create a shared space of vulnerability, each must open their hand in surrender, offering, and receiving, palm to palm, so that hands are clasped, fingers intertwined, thus creating a reciprocal space for creative action, within which generative possibilities may arrive.

Arendt's concept of natality invites each of us to wonder, who shall I become in the arrival of you? How might we nurture and cultivate creative spaces of shared vulnerability, surrender, compassion, that we might be in the presence of each other with tenderness?

JOYFULLY INTERRUPTING THE SCRIPT

We, you, and I are born in the midst of unfolding stories of ambition, love, hate, grief, joy, greed, arriving belatedly[6] in the stories interwoven through time. The future, suggests Hannah Arendt (1961), is predicted by the past. Thus, she calls educators to attend to the gap *between* past and future, *here and now*. The present is where stories we embody and enact may be rewritten into something new, unanticipated, thus changing future expectations.

In improvisation, participants are encouraged not to block, nor refuse an invitation, but to say *yes and* to each offering, with an offering in return. Arendt (1958) invites us, as educational leaders, to engage in the world's renewal with our students, conserving what matters. To improvise, with hope, integrity, care, compassion, not knowing what or who will arrive.

In all the heartbreak of stories as yet unfolding, small miracles arrive. Maxine Greene (1995) invites educators to release imagination so that ways of being present in creative action become possible. She writes, "... the role of imagination is not to resolve, not to point the way, not to improve. It is to awaken, to disclose the ordinarily unseen, unheard, and unexpected" (p. 28). To embrace the not-yet-known.

Leadership education through the arts invites an emergent curriculum, co-created in the presence of those who seek to learn, "enlarging the spaces of the possible" (Sumara & Davis, 1997, p. 299). To imagine leadership as a communal and creative offering of vulnerability is to invite openness, shared trust, a willingness to embrace the unexpected. As Amy Thomasson (2017) writes, vulnerability precedes trust; to earn another's trust one must first offer an act of vulnerability, to offer, metaphorically, an opening of one's hand to the closed fist of another. To be willing to risk so that the as-yet-to-become in the presence of each other may be enacted. To open one's fist in response to the opening of another's is to create dynamic spaces, fingers intertwined, of relational and creative possibility.

Learning how to create and cultivate shared action spaces of vulnerability in leadership education nourishes compassion, integrity, respect, and responsibility within an emergent community, as we communally lay down a path in shared leadership, step by step by step. This too is possible. But first, one must imagine opening a closed fist in the face of another's.

Our first commitment, then, that we, as educational leaders, might choose is to embrace Arendt's imagining of natality as an action space of renewal, and to ensure that the gap between past and present "remains a space of freedom and possibility" (Levison, 2001, p. 30; Meyer & Fels, 2014).

SKY'S OFFERINGS: POSSIBILITIES AND IMPOSSIBILITIES OF LEADERSHIP

The heart of our work together is to *mind the gap*, not the gap of a London tube station, but the gap *here and now* that Hannah Arendt (1961) speaks of in her writing. The gap is a liminal space of possibility between past and future. Our future, she proposes, is predetermined by the actions of our past *unless* we choose to reimagine *what is* and embody change in what we do *here and now* so that our future may be something other than what is ordained.

To mind the gap is to realize, recognize, and dare to interrupt scripts, practices, institutions, relationships, perceptions, and expectations that fuel and manipulate leadership and community in ways that diminish what is possible. To learn how to notice, to attend to the heart of Maxine Greene's call to educators for wide-awakeness, is to learn to embrace creative play within our everyday lives, to attend to the tug on the sleeve. *Leadership*, writes one of my students, *is stepping back so others can step forward. To enlarge the space of the possible. Creative leadership in compassionate action is a gift.*

Thus, embodied imagination realizes and recognizes a gap; through creative exploration arrives "a tug on the sleeve" (Fels, 2012) experienced as resistance, irritation, questioning, misgiving, delight, or dissonance that invites the possibility of asking *what if? what matters? so what? who cares?* In my search for creative leadership in compassion, the gap *serves* as inspiration and catalyst to ask, *what else is possible*? To invite embodied imagination as opportunity to interrupt the scripts my students and I perform, knowingly or not. To ask, who is the "we" performing these worlds we co-create? With what purpose, with what intent?

In the current call for imagination in leaders, communal discernment to the *why and how* of leadership is paramount. Caution and vigilance is ever required. Leadership may be inspired by an embodied imagination ill-begotten. Who, for example, could imagine the building of a wall between Mexico and United States of America? Who could imagine the burying of residential school Indigenous children in unmarked graves? Who could imagine the bombing of a theater with the word "children" written on the pavement?

The challenge, then, is to attend with wide-awakeness to the ambitions and values of those who choose to lead and those who are willing, or not, to be led. To question whose principles and whose interests are in play, and to interrogate one's own perceptions, expectations, illusions, and understanding. Our lived experience, individually and collectively, performs us. As educators and citizens, the desired imagination and creative action that you and I seek of our leaders, and of ourselves, necessarily turns the lens of inquiry on *our* desires, wants, and expectations. To unshackle from others' expectations, to reconsider one's habits of engagement, to entertain a willingness of uncertainty, not-knowing, attending to what arrives with critical consideration and compassionate reflection—such is educational leadership.

Arts in education offer experiential spaces of relationship, facilitating communal exploration, reflection, and witnessing, enlarging the space of the possible. In order to create and cultivate shared spaces of vulnerability within which creative action becomes possible, generosity of the heart's pulse needs to be in rhythm with communal compassion. We each have the potential for infinite creativity, which in the final analysis is love . . . (Tsao & Laszlo, 2019, p. vii).

(A POSSIBLE) CONCLUSION

May each leader to come into being nurture and cultivate an imaginative leadership in compassionate action with the spirit and teachings of

Embodying Imagination

a child's first encounter with rain, hands open to sky's offering. Take a moment, *here and now*, and witness a little girl, a toddler, experience rain for the first time.[7] Watch her delight, her joy, hands offered to falling rain.

> Here and now, a child's first encounter with Sky's offerings.
> Here and now, a moment, embodying curiosity, invitation, inquiry, joy.
> Here and now, the gift of a parent who responds, *yes, and*. . . .
> Here and now we witness imaginative leadership in a child's embrace of life's surprises.
> Celebrating humanity in relationship to all the joys of earth's offering.

Rain, snow, sunshine, then . . . bombs. Children are dying.

> *Imagine this. You are the leader of a country under attack. Inconceivably, your sovereign borders have been crossed by convoys of foreign tanks. A sky rains missiles. Schools, hospitals, residential homes are destroyed. Children, women soldiers, actors, athletes, neighbors, friends, fathers, grandmothers maimed, killed. Millions displaced. We are all players, spectators, participants, witnesses in a script written by an unhinged playwright,* now being performed.

What do you do? How to respond? Fist to open palm?

Fist to fist, wars, grievances, indignities, betrayals are enacted—a palimpsest of time, greed, hubris, and politics obscures heart's pulse. Here is a cruel leadership, imagined, enacted, and dangerous.

How might you and I embody imagination in ways that bring forth creative leadership in compassionate action? Will you and I be willing to step forward into educational leadership of vulnerable creativity, tenderness, joy, and forgiveness, in all the possible worlds that we might create together?

Palm to palm. Fingers interlaced.

Listen to a child's laughter, tears. See her dance in the rain, hands outreached to receive the sky's blessing. In the promise of natality, let us embrace love. So simple, and yet at this moment of time, so unimaginably, seemingly, impossible.

What if?

> *What if all the world's leaders could imagine, create, and nurture a shared sense of and responsibility, a communal chorus of "yes, and . . ." to all the possibilities and impossibilities that invite new ways of being in tender relationship, living together in peace on a fragile blue planet?*

What creative leadership might now arise from the wounds of human encounter?

What if each one of us received a poem, a dance, a song, a letter written in a child's hand, created by an unknown child from an unknown place? Can we imagine what such a child might offer?

If children were leaders, what possible worlds of renewal would they imagine into being?
Would we, you and I, be willing to say, "yes, and. . . ."?

Embodying Imagination

CULTIVATING CURIOSITY, CONVERSATION, AND IMAGINATION

After reading this chapter, what evokes your sense of wonder? What are you curious about?

For Consideration and Conversation

Fels and her students "focus on practices of listening, holding the space, taking care of one another, [and] documenting [their] learning in dialogue and writing." In what ways do these practices require imagination? How can you enact these practices within your own life personally and as a leader?

What institutional scripts do you work within as a leader? What instructions do you follow without interrogating? How might you playfully interrogate institutional scripts with and in your school community?

Cultivate Imagination With Cognitive Tools

Games, Drama, and Play

Fels explores the power of play—as a pedagogical tool—in experimental spaces of inquiry. How can games, drama, and play be used by educational leaders to promote affective connection with their team? What might that look like? What might it allow?

REFERENCES

Appelbaum, D. (1995). *The stop*. State University of New York Press.
Arendt, H. (1958). *The human condition*. University of Chicago Press.
Arendt, H. (1961). *Between past and future: Six exercises of political thought*. Viking.
Boal, A. (2003). *Games for actors and non-actors* (2nd ed.). Routledge.
Enlow, B. K., & Popa, A. B. (2008). Developing moral imagination in leadership students. *Journal of Leadership Education, 7*(2), 24–31.
Fels, L. (1999). *In the wind clothes dance on a line—Performative inquiry as a research methodology*. [Unpublished doctoral dissertation]. University of British Columbia.
Fels, L. (2002). Spinning straw into gold: Curriculum, performative literacy and student empowerment. *English Quarterly, 34*(1/2), 3–9.
Fels, L. (2004). Complexity, teacher education and the restless jury: Pedagogical moments of performance. *Complicity: An International Journal of Complexity and Education, 1*(1), 73–98. http://ejournals.library.ualberta.ca/index.php/complicity/article/view/8716/7036
Fels, L. (2010). Coming into presence: The unfolding of a moment. *Journal of Educational Controversy, 5*(1), Article 8. Western Washington University. https://cedar.wwu.edu/jec/vol5/iss1/8/
Fels, L. (2012). Collecting data through performative inquiry: A tug on the sleeve. *Youth Theatre Journal, 26*(1), 50–60.
Fels, L. (2015). Performative inquiry: Reflection as a scholarly pedagogical act. In W. Linds & E. Vettraino (Eds.), *Playing in a house of mirrors: Applied theatre as reflective pedagogical practice* (pp. 151–174). Sense.
Fels, L. (2016). Performing leadership: John Cage's 4'33" Reprise. *LEARNing Landscapes. 9*(2), 213–228.
Fels, L. (2020). Performing participatory action research: Stepping forth out of leadership. In K. Clausen & G. Black (Eds.), *The future of action research: A Canadian perspective* (pp. 253–270). McGill-Queen's University Press.
Fels, L., & Belliveau, G. (2008). *Exploring curriculum: Performative inquiry, role drama and learning*. Pacific Educational Press.
Fels, L., & McGovern, L. (2002). Intertextual recognitions through performative inquiry. In G. Brauer (Ed.), *Body and language: Intercultural learning through drama* (pp. 19–35). Greenwood Academic.
Greene, M. (1995). *Releasing the imagination: Essays on education, the arts and social change*. Jossey-Bass
Levison, N. (2001). The paradox of natality: Teaching in the midst of belatedness. In M. Gordon (Ed.), *Hannah Arendt and education: Renewing our common world* (pp. 37–66). Westview.
Meyer, K., & Fels, L. (2014). Imagining education: An Arendtian response to an inmate's question. *Canadian Journal of Education, 36*(3), 298–316.

Nilson, M., Fels, L., & Gopaul, B. (2016). Performing leadership: Use of performative inquiry in teaching organizational theories. *Journal of Leadership Education*, *15*(3), 170–186.

Sumara, D. J., & Davis, B. (1997). Enlarging the space of the possible: Complexity, complicity, and action-research practices. *Counterpoints*, *67*, 299–312. www.jstor.org/stable/42975255

Tarlington, C., & Verriour, P. (1991). *Role drama*. Pembroke.

Thomasson, A. (2017). *The gardener, the actor, and the educator: Six lessons towards creating and cultivating spaces of vulnerability between theatre for young audiences and education*. [Unpublished master's thesis]. Simon Fraser University.

Tsao, F. C., & Laszlo, C. (2019). *Quantum leadership: New consciousness in business*. Stanford Business Books.

Varela, F. (1987). Laying down a path in walking. In W. I. Thompson (Ed.), *GAIA, a way of knowing: Political implications of the new biology* (pp. 48–64). Lindisfarne.

Part III

IMAGINATION'S ROLE IN SOCIAL JUSTICE AND EQUITY

Imagination in Action
A Leadership Story

Family Stories Matter: Reenvisioning the Possible in Classrooms

Moraima Machado

> The goal of freedom is human creativity, the enhancement, and elaboration of life.
>
> —S. Nachmanovitch (1990)

When I was growing up in Venezuela, I often found myself on my mother's bed or at our dining room table listening to stories. We didn't have a television. My mom and Tia Elsita filled our space with all sorts of stories, from when they were growing up during politically turbulent times to more contemporary stories of their daily lives. The stories of our grandparents tapped into ancestral knowledge and shaped future generations, stories of *dichos, consejos,* joy, sorrow, love, and resilience. I do not recall when the learnings from those stories began to influence who I am as a mother, wife, sister, daughter, friend, colleague, and educational leader. But they did, and for that I am always grateful.

What I do recall is that in my career as a school leader, sharing my story was not something that I felt I needed to do—instead I felt that I needed to assimilate to the dominant culture; however, recently, as I undertook a project to bring the stories of families and children into the school, I felt the need to share my mother's stories as a foundation of my work. When we, as members of communities of color, enter the White-dominated educational system, we are compelled to leave our culture "at the door." There is no room for our voices. As a principal, I knew that I needed to tap into imagination and creativity to support teachers to bring the voices of students of color into the curriculum. As communities of color engage in counter-storytelling, their hopes, dreams, and aspirations for their children come to the forefront.

I invited a group of three teachers—a counselor, a parent, and a community member—to engage in a participatory action research project that entailed three successive cycles of inquiry over 18 months to bring the voices and stories of families of color into the curriculum. We were certain that providing a place for families to engage in a learning exchange and share stories and memories would lead to more innovative curriculum in the 5th-grade classrooms. And we were right!

Inspired by the learning exchange philosophy and work of Guajardo et al. (2016), I began with the self. I shared my story of growing up in a poor section of Caracas, Venezuela, and immigrating to the United States. Then, we invited parents to a Family Community Learning Exchange (FCLE) at our school to share their stories and histories. This work required imaginative thinking (Judson, 2018) to engage the families in drawing, thinking, and talking about their daily lives, their family histories, and the circumstances of their current experiences.

As students and teachers listened to one another's stories, the stories became more than a story. These stories constituted *testimonios*, a stronger word in Spanish for bearing witness, similar to what Emdin (2016) recommends in pedagogical approaches to replicate the cultural experience of the Black church. By testifying, the parents and families laid claim to stories of their power and gained a different kind of agency in the learning exchanges and, subsequently, so did the 5th-grade students in their classrooms. The relationship between teachers and students changed from hierarchical to horizontal, and the stories of the students became the foundation for creating a classroom community.

We used the stories shared by parents at the FCLE to create a curriculum of storytelling in the 5th-grade classrooms—what Muhammad (2018) names as critical literacy. The teachers and I realized that we had asked students to write emulation poems previously and the students had shared the "I come from a place" poems for many years. However, this time we observed a difference. In this case, the teachers understood that student *testimonios* as a process of witnessing—meaning public listening and relating to the stories—builds stronger community. As a result, teachers asked students for stories with the end goal of building community, and not an assignment. Alaina, a 5th-grade teacher, reflected on this shift:

> Instead of an assignment where you're bringing your story and you're teaching us about you, this identity project was more like we're creating

the community. You are part of this. You're bringing your story and bringing it into the classroom where the story is like the bonds that we're having. And I mean, the stories are who we are as a class.
—A. Lee, personal communication, December 5, 2020

What we learned throughout this project is that the storytelling process required changing relationships among participants from hierarchical to horizontal. For teachers and administrators to learn from families of color, we, as leaders, needed to be vulnerable, to let down the walls that separate us from the parent community, and to practice a different kind of listening. To do this, we engaged in the creative act of witnessing stories. Using FCLEs and protocols, we created a gracious space for deeper listening with our parent community (Guajardo & Guajardo, 2016; Hughes & Grace, 2010). Intertwined in the process of sharing one another's stories in family wisdom circles, we were able to see one another differently—not as professionals and parents interacting in a school setting, but as co-storytellers and listeners. The process humanizes the experience for everyone and sustains relationships in our work (San Pedro & Kinloch, 2017).

As school leaders with positionality, we have the power to change the dominant narrative if we so choose. To do this work, school leaders need a commitment to equity, a willingness to listen deeply to the stories of families, and the confidence to be vulnerable with their teachers, students, and parents. As leaders, we can open the schools to celebrate the richness of each story that passes through our doors. Unpacking with families the *sueños de generaciones*, the aspiration, dreams, wisdom, and knowledge handed down through generations, is an act of collective imagination and of courage. No longer do families need to experience leaving their culture, language, and history at the school door, but they can proudly share their history by co-creating a rich collective narrative.

REFERENCES

Emdin, C. (2016). *For White folks who teach in the hood-and the rest of y'all too: Reality pedagogy and urban education.* Beacon Press.

Guajardo, M. A., & Guajardo, F. J. (2016). La universidad de la vida: A pedagogy to last. *International Journal of Qualitative Studies 30*(1), 6–21.

Guajardo, M., Guajardo, F., Janson, C., & Militello, M. (2016). *Reframing community partnerships in education: Uniting the power of place and wisdom of people.* Routledge.

Hughes, P., & Grace, B. (2010). *Gracious space: A practical guide to working together* (2nd ed.). Center for Ethical Leadership.

Judson, G. (2018). Re-imagining school leadership: *Beginnings.* imaginED. www.educationthatinspires.ca/2018/02/15/re-imagining-school-leadership/

Muhammad, G. E. (2018). A plea for identity and criticality: Reframing literacy learning standards through a four-layered equity model. *Journal of Adolescent & Adult Literacy, 62*(2), 137–142.

Nachmanovitch, S. (1990). *Free play: Improvisation in life and art.* Tarcher/Putnam.

San Pedro, T., & Kinloch, V. (2017). Towards projects in humanization: Research on co-creating and sustaining dialogic relationships. *American Educational Research Journal, 54*(15), 373S–394S.

CHAPTER 7

Troubling Educational Leadership
Exploring Influences of Imaginative Practices on Equity and Social Justice

Zachary Thomas and James W. Koschoreck

Traditionally, in the age of accountability, leadership preparation programs have used "sanitized notions of educational leadership" to impart an idealized skill set of management techniques to lead educational buildings and systems efficiently (Dantley & Green, 2015, p. 822). Current trends in educational leadership seek to move beyond these notions of efficiency to expand equity and social justice in schools and learning by fostering attitudinal and behavioral changes that lead eventually to cultural improvement. Even as this focus on social justice leadership has helped to reorientate the purposes of leadership preparation programs, many of those efforts have existed alongside the traditional curriculum.

The coronavirus pandemic, the global economic crisis, and the sociopolitical upheaval resulting from racial and other inequities have given rise to a sense of urgency to reimagine how and why we provide public education. In this critical moment, educators are having to imagine solutions to problems we did not even know existed. By cultivating imagination in leaders, teachers, and students, we can take learning beyond what we already know.

As Enlow and Popa (2008) state, "imagination in a leadership context is a cognitive orientation to the world that emphasizes engaging alternative perspectives and creating new possibilities for action" (p. 24). Imagination, then, uses past ideas to create or formulate new future realities. Focusing on educational leaders as mediators of imagination and creativity (Judson, 2020), this chapter highlights the possibilities for creating socially just schools through imaginative leadership practices.

We have organized this chapter into four sections: (1) who we are and what we bring to this project, (2) what currently exists in public schools and leadership preparation practices in terms of skillsets, (3) how leadership can progress to a more equitable system based in social justice values, beliefs, and attitudes, and (4) how schools and leadership education can be (re)imagined through the application of imaginative and creative practices. We end with a poem as a provocation to imagine what is possible.

WE ARE

Because our epistemological understandings are inextricably interwoven with our social, political, and ethical positionalities, we begin this chapter by sharing appropriate and relevant aspects of ourselves that influence our thinking. As Takacs (2003) asserts,

> Simply acknowledging that one's views are not inevitable—that one's positionality can bias one's epistemology—is itself a leap for many people, one that can help make us more open to the world's possibilities. When we develop the skill of understanding how we know what we know, we acquire a key to lifelong learning. When we teach this skill, we help students sample the rigors and delights of the examined life. When we ask students to learn to think for themselves as thinkers—rather than telling them what to think and have them recite it back—we can help foster habits of introspection, analysis, and open, joyous communication. (p. 28)

We note, for example, that our ongoing commitment to critical reflection of ourselves and our professional practices—both in teaching and in leadership—has led to a reimagining of our pedagogies and our relationships in these times of a global pandemic and sociopolitical disruption. We have come to understand more deeply the importance of offering gracious space as so many struggle to make sense of the rapidly changing conditions of our political and social environments.

We navigate the oftentimes circuitous paths between theory and praxis in order to more fully appreciate the interconnection between the two. One of our fundamental beliefs is that a deep understanding of self allows for a fuller engagement with theoretical frameworks and literature, which thereby helps to bridge the seemingly insurmountable chasm between academic theories and praxis. As Guajardo et al. (2011) assert, "theoretical frameworks lay the groundwork for the student to engage in a multisensory process, analyzing his or her understanding of self as learner and fostering a greater awareness of the interdependence between theory and practice" (p. 152). In conformity with Khalifa's (2018) culturally responsive leadership model, the self-reflection we share in this section represents our belief in the fundamental recognition of this interdependence, which impels us to imagine new meaning(s) in these chaotic moments.

My (Thomas) experience in education comes from over 15 years of teaching in classrooms, museums, studios, and clinics. As an educator, I develop my programs to highlight innovation and exploration, the goal being something unexpected rather than a static target or objective. My epistemology has been cultivated through rigorous examination of what has been valued in learning and why. Every experience I have had in education over the years highlights my positionality as counter to reform in favor of transformation. If we simply move the pieces on the game we already have in place, we are still playing by the same rules; we, as school leaders, need to build a new board and start a new game with new rules allowing all players equal opportunity for success. Education needs to become something new. All my endeavors reflect my drive toward whatever creates possibility instead of creating outcomes. As Robinson and Aronica (2015) state in the introduction to their book *Creative Schools: The Grassroots Revolution That's Transforming Education*, "we have to do something else. The challenge is not to fix this system but to change it; not to reform it but transform it" (p. xxvi).

Moreover, I (Koschoreck) have been in the profession of educational leadership preparation for over 20 years. During that time, my pedagogy and scholarship have focused on issues of diversity, equity, and social justice—with a particular emphasis on matters of concern to the LGBTQIA+ communities (see, for example, Koschoreck & Tooms, 2009). The development of my epistemological standpoint has been highly influenced by the work of Sedgwick (1990). As she states so vigorously, "an understanding of virtually any aspect of modern Western culture must be, not merely incomplete, but damaged in its central substance to the degree that it does not incorporate a critical analysis of modern homo/heterosexual definition" (p. 1). Although the point of this chapter is not to embark on a critical analysis of heteronormativity in schools, these epistemological underpinnings do indeed lead to the assertion that imagination and creativity require us to think outside the traditional categories of analysis in educational leadership.

WE HAVE

The systematic forms of education—or "school learning in the classroom context" (Pereira et al., 2019, p. 46)—have involved recognizing problems, solving problems, and creating new problems. Schools in the United States largely maintain agendas laid forth by local and federal government officials (Hargreaves & Shirley, 2012; Urban et al., 2019). For example, the No Child Left Behind Act, and more recently, the implementation of Common Core State Standards, have streamlined education as a uniform process. Standardized tests and accountability inform the current discourses on American education (Giroux, 1997; Hutt & Schneider, 2018; Moran, 2015; Slattery, 2013). Over time, these discourses around the role(s) of public education in advanced Western societies are subject to change (Ball, 2021). Nearly every consecutive generation creates educational pathways building upon or diverging from previous ideology (Urban et al., 2019). This can be seen by looking at education reform policy shifts over time. The Child Development and Education Act of 1989 highlighted the need for head-start programs; then the Improving American Schools Act of 1994 resulted in the beginning of large-scale standardized testing in public schools. The No Child Left Behind Act of 2001 solidified school funding based on standardized testing, and in 2009 the Common Core State Standards Initiative emphasized bringing uniformity to standards in education (Hargreaves & Shirley, 2012; Urban et al., 2019).

In this way, education is both a measure of current social and cultural idealism and an institutional contributor that creates new cultural norms. Education can be viewed as a vehicle moving society toward that goal, which simultaneously moves further away. As such, education has one very important constant: continuous change. Amorphic in nature, it provides an ideal platform to develop imaginative leadership comfortable with ambiguity.

In the current system, educational leaders are called on to monitor teacher performance, student achievement, and results on high-stakes standardized tests. These systems of monitoring and surveillance create an environment that highlights "numerical metrics of effectiveness, quality, and productivity, as well as symbolic and material incentives for self-regulation" (Holloway & Brass, 2018, pp. 377–78). Practically, this notion of leader as enforcer of state and national policies oftentimes leaves little occasion to focus on "culturally responsive school leadership" (Khalifa, 2018) or "leadership for social justice" (Guillaume et al., 2020).

As Khalifa (2018) points out, however,

> A commitment to social justice and anti-oppression has become quite important to the field of educational leadership. [Culturally responsive school leadership] incorporates aspects of transformative and social justice leadership, mainly critical consciousness and praxis. Cultural responsiveness also focuses on pedagogy, curriculum, and instruction. (p. 24)

Leaders must be prepared to take time to focus on these important issues. Imagination and creativity serve in developing a focus on culturally responsive school leadership and are increasingly highlighted as pivotal for a well-rounded education (Krumm et al., 2018; Olivant, 2015; Roeper & Ruff, 2016).

At this point, it is important to note that imagination and creativity are not at all synonymous. As Tsai (2012) has rightly reminded us of Vygotsky's seminal work on imagination and creativity, "creative thinking involves the collaboration of imagination and thinking in concepts" (p. 16). In other words, creativity *requires* imagination to occur.

Educational leaders are now being asked to cultivate imagination and creativity in their schools. Many education reform professionals point to imagination and creativity as important for America's economic future (see, for example, Katz-Buonincontro, 2018). Developing imagination and creativity skills can bolster the ability of leaders, teachers, and students to perform tasks seamlessly (Roeper & Ruff, 2016). Leaders who exhibit higher levels of imagination are more able to employ complex thinking and wisdom in their daily lives. Imagination leads to increased personal growth and the development of social innovation, with creative thinkers being more able to use abstract thought, associations, deduction/induction, and metaphor in problem-solving (Płóciennik, 2018).

Educational leaders can help to develop and implement curricula that would facilitate the teaching and learning of imaginative practices. The importance of this cannot be understated. As Vincent-Lancrin et al. (2019) point out,

> Critical thinking and creativity are becoming increasingly important in the labor market and contribute to a better personal and civic life. People will increasingly have to contribute to and absorb innovation. Moreover, with artificial intelligence and robotics possibly leading to automation prospects for a sizeable share of the economy, skills that are less easy to automate such as creativity and critical thinking become more valued. Even if there was no economic argument, creativity and critical thinking contribute to

human well-being and to the good functioning of democratic societies. (p. 14)

Certainly, allowing for innovation and exploration will consequently produce better prepared leaders for the global educational community.

WE PROGRESS

Educational institutions are constantly attempting to progress toward something new and improved; imagination seats this flux as captain for the journey. Leadership for social justice requires imagination. Future educational leadership should focus on the changing educational environment as useful for cultivating novel ideas of learning, social justice, and cultural pluralism in schools. Recall once again that "imagination in a leadership context is a cognitive orientation to the world that emphasizes engaging alternative perspectives and creating new possibilities for action" (Enlow & Popa, 2008, p. 24). Leadership of the schools of tomorrow will need to enable change toward social and cultural renaissance. Equipping leadership with imagination and creativity provides buoyancy atop education's ever-changing agenda, allowing for a shift toward social justice and equity in schools.

Current educational leadership training programs fall short of both empowering imagination and addressing inequities in education. Social justice tends to be avoided in training of future educational leadership, and critical discourse is sidelined in subjects of race, gender, and discrimination (Guillaume et al., 2020). Subjects relating to social justice and equity are seen as threatening to current roles of education mentioned previously, namely student achievement and global competitiveness. It is paramount for future progress that educational leaders use critical analysis to increase understanding both of systematic oppression and of opposition to socially just educational practices.

Unfortunately, critique has become a process to fear. It is often a tool used to measure the effectiveness of leaders against goals that are unclear at best and oftentimes irrelevant. However, promoting generative critical dialogue directs us toward socially just leadership practices. Leaders utilizing imaginative and creative practices disavow fear from critique; rather, they view critical evaluation as a vehicle for progress. Leadership education led by imagination becomes constant critique and evaluation of purpose, creation of alternative pathways, and varied understandings of meaningful leadership (Enlow & Popa, 2008; Woodard, 2019).

Imagination that utilizes a critical perspective allows for understanding social justice in education outside of right and wrong (Woodard, 2019), which allows for leaders and educators to develop personal conceptions of this highly personal subject. This can lead to a critical evaluation of the future, conceptualized by what Dantley and Green (2015) call "historical imagination" (p. 828), or the process of leadership rooted in the reflection on future history of current actions. Ideally, by engaging in this process of historical imagination, leadership might create pathways toward increased social justice and equity. As evidenced by the work of Guajardo et al. (2018), through a critical focus on the ecologies of the self, the organization, and the community (pp. 59–63), individuals, schools, and communities can be infused with an imaginative lens of the possible.

Schools are the site of pervasively relational interactions among leaders and teachers, as well as among teachers and students and other school community members. This environment has limits determined by set goals and objectives laid out by educational institutions. For social justice and education to become symbiotic, relational work and imagination are necessary (Dyke et al., 2018). Leadership in education requires pioneering advancement toward social justice while facing social and political obstacles that discourage equity (Wang, 2020). Imagination can help move school leaders toward a better understanding of their personal values, conceptions, and biases, thus shifting them toward developing more equitable systems for students who are currently being deprived of equitable opportunities (Guillaume et al., 2020).

Leadership creates an environment of possibilities when approached with imagination and shuts down innovation and progress when limited by prescribed structured approaches. Imagination in leadership allows for the possible to become real, thereby opening alternative pathways to educational goals. Imagination allows for education to surpass now and here, creating something novel and new (Enlow & Popa, 2008). Leaders innovate while opening endless divergent dialogues with social and cultural ideas outside their own. This leadership does not harbor a particular position but maintains active participation in process.

The practice of imagination in leadership encompasses advocating and giving voice and mobility to those who have none. This requires dialogue with the "new possible" (Clayton et al., 2021) and priority for change (Ravitch, 2020). Imagination champions constant motion in all directions without the need for a predesigned terminus (Enlow & Popa, 2008). Creating new possibility becomes primary for leaders working toward equitable educational opportunities. As stated by Dyke et al. (2018) in the mission statement for the Social Justice Education Movement in 2015,

> We dream of socially and culturally just education systems free from colonization, capitalist exploitation, assimilation, and the erasure of histories and languages. Our future schools can and should honor the wisdom of our children, elders, educators, and families; center the self-determination of the oppressed; and fight for creativity, social justice, and community-flourishing. (p. 170)

This dream of new systems, institutions, and practices represents the exercise of imagination that leaders can bring to education in the 21st century; it behooves us to engage in the creativity to bring about these new realities. Imagination allows us to look forward, to what we could be.

WE COULD BE

Imagination among leadership creates openings and space that promote the possibilities for change. With the growing cultural shift toward equity and social justice in schools, the necessity for change has become increasingly evident. Shifting from traditional ideas to more imaginative openly explored concepts of what we are and what we are doing sometimes produces confusion, uncertainty, and ambiguity. Striving toward unknown goals requires risk without allowing fear to filter possibility.

CONCLUSION

To conclude, we present below a poetic summation of this important concept. Imagination and creative thinking guide our thinking as educational leaders. Allow the following synopsis to breathe in your creative imagination.

Shed all ideas confining free thought.
Remove barricades planted by cultures of fear.
Allow everything to be something

And nothingness to guide everything.
Standing in vast fields of our unconscious unleashed,
Distance becomes close enough to suffocate trepidation.
Eyes are opened by lack of closure.
Light becomes immersive
Moving through every thought as energy of possibility.
This is why.
This is how.
This is time.
Any direction leads to
Endless opportunity for everything.
What may be has no bearing on what will be.
Imagine a place
Encompassing all with only narrow focus on real.
Who really leads us when we have no conception
Of motion, tangible, or existential?
Leaders are those who brave new
Without checking for ghosts of past failures.
Imagination leads us all.
Thinking beyond timely possible realism.
Where are we going
May be less important than
We are going.
Worst of all
Is immobility of our minds
'Raging thirst for random
And inconceivable.
Ride the rocket.
Imagination can lead to anything, thus maintaining the ultimate solution for anything.

CULTIVATING CURIOSITY, CONVERSATION, AND IMAGINATION

After reading this chapter, what evokes your sense of wonder? What are you curious about?

For Consideration and Conversation

In what ways is your imagination as a leader constrained? What are the origins of those constraints?

Thomas and Koschoreck convey a sense of growth in their chapter structure by using the following subheadings—We Are, We Have, We Progress, We Could Be—and concluding with a poem. How does this imaginative structuring affect your understanding of imagination and transformation for positive social change?

Cultivate Imagination With Cognitive Tools

Cognitive Tool: *Humanization of Meaning*

Thomas and Koschoreck identify the transformative power of imagination. They also identify the challenges of this work, particularly in a context in which imagination can be undervalued if not misunderstood. What specific leadership stories can guide your work as a school community? What leaders *are inspired* and *inspire you* in terms of how they use their imaginations to respond to challenges, support community, and work for positive change?

REFERENCES

Ball, S. J. (2021). *The education debate* (4th ed.). Policy Press.
Clayton, P., Archie, K. M., & Steiner, E. (2021). *The new possible: Visions of our world beyond crisis.* Cascade Books.
Dantley, M. E., & Green, T. L. (2015). Problematizing notions of leadership for social justice: Reclaiming social justice through a discourse of accountability and a radical, prophetic, and historical imagination. *Journal of School Leadership, 25*, 820–837.
Dyke, E., Meyerhoff, E., & Evol, K. (2018). Radical imagination as pedagogy: Cultivating collective study from within, on the edge, and beyond education. *Transformations: The Journal of Inclusive Scholarship and Pedagogy, 28*(2), 160–180.
Enlow, B. K., & Popa, A. B. (2008). Developing moral imagination in leadership students. *Journal of Leadership Education, 7*(2), 24–31.
Giroux, H. (1997). *Pedagogy and the politics of hope: Theory, culture, and schooling: A critical reader.* Routledge.
Guajardo, M. A., Guajardo, F. J., & Locke, L. A. (2018). *Ecologies of engaged scholarship: Stories from activist academics.* Taylor & Francis.
Guajardo, M., Oliver, J. A., Rodríguez, G., Valadez, M. M., Cantú, Y., & Guajardo, F. (2011). Reframing the praxis of school leadership preparation through digital storytelling. *Journal of Research on Leadership Education, 6*(5), 145–161.
Guillaume, R. O., Saiz1, M. S., & Amador, A. G. (2020). Prepared to lead educational leadership graduates as catalysts for social justice praxis. *Journal of Research on Leadership Education, 15*(4), 283–302.
Hargreaves, A., & Shirley, D. (2012). *The global fourth way: The quest for educational excellence.* Corwin Press.
Holloway, J., & Brass, J. (2018). Making accountable teachers: The terrors and pleasures of performativity. *Journal of Education Policy, 33*(3), 361–382. https://doi.org/10.1080/02680939.2017.1372636
Hutt, E., & Schneider, J. (2018). A history of achievement testing in the United States or: Explaining the persistence of inadequacy. *Teachers College Record, 120*(11), 1–34.
Judson, G. (2020). Conceptualizing imagination in the context of school leadership. *International Journal of Leadership in Education.* https://doi.org/10.1080/13603124.2020.1818289
Katz-Buonincontro, J. (2018). Creativity for whom? Art education in the age of creative agency, decreased resources, and unequal art achievement outcomes. *Art Education, 71*(6), 34–37.
Khalifa, M. (2018). *Culturally responsive school leadership.* Harvard Education Press.
Koschoreck, J. W., & Tooms, A. K. (2009). *Sexuality matters: Paradigms and policies for educational leaders.* Rowman & Littlefield.

Krumm, G., Arán Filippetti, V., & Gutierrez, M. (2018). The contribution of executive functions to creativity in children: What is the role of crystallized and fluid intelligence? *Thinking Skills & Creativity, 29*, 185–195.

Moran, P. (2015). Reacting to crises: The risk-averse nature of contemporary American public education. *Policy Futures in Education, 13*(5), 621–638.

Olivant, K. F. (2015). "I am not a format": Teachers' experiences with fostering creativity in the era of accountability. *Journal of Research in Childhood Education, 29*(1), 115–129.

Pereira, S., Fillol, J., & Moura, P. (2019). Young people learning from digital media outside of school: The informal meets the formal. *Comunicar: Media Education Research Journal, 27*(58), 41–50. www.revistacomunicar.com/index.php?contenido=detalles&numero=58&articulo=58-2019-04&idioma=en

Płóciennik, E. (2018). Children's creativity as a manifestation and predictor of their wisdom. *Thinking Skills & Creativity, 28*, 14–20.

Ravitch, S. M. (2020). Flux leadership: Leading for justice and peace in & beyond Covid-19. *Penn GSE Perspectives on Urban Education, 18*(1). https://urbanedjournal.gse.upenn.edu/archive/volume-18-issue-1-fall-2020/flux-leadership-leading-justice-and-peace-beyond-covid-19

Robinson, K., & Aronica, L. (2015). *Creative schools: The grassroots revolution that's transforming education*. Penguin Books.

Roeper, G. A., & Ruff, M. (2016). Learning and creativity. *Roeper Review, 38*(4), 222–227.

Sedgwick, E. K. (1990). *Epistemology of the closet*. University of California Press.

Slattery, P. (2013). *Curriculum development in the postmodern era: Teaching and learning in an age of accountability*. Taylor and Francis.

Takacs, D. (2003). How does your positionality bias your epistemology? *Thought & Action, 19*(1), 27–38.

Tsai, K. C. (2012). Play, imagination, and creativity: A brief literature review. *Journal of Education and Learning, 1*(2), 15–20.

Urban, W. J., Wagoner, J. L., & Gaither, M. (2019). *American education: A history*. Routledge.

Vincent-Lancrin, S., González-Sancho, C., Bouckaert, M., de Luca, F., Fernández-Barrerra, M., Jacotin, G., Urgel, J., & Vidal, Q. (2019). *Fostering students' creativity and critical thinking: What it means in school*. Educational Research and Innovation, OECD Publishing.

Wang, F. (2020) Social justice leadership and *The Art of War*. *Critical Studies in Education, 61*(1), 86–100.

Woodard, J. (2019). The power of creation: Critical imagination in the honors classroom. *Journal of the National Collegiate Honors Council, 20*(1), 39–43.

CHAPTER 8

Rewilding Imagination
Reorienting Eco-Leadership in Education

Mark Fettes and Sean Blenkinsop

> Imagination is understood to be a quality of mind in settler culture. In Haudenosaunee/ Mohawk tradition, the same quality is understood to be animal and spiritual helpers manifesting their presence in one's life. . . . [The settler conception of] imagination dominates where fear of the unknown, uncertainty of memory, and placelessness thrive.
>
> —Sheridan & Longboat, 2006, p. 365

THE ABERRANT SETTLER IMAGINATION: A PROBLEM FOR SCHOOL LEADERSHIP

What is educational leadership for? Beyond managerial concerns of budgets, policy, staffing, buildings, and grounds, educational leadership is essentially about fostering human relationships and development within a given social and cultural (and ecological) context. How school leaders think about the personal and collective journey from childhood to adulthood is hugely consequential for the kinds of education that they enable and encourage.

Such thinking does not take place in a vacuum. Embedded within the institution of modern schooling are values and assumptions shaped by (among others) colonization, industrialization, urbanization, and the insidious commodification of daily life. Even when school leaders do not consciously share those values and assumptions, they will likely be influenced by them. Schools, in many ways, can be seen as a "crystallization" (Vygotsky, 2004) of the modern Western imagination. As argued in this chapter, this is deeply problematic for educational leadership in the present era of ecological crisis, climate change, and efforts to reconcile with Indigenous peoples, among other challenges.

Fortunately, however, there is an alternative. It stems from an understanding of imagination as fundamentally *more than human*—as embedded in land and the intricate dance of "all our relations." Such a conception asks us to rethink our beliefs about human development and hence about what school leaders should be trying to accomplish. Indeed, it may lead us to seek alternatives to schools, as we know them today.

What are our present schools like? Well, first of all, they are overwhelmingly human-centered. Apart from the odd potted plant or aquarium, virtually everything one sets eyes on within a school building is the product of human labor and instantiates (a particular set of) human values. Furthermore, it is an environment designed to encourage particular kinds of attention to particular topics and remove potential sources of distraction—that is, to minimize the possibility of unplanned and spontaneous discovery.

Second, and as a necessary complement to this simplification, schools are physically surrounded by boundaries, typically in the form of walls or fences. Although it is impossible fully to separate a school from its surrounding communities and living systems, the boundary nonetheless communicates the fact that *school is a different place*, a place that is not *of* the place where it is located. Schools are more similar to one another than they are to the buildings and spaces that adjoin them. To step onto school grounds is to enter into a kind of cultural hyperspace, a realm that is intricately connected to everywhere and yet nowhere in particular.

Third, schools are *evaluative* spaces. This is straightforwardly true of the school's instructional mission, exemplified by report cards and grades. But it also holds in more subtle ways; in the feedback students (and staff) receive on their attire, comportment, behavior, language use, food preferences, knowledge of social norms, likeability, willingness to conform, and so on. It is difficult to think of another social setting where one is so constantly subjected to the judgment of others. This is especially problematic when one considers widespread systemic bias at the level of society as a whole in areas such as gender, race, religion, language, sexual orientation, and ability. Schools are places where social and cultural hierarchies are inculcated and reinforced, sometimes as deliberate policy, but often simply in their operation as hothouses of peer pressure and normative messaging.

Fourth, schools are divorced from the realm of physical and collective labor, such as that involved in obtaining food, water, shelter, and clothing, as well as caring for the very young, the very old, and the infirm. Physical education is focused on games and sports rather than any activities with a tangible, lasting outcome or with benefits for nonparticipants. The body—physical strength, vigor, and skill—is regarded from the viewpoint of individual health and capability, but not as an important contributor to community well-being.

Fifth, schools normalize a particular kind of individual consciousness, an understanding of the self as autonomous and self-fashioned, rather than a collective consciousness, which manifests itself in the kinds of learning and performance that are most valued in school settings. As student populations become increasingly diverse, this tendency is actually reinforced: what other inclusive understanding of excellence could there be, other than the opportunity for each student to succeed on their own individual merits? In this way, schools shape a notion of what it means to live a successful life that is oriented to such measures of individual achievement as credentials, income, status, and material possessions.

School leaders, almost by definition, exemplify and model these dominant values. They are seen (and often see themselves) as individual success stories. They spend their days in human-dominated settings, speaking and listening, reading and writing, but rarely calling on other physical, practical, or artistic skills. They speak on behalf of the larger education system and ensure that their school or school district is in line with public (and parental) expectations and understandings of what schools should be like. They enforce the grading and classification systems and processes that tell children and their families whether they are succeeding at school. It is possible to do all this more or less skillfully, more or less humanely and compassionately, but it is hard to opt out of any of it; it comes as a package.

Consider, then, a sixth way of characterizing schools: as places of domestication, typified by a high density of bodies, relative lack of movement, repetitiveness, and a significant degree of boredom. Schools in these respects resemble the feedlots designed for raising domesticated animals, although here the "feed" is for mental rather than physical development. The "wildness" of the child appears to the domesticating mind as a problem to be remedied through the application of confinement, routine, and predictability, using a mixture of rewards and punishments. In this light, school leaders appear as the equivalent of drovers, shaping a herd identity that tends toward passivity, conformity, and dependency. While this may appear as a shocking exaggeration to educators working in settings of relative wealth and privilege, it is a sadly apt description of many schools in contexts that are working-class, racialized, postcolonial, or otherwise characterized by relations of oppression and marginalization. It seems legitimate to ask as school leaders: is this a difference in kind, or only in degree?

Regarded in this light, schools in general offer unpromising soil for imagination to flourish (see Judson, 2021). There is, indeed, a long history of hostility to imagination in the Western educational tradition (Egan, 1997, 2002), but even when its importance and relevance are reassessed, ideas about the role it might play in education will likely be constrained by these six features of institutional schooling. That is, imagination will be thought of as a capacity that is uniquely human; that is untethered from the particularities of place and ecology; that is to be judged by shared (i.e., dominant) cultural standards; that is essentially separate from the body and its needs, and from the world of manual labor; that is individual in nature, and whose value is realized through individual excellence; and whose potential wildness is to be resisted and controlled. Ultimately this suggests that imagination will be developed and deployed in ways that reinforce the very worldview that has produced our current civilizational crisis.

THE HAUDENOSAUNEE IMAGINATION: AN INVITATION TO LEAD DIFFERENTLY

The alternative we develop in this chapter is inspired by an article by Joe Sheridan and Roronhiakewen "He Clears the Sky" Dan Longboat (Sheridan & Longboat, 2006), whose ideas we first encountered at a Vancouver conference on "Educating Imaginative Minds" in 2004. As the article notes, "normative assumptions" at the conference included the belief that imagination belongs to "the exclusive domain of human cognition" (p. 366). We wish to acknowledge the accuracy of this observation as it applies to ourselves. Even while exploring the role of the imagination in environmental and "sustainability" education (Blenkinsop & Fettes, 2007), in place-making (Fettes & Judson, 2011), in ecological schooling (Blenkinsop, 2012), and in the land-based revitalization of Indigenous languages (Fettes, 2017), much of our work has reproduced this focus on imagination as a human trait.

In contrast, Sheridan and Longboat (2006) challenge the very notion of "human" thinking set apart from "the unity, interrelation and reciprocity between language and psychology, landscape and mind" (p. 366). Their article advances two parallel arguments. One is a critique: they suggest that Western or modern conceptions of mind and imagination are a way of naturalizing both anthropocentrism and the conceits of "cultures colonized by . . . the interior sources of their intelligence" (p. 366). Once the mind is conceived as isolated from the world, as a purely human-cultural achievement, the work of educating the mind will tend to confirm beliefs in human superiority and, by extension, in the superiority of those groups of humans who think this way. "Aberrant imagination imperiled Mother Earth and now seeks to replace her to perpetuate itself. . . . Without everything to think with and through, imagination thinks only of itself" (p. 371).

The second, complementary argument running through the paper develops an alternative vision of how imagination works and what it is for, drawing on the specific traditions of the Haudenosaunee, the Six Nations Iroquois Confederacy. Imagination itself, Sheridan and Longboat (2006) say, is not a Haudenosaunee concept, yet "understood as a blessing, imagination is the ongoing invitation to give thanks at remaining part of Creation's bestowal of belonging" (p. 370). That is, imagination can be understood as "a quality of consciousness that reminds consciousness of its spatial and temporal belonging within Creation's spiritual ecology . . . [It is] the cognitive and spiritual condition of entwining with local and cosmological intelligences" (p. 370). A crucial aspect of these intelligences is that they unfold cyclically over deep time, in contrast to "the anthropocentric present" that supports only a starved and tenuous realism "limping on the singularity of a receding future bereft of the eternal" (p. 374).

This is high-flown language, and the concept is not an easy one to grasp if one approaches it from typical Western premises. Our first priority, then, is to establish its relevance to contemporary issues of schools and school leadership.

We begin with the conversation around schools as colonial institutions. In Canada, awareness has been growing of the historical role of schooling in the violence perpetrated on Indigenous peoples—first and foremost through enforced attendance at residential schools, but also through provincial school systems. In our province of British Columbia, and in others across the country, educational leaders are being asked to consider changes to curriculum, staffing, pedagogy, scheduling, and community involvement in mainstream schools. Yet it is still rare to see explicit connections being made, at the level of school leadership, between this conversation and the colonization of nature or land. Canada's Truth and Reconciliation Commission did, in fact, recognize this link in its summary report, although it failed to make it into the Calls to Action that are the Commission's best known statement of what reconciliation entails in practice:

> Reconciliation between Aboriginal and non-Aboriginal Canadians, from an Aboriginal perspective, also requires reconciliation with the natural world. If human beings resolve problems between themselves but continue to destroy the natural world, then reconciliation remains incomplete. This is

a perspective that we as Commissioners have repeatedly heard: that reconciliation will never occur unless we are also reconciled with the Earth. Mi'kmaq and other Indigenous laws stress that humans must journey through life in conversation and negotiation with all creation. Reciprocity and mutual respect help sustain our survival. It is this kind of healing and survival that is needed in moving forward from the residential school experience. (Truth and Reconciliation Commission of Canada, 2015, p. 123)

Sheridan and Longboat's article is an eloquent elaboration of this idea. We read them as saying that the North American colonizers understood the importance of this connection to land and place even while they denigrated and dismissed it. When policies were put in place to separate Indigenous people from the land, to exclude Indigenous languages from schooling, and to render the land invisible and voiceless in educational settings, the goal was to actively separate human from more-than-human as an essential dimension of the colonial project. And so the time is ripe for educational leaders to consider how those relationships can be rebuilt as part of the work of reconciliation.

Alongside this Indigenous-informed conversation, there is another conversation centering on anthropocentrism—the prioritizing and centralizing of human needs and values in schools. The ecological and climate crises are challenging the modern ontological positioning that allows us to shape and exploit every other living being as a resource for our own benefit (Serres, 1995). Perhaps it is time to acknowledge that anthropocentrism is *making us stupid*—to put it another way, that it is *anti-educational.* Sheridan and Longboat (2006) suggest that "as biodiversity wanes, so wanes the capacity for thinking with nature and beyond species-specific consciousness" (p. 371). An analogy might be to remove most of the books from a school library, leaving students and teachers impoverished in terms of both knowledge and imagination. For educational leaders, this is an issue that goes to the heart of what schools are for. If we are educating for wide-ranging and flexible intelligence and for ecological citizenship, the offerings and gifts of the larger community (human and more-than-human) need to be seen, recognized, and included.

Currently, a third educational conversation concerns individualism, influencing our ideas of human development. Developmental models often begin with an account of the infant/child as deeply relational and connected to their surroundings, but posit that developing a sense of autonomous selfhood requires the growing child to pull away from those primal attachments, recognizing its individuality and separateness. Only once autonomy is established can the maturing adult turn back toward relationship, a return to childishness as it were, but with the wisdom of the journey. Such a conception of the process is clearly influenced by modern culture, including the practice of sending children to school for many hours each day throughout the formative years of their lives, separating them from the domestic, primarily maternal domain.

The Haudenosaunee understanding of development is very different. According to Sheridan and Longboat, the very notion of the autonomous individual human has no place in North American Indigenous tradition. Instead of going through a process of separation and return, the child is always already *in relation* to family, to kin, to community, to place. Even those most seemingly private operations, one's thoughts and imaginings, are a relational space, a place of gifts and exchanges, and one actually gets wiser over time through better recognition of these offerings. Ultimately, in the Haudenosaunee worldview, there is no individual, no thinking, and no maturation in the absence of place—*place* in the sense of "living communication within a sentient landscape" (p. 369). When one contrasts this with the Western tradition, it is noteworthy that there is no sign of gifts or animal and spirit helpers in *cogito, ergo sum*.

One of the most influential Western proponents of a relational approach to education, Nel Noddings, claims in her work on "the ethic of care" (2013) that in order for us to enter into a caring relationship, care must be acknowledged by the cared-for. It follows for Noddings that humans cannot have a caring relationship with the natural world, because the denizens of the natural world are unable (in general) to acknowledge the care being offered by humans. Yet Sheridan and Longboat (2006) invert this discussion. According to them, *care for humans* is abundant in the natural world; it is humans who fail to recognize the care being offered. "Humans think at their best if they know they are the last beings created. Literally, after all, humans are totally dependent on everything else" (p. 369). The first step toward maturity would be to acknowledge that we are being cared for; we might then begin to exercise appropriate care in return. To lead in light of *this* understanding, then, requires educators to take this very step—to own our indebtedness and immaturity in the face of the Earth's vast intelligence, and to ask how, through leadership, we might support ourselves and others to learn from it more humbly and fully.

NATURE AS FIRST TEACHER: OUR ORIGINAL DEVELOPMENTAL PATH

Sheridan and Longboat's critique in some ways runs parallel to that of environmental philosopher Paul Shepard, who argues in *Nature and*

Madness (1982) that modernity (and indeed the mainstream of human cultural development since the invention of agriculture) both fosters and rewards a kind of enduring psychological adolescence. Shepard traces this in the form of six lasting shifts in human-nature relationships, and a quick survey of these will add further depth to Sheridan and Longboat's account and help set the scene for our concluding discussion of how educational leaders might respond.

First, Shepard (1982) invites us to think about *attention*, the "casual way in which we pay heed" (p. 21). In humanity's evolutionary origins as small bands of hunter-gatherers, we became skilled at scanning complex and intricate environments in which food and other resources were transient and scattered. It was important to notice what was available and when; to understand the behavior and interaction of many different beings, how they might act to draw, hide, repel others. These cues were often subtle and cumulative. Through a long process of asserting human control over nature, involving farming, urbanization, and the overall shift to planned and built environments, attention gradually took on a more adolescent psychic quality of focus. Shepard describes this as a kind of singularity of awareness that goes hand in hand with *ownership, management, and hierarchical leadership,* rather than *participation and reciprocity.*

Second, Shepard notes the shifting meaning of *place or territory.* Hunter-gatherers tend to be familiar with a relatively large territory through which they move with the seasons. As agricultural and urban communities were established, their occupants came to live their lives in much more restricted surroundings characterized by younger, simplified ecological systems. This was no longer immersion in a succession-filled, eventually old-growth and biodiverse world; indeed, to some extent, that wild world became framed as the Other, a threat calling for defensiveness rather than participation. In this way Shepard's (1992) third shift, *duality*, got under way as well: animals were classified as wild or tame, plants were weeds or crops, lands were yours or mine, acts were human or divine, things were good or bad. Over time, knowledge became increasingly siloed, while rationality was detached from place, body, and relationship. Again, Shepard sees this simplification of both place and value as mapping onto the adolescent psyche.

The fourth shift Shepard calls *trophic pattern*. In place of the gifts of the land, a sense arises of productivity as the fruit of human labor, with Nature or Mother Earth as a necessary but unreliable partner needing skill and labor to subdue and control. At the same time, the need to accumulate stores against times of scarcity helps to catalyze a shift in values toward *possession,* a "more is better" mentality completely foreign

Rewilding Imagination

to mobile hunter-gatherers. For Shepard, both these shifts encourage a kind of adolescent ego inflation. It was not long, he suspects, until ownership of sources of value (including knowledge and expertise) equated to greater prestige and power, and *belongings* became a primary token of *belonging*.

The final shift in Shepard's list is *domestication*—another move away from the wild, the unpredictable, the spontaneous and the dangerous, toward control and oversight. Cows were bred for docility, chickens for reduced mobility, and sheep for maximum production and minimum complexity. For Shepard, this move to infantilize the animals in closest contact with humans at the same time reinforced a developing sense of human superiority. People surrounded themselves with beasts designed for human purposes and dependent on human care. This creates, in another echo of Sheridan and Longboat, a kind of tautological loop whereby the product of human colonization is said to confirm the human's rights to colonize.

All of these psychological patterns are still with us in modern North America, transmuted and amplified in countless ways, including through the characteristic patterns of schooling noted earlier. The curious feature of this developmental account is that, in contrast to the prototypical modern narrative of continuous progress, it suggests a process of gradual but steady psychological *regression*. Seen through Shepard's lens, the modern West has not only become more stupid as a civilization over time; it has created institutions—public schools—to accomplish this stupidification still more thoroughly and efficiently. But educational leaders are *trained not to see this*—for how could they do their job otherwise?

Perhaps surprisingly, Sheridan and Longboat (2006) cherish a degree of hope. "When North Americans rely on their primal intelligence, they can intuit that *to be here* is to encounter sentient temporal and spatial landscapes" (p. 369); "The tongue that settlers hear as imagination is the budding of the autochthonous archetype that . . . is learning to think as the continent thinks" (p. 370). Yet they are pessimistic about achieving this through formal education: "it is . . . unlikely that essentially wild imaginations can be forced, evoked, or nurtured in school settings," which "[re-create] minds as buildings rather than as hunters or bush dwellers" (pp. 375–376). We would, of course, agree with this conclusion if schools remain just as they are. Yet this is where the opportunities for leadership arise.

A few years ago, we were involved in the development of a public elementary school in British Columbia where virtually all teaching and learning takes place outdoors throughout the year, with nature understood as co-teacher (Blenkinsop, 2012; Blenkinsop & Beeman, 2010; Jickling et al., 2018). Ten years further on, the school is still thriving. Essentially, this school serves as a prime example that it is *possible* to make quite different choices about how public education is conceived of and delivered. Furthermore, our research with children at the school (Blenkinsop & Piersol, 2013) bears out Sheridan and Longboat's suggestion that the sentient world can make its presence felt to modern settler minds.

Here is Raven (her chosen nature name), a 4th-grade student at the school, describing what it is like to talk to plants:

> *Researcher:* "So do you hear the plant?"
> *Raven:* "Yeah, but you have to hear it through your heart."
> *Researcher:* "I was going to ask where you hear it . . . do you hear it in your heart?"
> *Raven:* "Little words curl into your mind. You have to know that you're not thinking."

On another occasion, Raven elaborated further:

> *Researcher:* "Do you feel like you have 'conversations' with the natural world?"
> *Raven:* "It's not exactly like that, it's not 'speaking,' it's more like energy or signals. You don't hear it out loud. It's something that your mind and only your mind can understand because nature is that open to any language. So if you were just thinking, not even in your language, just showing pictures, it would still work."
> (Blenkinsop and Piersol, 2013, p. 53)

For Raven, it is self-evident that the natural world speaks—it is not even a debatable point. This leads her (in these and other dialogues with the researcher) to a conception of mind as a place of conversation, fluid discussion, with myriad beings speaking myriad languages in myriad voices. Rather than supposing that this particular 9-year-old girl is exceptional, it seems to us more likely that this capacity of ecological imagination is part of our human inheritance and that its suppression in settler culture is systematic—an expression of a collective will not to know (Gilligan, 1982). If risk-taking educational leadership can support students and staff to immerse themselves in the outdoors, to build relationship with place over time, and to articulate their experiences through a variety of means, we believe this ancient pathway of human development can be reactivated.

REWILDING IMAGINATION: A NEW CONCEPTION OF SCHOOL LEADERSHIP

In our recent work on education for eco-social-cultural change (Blenkinsop & Fettes, 2021), through a critical review of the literature, interviews with selected educators working on transformative change, and extended creative dialogue with four other co-researchers, we identified four distinctive, mutually complementary sets of competencies, capacities, and capabilities found in a range of educational settings. We then reflected on these findings in light of the teachings of the Four Directions, a tradition shared by a number of Indigenous nations for orienting the mind toward holistic understanding (Cruden, 1995). We should say here that we are not claiming to be *applying* these teachings; rather, we want to humbly acknowledge that they have helped us glimpse how our painstakingly gained insights may be merely a reflection of a deeper pattern, one of potential value for reorienting eco-leadership in schools.

In the East, we locate the *critical educator-leader,* whose mission is to shake up entrenched assumptions and cultivate critical self-awareness and reflection at the individual, group, and systemic levels. Critical educators and leaders may assume different roles, depending on their own positionality and the needs and possibilities of the situation where their work unfolds. One role is that of activist, critiquing existing relationships and norms, and mobilizing resistance to injustice and oppression. Another role is as an ally, walking humbly alongside the historically marginalized and disempowered, helping to open and hold space for their voices and practices. A third role is that of advocate, articulating and advancing alternatives to the status quo for a range of potential audiences, including those not yet convinced of the need for change.

Turning to the South, we encounter the work of the *community educator-leader* who facilitates relationship-building and collective flourishing—involving children, caregivers, knowledge-holders and elders, and a spectrum of diversity encompassing both the human and the more-than-human. Such work is founded on belief in the capacity of self-governing groups of individuals to take responsibility for their actions, participate in community-building, and collectively resolve complex problems together. Belonging, inclusion, and shared purpose are vital dimensions of this work, which generally requires articulation of a shared vision, based on core values, and the cultivation of participants' understanding of their own commitments, personal contributions, and shared responsibility.

In the West, we find the *change educator-leader*. While all of these positionalities involve leading for change, this one is especially concerned with how change is *experienced* by participants, in particular the challenges entailed by uncertainty, risk, discomfort, disruption, and loss. One of the greatest barriers to change is fear and the retreat from pain; thus, change educator-leaders seek to help people turn toward and move through fear and pain into new possibilities of growth and flourishing. At the collective level, this requires the creation of safe-enough spaces where participants are supported to share their pain and grief, learn from past failures and disasters, experiment with new self-understandings and practices, and articulate their evolving understanding of their needs, desires, and possibilities.

Finally, the North is the direction of the *coeur/care educator-leader*, whose core vocation is to support and nurture well-being: mental, physical, social, and emotional. This work involves both connecting with and building on the strengths that people already have as individuals (i.e., the cultivation of resilience) and weaving new connections with human and more-than-human others and with the sacred. Coeur/care educator-leaders promote, encourage, and celebrate practices of connection, thoughtfulness, kindness, and gratitude. They foster a growth mindset: the belief that abilities, intelligences, and skills can be developed through intentional effort. Coeur/care spaces are inclusive environments that respond to the diverse needs of participants, their families, their communities, their contexts, and the denizens and beings that make up these more-than-human places.

Even as they are now, schools offer evidence of all of these educator-leader stances, which we recognize from our own work with teachers and administrators in graduate programs. However, schools are clearly not *designed* for this kind of transformative teaching and leadership, and it is rare to see it intentionally and wholeheartedly supported and cultivated. This, we propose, is the challenge posed by Sheridan and Longboat's conception of imagination.

As *critical* educators, educational leaders can educate themselves and others in the land-based teachings offered by Indigenous knowledge-holders, both locally and on a wider scale (e.g., Kimmerer, 2013; Simpson, 2017; Styres, 2017). They can also learn to attend better, both to the more-than-human (e.g., Hass, 2013; Young, 2012) and to children (e.g., Davies, 2014; Egan & Judson, 2016). If imagination is a gift, then leaders need to be listening for the world not only within their own thoughts but also within the words, ideas, and imaginations of others. Eco-imaginative leadership must recognize that humans are not the center of the universe, that modern adult humans are not the center of the human world, and that White, educated, straight Western men are not the prototype for human development. Working against these tropes implies educating oneself in the literature, language, and experience of anticolonial and antiracist, feminist, and queer movements and bringing that more expansive (self-) understanding to the work of becoming autochthonous to place.

As *community* educators, educational leaders can nurture the positive, supportive, mutually beneficial relationships that comprise the heart of every strong school (and nongovernmental organization [NGO], community organization, etc.), and extend and open them to include the land and its myriad wise beings. Sheridan and Longboat (2006) aver that accepting the "coevolutionary nature" of "mind, spirit and land . . . guides imagination in its duty to integrate nature's realities and ensure the perpetuation of those realities and so all of Life" (p. 369). This helps clarify the active, even activist, nature of this work for the eco-imaginative leader, who is working within structures where this kind of integration with the natural world has not only never been considered, but—as argued earlier—has been intentionally left out. Helpful, too, is Sheridan and Longboat's emphasis on the importance of mythology—"what happens when imagination grows up" (p. 376). This is a reminder that communities need shared stories in order to thrive, and the stories of communities deeply rooted in place are needed to invoke the full range of wisdom that sits therein.

As *change* educators, educational leaders must start by recognizing their own grief and culpability, and the forms of resistance, distraction, and denial present in their own struggle in becoming attuned to land and place. Without compassion for themselves, they will find it hard to extend compassion to their staff, students, and families as they, too, struggle to shift old habits and engage in new ways of being. There is a balance to be held along the East-West axis, between the brightness of new insight and the letting-go of old assumptions, between the clarity of critical thought and the depth of emotional anguish—for we are now all fated to live in an age of great loss and upheaval. Pacing, rhythm, and humility are of vital importance, for no one can flourish under conditions of constant stress and trauma. Spaces of peace, calm, slowness, and stillness are essential to the work.

As *coeur/care* educators, educational leaders can work with the imagination as a gift-filled, place-shaped space of personal and group development in which they, too, take part. This includes seeking out and spending time with elders and wise teachers, human and more-than-human—especially in outdoor settings where the imagination can more readily be released from its colonial domestication. Simple practices such as sit spots and listening walks can allow one to receive more of the gifts being offered (cf. the "place-thoughts" of Watts, 2013), to recognize them as such, and to take small but genuine steps toward reconciling mind, body, spirit, and landscape, toward autochthony. Local Indigenous practices of reciprocity and gratitude with our more-than-human kin are often relatively accessible and willingly shared. Diverse art practices can be adapted to similar ends. Here, too, there is a balance to be held along the North–South axis so that the robust intertwining of community remains open to ongoing, ever-deepening, and sometimes challenging and disruptive learning.

CONCLUSION

Sheridan and Longboat (2006) suggest that imagination, properly understood, "is showing us the way to the quintessential human condition—the paradise of one's surroundings and one's place there" (p. 379). Seen from their perspective, schools as we currently know them are a long way from that paradise. We find it heartening, however, to contemplate the imaginative work calling to be done—work that is demanding and difficult, to be sure, but that is also filled with relationships, gifts, and joy. What greater vocation could there be for educational leaders than to help all of us "neo-Americans" "out of [our] problems and into how things should be" (p. 379)?

CULTIVATING CURIOSITY, CONVERSATION, AND IMAGINATION

After reading this chapter, what evokes your sense of wonder? What are you curious about?

For Consideration and Conversation

Fettes and Blenkinsop describe four leadership positionalities with reference to an Indigenous framework of the Four Directions. These include: the change educator-leader, community educator-leader, critical educator-leader, and coeur/care educator-leader. Using the descriptions of each of these stances, conduct a critical self-evaluation of your own leadership. Which of these stances do you already embody, and to what extent? What are some concrete examples? Which areas would you like to strengthen, and what concrete actions can you take to begin doing so?

This chapter brings into focus what must transform, or shift, in order to move to a more land-based, holistic version of education. Which one of the shifts described by the authors resonates with you the most? Why? What barriers or opportunities exist in your leadership context to work toward this kind of transformation? What is an actionable next step you could take to shift your school and/or your leadership in this direction?

Cultivating Imagination With Cognitive Tools

Meta-Narratives

Fettes and Blenkinsop offer a new meta-narrative within which we can explore and examine our ideas and theories of educational leadership. What is your emotional response to exploring educational leadership through the Four Directions? How does this framework offer something new to your understanding? How might exploring different frameworks or meta-narratives allow for new possibility?

REFERENCES

Blenkinsop, S. (2012). Four slogans for cultural change: An evolving place-based, imaginative and ecological learning experience. *Journal of Moral Education, 41*(3), 353–368.

Blenkinsop, S., & Beeman, C. (2010). The world as co-teacher: Learning to work with a peerless colleague. *Trumpeter, 26*(3), 26–39.

Blenkinsop, S., & Fettes, M. (2007). Developing the scientific imagination: A key to sustainability? In D. B. Zandvliet & D. L. Fisher (Eds.), *Sustainable communities, sustainable environments* (pp. 37–46). Sense.

Blenkinsop, S., & Fettes, M. (2021). *Living within the earth's carrying capacity: Towards an education for eco-social-cultural change*. Report submitted under the Knowledge Synthesis Grants program of the Social Sciences and Humanities Research Council. www.circesfu.ca/wp-content/uploads/2021/06/Final-Report-Blenkinsop-Fettes.pdf

Blenkinsop, S., & Piersol, L. (2013). Listening to the literal: Orientations towards how nature communicates. *Phenomenology and Practice, 7*(1), 41–60.

Cruden, L. (1995). *The spirit of place: A workbook for sacred alignment*. Inner Traditions/Bear & Co.

Davies, B. (2014). *Listening to children: Being and becoming*. Routledge.

Egan, K. (1997). *The educated mind. How cognitive tools shape our understanding*. University of Chicago Press.

Egan, K. (2002). *Getting it wrong from the beginning: Our progressivist inheritance from Herbert Spencer, John Dewey, and Jean Piaget*. Yale University Press.

Egan, K., & Judson, G. (2016). *Imagination and the engaged learner: Cognitive tools for the classroom*. Teachers College Press.

Fettes, M. (2017). Land and the living roots of language: From rights to reconciliation. *Tusaaji: A Translation Review, 5*(5), 1–16.

Fettes, M., & Judson, G. (2011). Imagination and the cognitive tools of place-making. *Journal of Environmental Education, 42*(2), 123–135.

Gilligan, C. (1982). *In a different voice: Psychological theory and women's development*. Harvard University Press.

Hass, R. (2013). Introduction. In A. Fisher-Wirth & L-G. Street (Eds.), *The ecopoetry anthology* (pp. xli-lxv). Trinity University Press.

Jickling, B., Blenkinsop, S., Timmerman, N., & Sitka-Sage, M. (2018). *Wild pedagogies: Touchstones for re-negotiating education and the environment in the Anthropocene*. Palgrave Macmillan.

Judson, G. (2021). Cultivating leadership imagination with cognitive tools: An imagination-focused approach to leadership education. *Journal of Research on Leadership Education*. https://doi.org/10.1177/19427751211022028

Kimmerer, R.W. (2013). *Braiding sweetgrass. Indigenous wisdom, scientific knowledge and the teachings of plants*. Milkweed Editions.

Noddings, N. (2013). *Caring: A relational approach to ethics and moral education*. University of California Press.

Serres, M. (1995). *The natural contract.* University of Michigan Press.

Shepard, P. (1982). *Nature and madness.* University of Georgia Press.

Sheridan, J., & Longboat, D. (2006). The Haudenosaunee imagination and the ecology of the sacred. *Space and Culture, 9*(4), 365–381.

Simpson, L. (2017). *As we have always done: Indigenous freedom through radical resistance.* University of Minnesota Press.

Styres, S. (2017). *Pathways for remembering and recognizing Indigenous thought in education: Philosophies of iethi'nihstenha ohwentsia'kekha (land).* University of Toronto Press.

Truth and Reconciliation Commission of Canada. (2015). *Honouring the truth, reconciling for the future: Summary of the final report of the Truth and Reconciliation Commission of Canada.* Truth and Reconciliation Commission of Canada. https://publications.gc.ca/collections/collection_2015/trc/IR4-7-2015-eng.pdf

Vygotsky, L. (2004). Imagination and creativity in childhood. *Journal of Russian and East European Psychology, 42*(1), 7–97.

Watts, V. (2013). Indigenous place-thought and agency amongst humans and non-humans (First Woman and Sky Woman go on a European world tour!). *Decolonization: Indigeneity, Education & Society, 2*(1), 20–34.

Young, J. (2012). *What the robin knows: How birds reveal the secrets of the natural world.* Houghton Mifflin Harcourt.

CHAPTER 9

Disrupting Deficit Through Radical Reimaginings of Urban Student Subjectivities and Knowledges

Kathryn Strom, Kara Viesca, and Jessica Masterson

For many educators, the term "urban" is not an adjective denoting a metropolitan or densely populated city, but rather is shorthand for race, class, language, culture, and any other significant factor in minoritizing students, families, and communities (Milner, 2012). "Urban" thus becomes racialized code and is applied to low-income neighborhoods housing mainly Black and Brown families, and their schools, as dangerous spaces filled with "others" on the fringes of society. These deficit-based perspectives (Sharma, 2016; Walker, 2011) locate the problem with the individual student through narratives that focus on solving the "achievement gap" through personal responsibility and "grit" (Gorski, 2016).

Such a pathological perspective reinforces racist stereotypes and places the focus on the human actors, blaming them for a variety of issues and acting as if they have the complete agency to change their realities. This thinking ignores the socio-materiality of urban communities, and the ways that students are produced in complex ways by them, along with the larger historical and contemporary systems of capitalism and racism that shape low-income areas and their residents (Sondel et al., 2019). By obscuring these factors and focusing on individuals, these human-centric perspectives ultimately reproduce and sustain white supremacy, colonialism, and income/class-based inequalities.

We, like many researchers, advocate disrupting these deficit perspectives and pursuing systemic change in urban education. However, merely critiquing the deficits and educational systems that reproduce them is not enough—we have to *create* alternatives. To do that, educational leaders, teachers, and researchers must be able to think beyond what we already know, beyond what is in front of our faces, and envision what is not-yet. That is, we must use the powers of imagination and imagine *otherwise*.

In this chapter, we argue that critical posthuman concepts offer tools for school leaders and other educators to imagine otherwise. We illustrate these possibilities by considering the material-affective realities of urban neighborhoods in relation to schooling through a relational, multiplistic, and difference-rich ontology. We first describe critical posthumanism (Braidotti, 2013, 2019), alongside the notion of imagination. We then detail the methodological approach and delve into two fragments of "glowing" data (MacLure, 2013a, b) that demonstrate the agency of urban neighborhoods; the objects, sounds, and events that comprise them; and their role in the co-constitution of students' subjectivities, knowledges, and classroom experiences. We conclude with brief recommendations for leaders and teachers seeking to imagine-otherwise in urban schools.

CRITICAL POSTHUMANISM AND IMAGINING OTHERWISE

The reductionist, positivist, human-centered logic that tends to dominate Western thinking and scholarship constructs harmful narratives about students (Kayumova & Buxton, 2021; Strom, 2015) and promotes a simplistic understanding of teaching in "urban" settings that upholds longstanding patterns of inequity (Colmenares, 2021; Strom & Martin, 2017). Critique is not enough, however: we must also create affirmative "counter-actualizations" (Braidotti, 2013, p. 165). This requires thinking outside commonsense thinking, and particularly beyond ideas that we exist as bound encapsulated bodies separate from everything; that the schoolhouse exists separate from the neighborhood; and that kids come to school already as formed entities.

Thinking differently requires conceptual creativity and experimentation, which in turn require both individual and collective imagination. Braidotti (2011) describes imagination as a "creative re-working" process (p. 248), echoing Judson's (2020) assertion that imagination is not synonymous with creativity, but rather enables it. Judson also argues for the centrality of imagination in the work of educators, particularly those who seek to disrupt current inequitable status quos of harm for students. These leaders must think outside the confines of White, Eurocentric, heteropatriarchal, neurotypical, and ableist logics, while simultaneously envisioning future possibilities for transformative change. Moreover, they must engage in "collective re-imagining, or a shared desire for transformations" (Braidotti, 2013, p. 205), to begin to think differently, because moving away from the trappings of White thinking-being shakes the very foundation of our ideology in the West (and particularly in the United States). In this study, we argue that a critical posthuman lens (Braidotti, 2013, 2019) provides conceptual tools to think differently about students living and learning in high-poverty urban environments and thus to imagine affirmative alternatives. These conceptual tools include notions of immanence, multiplicity, shared agency, assemblage, lines of flight, and posthuman subjectivity, as explained next.

Critical posthumanism (Braidotti, 2013, 2019) draws on a neo-materialist interpretation of Spinoza (e.g., Deleuze, 1988; Deleuze & Guattari, 1987) and critical feminist philosophy (e.g., Braidotti, 1994; Haraway, 1988). It moves away from a dualistic perspective that divides the world into discrete, static categories (e.g., this/that, self/other, man/woman) and toward an understanding of the world as *immanent*, or composed of matter that is connected, alive, and constantly morphing (Braidotti, 2013; Deleuze, 1988). This shift also entails replacing the individual human as the central referent for reality with *multiplicity*. This means we do not exist as single, isolated actors, but rather are part of larger aggregates of matter (e.g., humans, objects, places, nonhuman organisms) and forces or incorporeal elements (e.g., power, affect, knowledge).

These shifts also disrupt the notion that agency belongs to humans who have free will and control themselves and their environments, and shift to an understanding of *shared agency*: all elements in an assemblage, including nonhuman and incorporeal (Bennett, 2010) ones, act. *Assemblages* are constantly moving and changing clusters of heterogeneous elements that work together to do something (Strom, 2015), and this heterogeneity—all the different parts working together—is a creative force. This makes assemblages *sympoietic* (Haraway, 2016): they are co-making, or becoming-different, always in relation to the inside and outside. These material and discursive components co-constitute each other, co-creating the other in a recursive process that Barad (2007) refers to as *intra-action*.

Critical posthumanism also always entails a political analysis: multiplicities are shaped not just by human and nonhuman elements, but also by flows of power seeking to bind activity to the status quo, and mutant, subversive flows (Deleuze & Guattari, 1987). Although these mutant flows—also known as *lines of flight*—are always recaptured by the dominant power forces, lines of flight shuffle the segments of the system and produce change. Critical posthumanism also has an ethico-political component: it is an antitranscendent approach, meaning that nothing can be extracted as universal and correct. Knowledge and practices are always situated (Haraway, 1988), because they are produced by specific assemblages, and the components of those assemblages necessarily affect the knowledge/practices that are generated. Therefore, it is an ethical imperative to practice a *politics of location*, whereby those involved in production of knowledge/practices situate themselves historically, socioculturally, geopolitically, and so on (Braidotti, 2013).

The question of the subject in critical posthumanism is also a political one. While we acknowledge that some posthuman analyses seek to remove the subject altogether and focus on the nonhuman, we argue that doing so reproduces the "god trick" of being the voice from everywhere and nowhere (Braidotti, 2018; Haraway, 1988). To include the human (researcher) subject is to practice a politics of location. To include the human (participant) subject is to account explicitly for those who have been historically afforded the rights assigned to those judged to be human, and for those who have never had the chance to fully be considered human (Braidotti, 2013). However, the critical posthumanism subject is not the conscious, completely agentic subject of rational humanism, but rather multiplistic, mobile, and creatively produced by material, discursive, and affective forces and elements (Braidotti, 2019). We contend that this processual, relational subject needs to be included in analyses, as part of larger assemblages that also account for nonhuman and affective elements.

Critical posthumanism has many implications for the ways we think about students, schooling processes, and teaching in urban settings—and the ways we can imagine otherwise to create alternatives. For one, the inside/outside boundary of the schoolroom is porous, and the lives of students outside the classroom are part of the multiplicity of elements that influences what happens inside the classroom. Further, students themselves are multiplicities who are not preexisting subjects, but are produced by assemblages of *home-neighborhood-school-plus*. Dominant discourses/practices tend to privilege the human actors in the teaching-learning situation (e.g., the students learn, the teachers teach), and these human actors are assigned complete agency: they control their successes and failures. This individualistic stance renders students as context-free individuals who make a choice whether to learn and draws a causal connection between teachers' work and students' learning.

However, there are many nonhuman actors in classroom assemblages that affect the processes of teaching and learning that occur. We suggest that some of the most notable nonhuman actors include objects, events, and sounds from the urban neighborhood just outside the window of the classroom. Employing a posthuman perspective to consider these nonhuman actors and the ways they construct knowledge and subjectivity can provide "visionary fuel" to disrupt deficit perspectives of our students and engage in radical reimagining.

METHODOLOGICAL APPROACH

In this chapter, we focus on a material-affective analysis of two "glowing" (MacLure, 2013a, b) data fragments drawn from a larger ethnographic study of elementary, middle, and high school classrooms in schools in two U.S. states. The data fragments come from observations in a 6th-grade classroom at Sweetbriar Elementary (a pseudonym), a public elementary school in a highly diverse city in the western United States. The school serves a population of approximately 600 students, of which 80% are Latino, with small percentages of Asian, Black, Filipino, Pacific Islander, White, and multiracial students. Approximately 60% of the school's population are multilingual learners, and 80% of the students receive free or reduced lunch. The neighborhood surrounding Sweetbriar Elementary has the highest poverty rate in the city, with approximately 36% of children under the age of 6 living below the absolute poverty line.

The 6th-grade class was taught by Isabella, a bilingual Latina in her early 30s. The class of 34 students was representative of the larger school population, with the vast majority of the students in the class Latino and multilingual. One of us conducted an 80-minute observation approximately once per week during the spring semester ($n=11$), which included a short conversation afterward with the teacher regarding the class. Data sources included observation notes, student artifacts, and transcripts of post-class conversations.

After each observation, we created an analytic memo that included (a) a detailed summary of the class; (b) an "assemblage" analysis that considered elements such as the teacher, students, contextual elements, and pedagogy; (c) a pedagogical analysis of the lesson utilizing a six-point framework grounded in critical sociocultural theory (Teemant et al., 2014); and (d) notes regarding the teacher debrief. Foregoing a traditional analytic coding process, we focused on what MacLure (2013b) calls "hot spots" or "glowing" data, which

> . . . can be felt on occasions where something—perhaps a comment in an interview, a fragment of a field note, an anecdote, an object, or a strange facial expression—seems to reach out from the inert corpus (corpse) of the

data, to grasp us . . . they exert a kind of fascination, and have a capacity to animate further thought. (p. 228)

These glowing fragments of data are affective intensities (Ringrose & Renold, 2014) that refuse to fit into a neat analytic category or theme, exceeding the tidy lines of traditional qualitative analysis, drawing our attention back again and again as we resisted reductive sense-making (MacLure, 2013a) and leaned into this space of imagination and possibility.

We focus on two hot spots—a lockdown incident and an assignment from a poetry unit—as fertile sites for engaging in imagining-otherwise with posthuman concepts. Both data fragments not only contain powerful language and images that hint at the production of student subjectivities and knowledge by their neighborhood, but also produce hauntings from our own pasts, when the three of us (the authors of this chapter), White women from working- or middle-class backgrounds, were classroom teachers. As we analyzed data, we felt echoes of the high-poverty, highly diverse neighborhoods, classrooms, and students of the schools in which we taught. In our discussions, we wondered if we also reproduced the deficit narratives that tend to accompany contextual analysis of urban schools. In the next section, we use ideas constructed from these glowing data fragments to delve further into these questions, considering the role of the urban neighborhood in producing students and learning environments.

Campus Lockdowns

On a dreary day in early February, Isabella notified students that a lockdown drill would be happening later that day. In a lockdown drill, teachers lock their doors, turn off the lights, and draw their blinds. Held periodically throughout the year, the drills help students understand and practice what to do in an active shooter situation. That day, the drill would be happening during recess, so students would be outside on the playground when the alarm rang. The students had been through lockdown drills before, but they had always happened when students were in a classroom. Isabella informed students that if they were outside when the alarm sounded, they should run to the nearest classroom and "shelter in place" until notified otherwise. She explained, "The point is to get somewhere where you can hide and stay quiet."

After her announcement, students raised various "what if" questions. One student asked, "What if [a student is] in the bathroom and all the classrooms are already locked?" Another student commented on the likelihood that chaos would ensue from students running from the playground to different classrooms: "It's going to be a mess!" Isabella agreed, acknowledging that she was not sure what the drill was going to look like, and that was why they needed to practice.

After the class ended, Isabella told us two actual lockdowns had already occurred at Sweetbriar this year. One of them, she shared, which had happened just the previous week, was triggered by an active shooter situation at the apartment complex across the street from the school. Isabella's classroom was located in a "portable," a cheap, movable pod sometimes referred to as a "trailer." Although intended as a temporary space because of their flimsy construction, in many urban schools, portables often end up serving as permanent classrooms. Isabella's room was one of about 10 or so portables that made up the outer layer of the campus. Her classroom window faced the street, directly across from the apartment complex.

Recalling the incident, Isabella described "sheltering in place" with her students in her classroom: she locked the doors, turned out the lights, and instructed all students to remain as still and quiet as possible. Although she drew the blinds so students could not see what was happening, the thin walls of the portable could not keep out the sounds of the police activity, sirens, and shouts. These sounds easily filtered through the inadequate barrier between the students and the outside, frightening and upsetting students. Isabella remembered,

> You could hear the police trying to convince the person to come out, with their hands up. It was very real for the students. It was quite scary [for them]. It was scary for me as well. I had two girls crying. After that it was "shelter in place," [and] they calmed down a bit.... I moved students away from the window because the house is really across the street, and they could come out shooting. Thank God we were only there for an hour. We had no idea how long it would last. We [the teachers] saw the man come out of the house and get down on the floor.

The lockdown drill and the actual lockdown that Isabella recounted both point to the porosity of the inside and outside of schools. Often, schools treat the boundary of the school walls as an impermeable, protective barrier that creates a neutral space in which students and teachers can focus on the business of teaching and learning. By doing this, students and teachers are constructed as autonomous individuals with complete agency; that is, they have total control over how they teach and learn (Dernikos, 2019). This corresponds with the popular "No Excuses" rhetoric often heard in urban schools, which views any other factor besides student and teacher effort as an excuse, or a distraction, that amounts to giving up on kids of color. This rhetoric is an individualistic, a-historical, a-contextual perspective of education that, ultimately, enables school systems to blame students and/or teachers for failing to meet academic benchmarks (Sondel et al., 2019).

However, as this vignette shows, the outside *matters*. Students do not exist in a vacuum. They are part of connected multiplicities, embodied and embedded (in their neighborhoods; Braidotti, 2013). The things that happen in that neighborhood shape their subjectivities as well as their experiences in the classroom, as this data fragment shows. On one hand, the school engaging in drills is an acknowledgment by the system of the porous nature of schools—they are responding to potential danger by preparing the teachers and students to stay as safe as possible in a lockdown event. However, typically little effort is taken beyond the drills to account for how the local geography actually shapes processes of teaching and learning in classrooms, student subjectivities, and/or operations at the larger school level (Leander et al., 2010).

This vignette also points to sound as an agentic actor in urban neighborhoods and schools. Sound is a resonance, which Gershon (2013a) defines as "affective knowledge that strongly informs how one 'is' and one 'knows'" (p. 258). Sounds are affects that work on bodies, diminishing or augmenting their capacities, forming them into particular identifications, producing particular understandings of the world. Affects of sound are also political and racialized (Dernikos, 2019; Gershon, 2013b); for example, the sounds of police activity outside the classroom window are more likely to be heard in low-income areas populated by Black and Brown children, thus shaping the knowledge and bodies of kids of color. Further, the sounds of police negotiating with the active shooter leaked into the students' space via the thin walls of the portable classroom, which is a structure less likely to be found in wealthy schools. During the lockdown, these sounds created powerful affects flowing through the classroom and bodies in it (students were frozen in fear, some crying).

This vignette also demonstrates that, taken together, the sounds, events, and spaces of the neighborhood shape students' knowledge and sense-making skills. When Isabella brought up the lockdown drill that was to occur later that day, students demonstrated their ability to engage in complex meaning-making by interpreting or analyzing the situation and showing an ability to imagine future problems or outcomes based on that analysis. For example, one student clearly imagined the chaos that could ensue when the alarm sounded while students were at recess with no directions where to go, predicting, "It's going to be a mess!" Another student imagined a scenario where she might be using the restroom and would need to know where to go from there. The ability to analyze a future situation is a highly complex skill, one that Freire (1985) described when he talked about literacy as both reading the word and reading the world. He argues:

> The act of reading cannot be explained as merely reading words since every act of reading words implies a previous reading of the world and a subsequent rereading of the world. There is a permanent movement back and forth between "reading" reality and reading words-the spoken word too is our reading of the world. (p. 18)

By connecting reading words with reading the world, Freire illustrates the complex, contextualized, co-constructed nature of meaning-making between words on a page and life experiences. The students in this discussion of a lockdown drill illustrate strong abilities to read the world. However, these abilities do not appear to be tapped into substantively or connected to the words they read on the page in their classrooms. In fact, seeing these children as highly literate at reading the world sits at odds with Sweetbriar's reported literacy outcomes as measured by standardized tests. According to 2018 outcomes at the elementary school, only 25% of the students were proficient in literacy. So, while the 6th-grade students in Isabella's classroom were positioned by the school system as having poor literacy skills, they could clearly draw on their experiences in the neighborhood to show that they actually had very complex thinking and real-world literacy skills. We can employ the notion of *shared agency* of the neighborhood, including the nonhuman objects, events, and sounds associated with it, as teachers. That is, these nonhuman actors provide a site for learning and developing meaning-making abilities for the students in Isabella's class. From a leadership perspective, such an act requires a radical reimagining, moving beyond the idea that only human actors are agentic. Doing so, however, reframes the neighborhood from a site of deficit to a productive assemblage contributing to students' valuable literacy skills.

"I Am From" Poems

As part of their poetry unit, students constructed their own poems using a sentence-frame template that prompted them to think of items from their neighborhood and yard, items that were found around their homes, and items that were important in their lives. These poems were intensely affective, provoking in us sadness and outrage, yet also wonder of the resiliency, knowledge, and cultural heritage of these

11- and 12-year-olds. Below, we share two of the poems. We also reference other poems that we viewed while students were writing but were not able to capture in their entirety.

Poem 1: I am from [city name] and Mexico

I am hanging TVs,
PlayStation,
And XBox.
I am from sport balls and
Kids on their phones,
And touch screen tech.
I am from guns and knifes [sic]
Use[d] cigs on the floor and abandoned houses.
I am from it rains
Cats and dogs.
I am from tacos,
And child support,
And [parents' names].

Poem 2: I am from [city name] and Flip Phones

I am from broken homes
And broken fences
I am from popped balls around the yard
And broken bottles
I am from 7 eleven
And big leafless trees
I am from a world of surprises
And a home with no entertainment
I am from beans and rice
And my little brother
I am from [parents' names].

During the observation, Isabella brought two poems over to where one of us was sitting in the corner of the room, which immediately captured the researcher's attention. She walked around the room and peeked at other students' poems. At first glance, they offered stories told through the detritus found in a high-poverty neighborhood. Students wrote about things that were broken: broken homes, broken fences, broken bottles, popped balls. They also wrote about things perhaps associated with "bad" neighborhoods: used cigarettes on the floor, abandoned houses, leafless trees, dog poop. They also wrote about dangerous items, things that hinted at the violence just under the surface of the places they live: guns and knives, cocaine.

Activating a posthuman imaginary, these objects commonly found in urban, high-poverty neighborhoods are more than inert, passive items. They work together with the homes and other physical elements of the neighborhood to create a collective feeling that shapes our perception of a neighborhood as "good" or "bad," "rich" or "poor," and so on. These objects are indicative of power flows, existing in places where the human residents, particularly in the United States, are more likely to be lower-income and Black and Brown. Further, the objects in the poem affect human bodies in the classroom, inviting students to identify them as representative of their homes, of themselves, invoking feelings of familiarity and connection in students. They may also provoke a multitude of affective reactions from the readers of the poems—perhaps shock, disgust, sadness, anger, concern, or pity. These items demonstrate what Bennett (2010) calls "thing-power": "the strange ability of ordinary, man-made items to exceed their status as objects and to manifest traces of independence or aliveness" (p. xiv). Like neighborhood events such as the lockdown drill discussed previously, these items produce student subjectivities in particular ways, as well as shape their ways of knowing-being.

It would be relatively easy to construct yet another deficit or pity-based narrative from these poems. The objects chosen by the students to express how they saw themselves—weapons, excrement, drugs, broken or forgotten things—produce powerful but mostly negative affective relations, as noted above. Returning to the poems with a posthuman perspective, however, creatively reworks the analysis: while the students in this class may be produced by these items associated with violence and dereliction, they are also an assemblage of place-based knowledge, technological know-how, and rich cultural traditions. For instance, the poems show the agency of technology in constructing student identity: "I am hanging TVs, PlayStation, and Xbox . . . I am from . . . kids on their phones, and touch screen tech." The poems also show the influence of home, culture, and language: "I am from beans and rice"; "I am from tacos"; "I am from go away and *cayate*."

While we would never argue that students and families living in unsafe, impoverished conditions is desirable, the objects of urban poverty that surfaced in these poems did so in ways that also illustrate a rich complexity in student understanding and reading of their world—similar to the highly developed analytic skills demonstrated by students in the previous vignette. For example, one student wrote, "I am from MacDonald's [sic], where the rich kids say it's peasant food." This statement demonstrates the student's sociopolitical understanding that

McDonald's, with its value menu, chemically produced foods, and association with poor eating habits, is considered inferior fare by some from wealthier communities. It also provides another angle for reimagining the neighborhood in a more assets-based way: as a site of learning, of problem-posing, of world reading that can relate to word reading (Freire, 1985) to understand power and inequities.

The nonhuman actors discussed in these poems clearly produce student subjectivities. However, we did not see these nonhuman actors taken up to support strong learning/teaching assemblages in this classroom; other than having student volunteers read their poems aloud, Isabella and her students did not discuss the nonhuman elements that appeared in the poems. This is not surprising—often there is substantive silence around the complex reality that living in impoverished neighborhoods produces tangible hardships while also generating conditions for strong literacy capabilities, as demonstrated in the previous section. We have to wonder, what would happen if that silence were disrupted? If teachers and leaders reimagined classrooms as spaces where the nonhuman actors that are such important elements in teaching/learning assemblages in schools and that substantively produce student subjectivities were more visible and interacted with purposefully? We think through these possibilities in the discussion below.

DISCUSSION

In the two data fragments discussed above, we radically reimagine subjectivity from a posthuman perspective, viewing it as co-produced or co-constituted by objects, spaces, events, sounds, discourses. From these analyses, we argue that the urban neighborhood and its objects exerted *thing-power* (Bennett, 2010) that serves as a subject-producing force, as evidenced by the poems. The sonic affects (Gershon, 2013a) produced by events like the active shooter lockdown also shaped the students and their world. This materially informed radical reimagining shows that students' subjectivities are multidimensional. They are composed of the material realities of their neighborhoods and markers of poverty, yes, but also rich cultural traditions/language and complex technological tools. However, such a perspective presents a significant disruption to the ways that teachers and leaders think about teaching, learning, and students, and we need to support leaders to make this shift. Accordingly, in this final section, we offer recommendations for helping leaders engage in this radical reimagining of education by infusing key ideas into their preparation and ongoing support.

In our leadership preparation programs, we need to tackle the rational thinking that undergirds the ways leaders (and anyone socialized into a Western, White perspective) think. For example, educators tend to view Black and Brown students from high-poverty neighborhoods as one-dimensional—as either problems to be fixed or as objects of pity. Such perspectives contribute to the dehumanization of Black and Brown students (Baldridge, 2014), which positions them as undeserving of the same rights afforded those who do qualify as human (Braidotti, 2013). By this logic, site and district leaders can justify the outdated facilities, lower-quality teachers, and lack of resources that often characterize urban schools.

They can also rationalize the unequal distribution of childhood innocence. Although dominant narratives hold that children are to be sheltered from harm, students in high-poverty urban areas are often denied that. As shown by the vignettes, urban students often deal with what are usually considered "adult" issues from a young age (Burton, 2007), including violence, and that affects what happens in school as well—although schools are supposed to be places where students are protected. However, as the lockdown incident shows, schools are porous in multiple ways. Although the teacher tried to protect her students from what was happening outside by closing the windows and turning out the lights, the sounds of the active shooter situation seeped in through the thin walls of the portable, creating a collective wave of anxiety and fear through the class—one that was not addressed in any meaningful way before the children were expected to go back to business as usual.

A major concept that educational leadership preparation programs should emphasize, then, is this porousness of the inside/outside of schools. However, the conditions of urban neighborhoods are often seen as taboo subjects—although the context of urban poverty may be acknowledged by teachers and leaders, it is not typically seen as a site for learning. This presents a paradox; although the students are immersed in their material urban environments, and it produces them as particular subjects, we pretend that these conditions do not exist outside the classroom, treating the school walls as barriers that keep the inside as neutral space where students can concentrate solely on learning (Dernikos, 2019). This pretense creates disconnects between what is emphasized in schools and the daily realities of students living in urban neighborhoods.

Educational leaders also need to grapple with *affect*, an aspect of urban education that educators typically ignore altogether or expect students to leave at the school door (Dernikos et al., 2020). Dominant narratives render the work of schooling as solely intellectual; it takes place in the brain and is supposed to be rational. Because of this belief, many believe that feelings, and the things that make feelings feel (Gregg & Seigworth, 2010), are not supposed to have a place in educational activity. The sounds of the neighborhood, the items on the ground, the conditions in which the students live—all these create powerful affective relations. Take, for instance, the responses of the students to the active shooter lockdown—terror, sobbing, panic. Although the lockdown lasted an hour, the affects of the event, and the sounds and movements associated with it, would be felt in the bodies of the students and Isabella for a long time afterward, and it would become an active force in the shaping of subjectivities, knowledges, and worldviews. Yet, after that hour, the students were expected to go back to business as usual, asked to shove aside the terrifying and gut-wrenching experience and concentrate on learning. Not acknowledging these affects, and instead expecting the students merely to carry on with learning curriculum disconnected from their lives outside the heavy metal fence of the school, is another method of dehumanizing students.

Explicitly working with leaders to deconstruct dominant thinking/discourses, to understand the way these operate via dualisms and hierarchies, and to identify the ways those harm students is a first step. However, we also have to find entry points into this radical reimagining, into ways of thinking that construct our students and school settings from difference-affirmative positionings that can help educational leaders develop not only a more complex perspective, but also an assets-based, collectivist way to disrupt individualistic, human-centric, a-contextual, deficit-based perspectives that produce students as less-than-human.

One type of entry point, we suggest, could be vignettes and classroom artifacts like those shared in this chapter. For instance, educational leaders could examine the lockdown incident and poems from a posthuman lens to analyze the ways that students demonstrated deep, complex, high-level understandings that were generated from their everyday intra-actions with their environments. Although the lockdown event and the poems do reveal the dangers and tough conditions of the urban neighborhood, educational leaders can be supported to become attuned to the brilliance that students have been taught from their material surroundings—knowledge that is generally not recognized by schools as legitimate, or existing at all, as their neighborhoods are typically seen as something to overcome, or something to leave behind, rather than rich sites of learning. With support, leaders could then work with teachers to utilize a problem-posing pedagogy (Freire, 1970) that used students' everyday lives—especially the objects, sounds, and events of their community—as curriculum. This curriculum could take up the social inequities of which students already are very aware and problematize them to gain deeper understanding and generate social action.

CONCLUSION

In sum, a critical posthuman perspective helps to illuminate the harm of dominant narratives while offering tools for radically reimagining the subjectivity of urban students as more-than-human to gain much more complex and assets-based understanding. This reimagining through a posthuman lens can not only help leaders see students as more than their high-poverty neighborhoods, but also help them to consider the agency and affectivity of the neighborhood and its objects, events, and sounds in the process of schooling. These nonhuman actors not only produce students in particular ways, but also generate particular schooling experiences, knowledges, and ways of knowing/being in the world. If taken seriously by educational leaders and teachers as curriculum, such urban-neighborhood-knowledges could help leaders imagine ways of teaching-otherwise and learning-otherwise that move toward collective justice.

CULTIVATING CURIOSITY, CONVERSATION, AND IMAGINATION

After reading this chapter, what evokes your sense of wonder? What are you curious about?

For Consideration and Conversation

This chapter draws attention to the porous nature of schools. How does this porosity enrich your school community? How does it present challenges? As a leader, how can you account for this porosity in your relationships and actions?

Within the relational conception of educational leadership that Strom, Viesca, and Masterson propose, what material, more-than-human influences must be acknowledged by leaders and how?

Cultivate Imagination With Cognitive Tools

Revolt and Idealism

Strom, Viesca, and Masterson call leaders to radically reimagine urban education, to replace harmful deficit-focused narratives with complex and asset-focused understanding of learners and learning. Think about your school community. Identify a deficit-focused narrative that negatively impacts students that you would like to disrupt. Reveal a policy, process, or practice (small or large) that sustains this deficit-focused way of understanding students in your school. How can you "break the rules" or disrupt what is to create a more equitable and socially just learning environment? How does "breaking the rules" support student learning and support asset-focused understanding of your school community? How can the rules be radically reimagined to enrich the school community?

REFERENCES

Baldridge, B. J. (2014). Relocating the deficit: Reimagining Black youth in neoliberal times. *American Educational Research Journal, 51*(3), 440–472. http://doi.org/10.3102/0002831214532514

Barad, K. (2007). *Meeting the universe halfway.* Duke University Press.

Bennett, J. (2010). *Vibrant matter: A political ecology of things.* Duke University Press.

Braidotti, R. (1994). *Nomadic subjects: Embodiment and sexual difference in contemporary feminist theory.* Columbia University Press.

Braidotti, R. (2011). *Nomadic theory: The portable Rosi Braidotti.* Columbia University Press.

Braidotti, R. (2013). *The posthuman.* Polity Press.

Braidotti, R. (2018). Affirmative ethics, posthuman subjectivity, and intimate scholarship: A conversation with Rosi Braidotti. In K. Strom, T. Mills, & A. Ovens, *Decentering the researcher in intimate scholarship: Critical posthuman methodological perspectives in education* (pp. 179–188). Emerald Publishing Limited.

Braidotti, R. (2019). *Posthuman knowledge.* Polity Press.

Burton, L. (2007). Childhood adultification in economically disadvantaged families: A conceptual model. *Family Relations, 56*(4), 329–345. http://doi.org/10.1111/j.1741-3729.2007.00463.x

Colmenares, E. E. (2021). Exploring student teachers' "stuck moments": Affect[ing] the theory-practice gap in social justice teacher education. *Professional Development in Education, 47*(2–3), 377–391. http://doi.org/10.1080/19415257.2021.1879229

Deleuze, G. (1988). *Spinoza: Practical philosophy.* City Lights Books.

Deleuze, G., & Guattari, F. (1987). *Capitalism and schizophrenia: A thousand plateaus.* University of Minnesota Press.

Dernikos, B. (2019). *The call of "things": Exploring sonic vibrations and "noisy bodies" in readers workshop.* Paper presented at the American Educational Research Association Annual Meeting in Toronto, Canada.

Dernikos, B., Lesko, N., McCall, S., & Niccolini, A. (2020). *Mapping the affective turn in education: Theory, research, and pedagogy.* Routledge.

Freire, P. (1970). *Pedagogy of the oppressed.* Continuum.

Freire, P. (1985). Reading the world and reading the word: An interview with Paulo Freire. *Language Arts, 62*(1), 15–21. www.jstor.org/stable/41405241

Gershon, W. S. (2013a). Vibrational affect: Sound theory and practice in qualitative research. *Cultural Studies ←→ Critical Methodologies, 13*(4), 257–262. http://doi.org/10.1177/1532708613488067

Gershon, W. S. (2013b). Sonic cartography: Mapping space, place, race, and identity in an urban middle school. *Taboo: The Journal of Culture and Education, 13*(1), 21–45. http://doi.org/10.31390/taboo.13.1.04

Gorski, P. C. (2016). Poverty and the ideological imperative: A call to unhook from deficit and grit ideology and to strive for structural ideology in teacher education. *Journal of Education for Teaching, 42*(4), 378–386. http://doi.org/10.1080/02607476.2016.1215546

Gregg, M., & Seigworth, G. J. (Eds.). (2010). *The affect theory reader*. Duke University Press.

Haraway, D. (1988). Situated knowledges: The science question in feminism and the privilege of partial perspective. *Feminist Studies, 14*(3), 575–599. http://doi.org/10.2307/3178066

Haraway, D. J. (2016). *Staying with the trouble: Making kin in the Chthulucene*. Duke University Press.

Judson, G. (2020). Conceptualizing imagination in the context of school leadership. *International Journal of Leadership in Education*, 1–13.

Kayumova, S., & Buxton, C. (2021). Teacher subjectivities and multiplicities of enactment: Agential realism and the case of science teacher learning and practice with multilingual Latinx students. *Professional Development in Education, 47*(2–3), 463–477. http://doi.org/10.1080/19415257.2021.1879225

Leander, K. M., Phillips, N. C., & Taylor, K. H. (2010). The changing social spaces of learning: Mapping new mobilities. *Review of research in education, 34*(1), 329–394.

MacLure, M. (2013a). Classification or wonder? Coding as an analytic practice in qualitative research. In R. Coleman & J. Ringrose (Eds.), *Deleuze and research methodologies* (pp. 164–183). Edinburgh University Press.

MacLure, M. (2013b). The wonder of data. *Cultural Studies ←→ Critical Methodologies, 13*(4), 228–232. http://doi.org/10.1177/1532708613487863

Milner, R. (2012). But what is urban education? *Urban Education, 47*, 556–561. http://doi.org/10.1177/0042085912447516

Ringrose, J., & Renold, E. (2014). "F** k rape!" Exploring affective intensities in a feminist research assemblage. *Qualitative Inquiry, 20*(6), 772–780. http://doi.org/10.1177/1077800414530261

Sharma, M. (2016). Seeping deficit thinking assumptions maintain the neoliberal education agenda: Exploring three conceptual frameworks of deficit thinking in inner-city schools. *Education and Urban Society, 50*(2), 136–154. http://doi.org/10.1177/0013124516682301

Sondel, B., Kretchmar, K., & Dunn, A. H. (2019). "Who do these people want teaching their children?" White saviorism, colorblind racism, and anti-blackness in "no excuses" charter schools. *Urban Education*. http://doi.org/10.1177/0042085919842618

Strom, K. J. (2015). Teaching as assemblage: Negotiating learning and practice in the first year of teaching. *Journal of Teacher Education, 66*(4), 321–333.

Strom, K. J., & Martin, A. D. (2017). *Becoming-teacher: A rhizomatic look at first-year teaching*. Springer.

Teemant, A., Leland, C., & Berghoff, B. (2014). Development and validation of a measure of critical stance for instructional coaching. *Teaching and Teacher Education, 39,* 136–147. http://doi.org/10.1016/j.tate.2013.11.008

Walker, K. L. H. (2011). Deficit thinking and the effective teacher. *Education and Urban Society, 43*(5), 576–597. http://doi.org/10.1177/0013124510380721

Postscript and Possibilities

Laurie Anderson

> Unlike a fountain that circulates the same water in an enclosed, perpetually recycling system, a human being circulates thoughts in an unlimited reservoir of self. Don't limit yourself to being a mere fountain when you contain an ocean.
>
> —Vera Nazarian, 2010

My initial invitation to this book party was to write a chapter on the links among leadership, imagination, and contemplative education, and more pointedly, how the latter could enhance the former two. Work, COVID, life in general, and a grueling asynchronous four-credit math course I signed up for nixed that ambitious goal. The second invitation was to write a concluding chapter, an opportunity I seized immediately. When I semifacetiously mentioned to the book's co-editors, Gillian and Meaghan, that critiquing others rather than creating something myself made the second option infinitely more appealing, they quickly corrected my faulty thinking.

Your task is not to opine, Laurie, they said, but to identify themes, reveal connections, and suggest ways forward. Your job is to illuminate, weave, and, in keeping with the central theme of the book, imagine. In short, attempt to manifest the imaginative leadership explored throughout this text. This chapter therefore cannot be the conventional "closure" type: bringing everything together and wrapping it up with a nice tidy bow. No, the call to lead with imagination that weaves throughout the book summoned me to take a different tack. Begging your indulgence, I take grammatical license and call that approach "opensure" (Burkeman, 2012; Wheatley, 2006).

There are clearly times and situations in leadership where closure is appropriate. A project or event is wrapped up; a difficult conversation has resolved a thorny issue; the books are literally closed on a budget reconciliation; a seemingly interminable challenge of some sort reaches a conclusion: closure provides a sense of satisfaction and represents a small victory. Arguably, we, as school leaders, do not get enough closures these days, so acknowledging them when we do makes sense.

Opensure, on the other hand, means that the door remains open, the antenna remains up, the sensors active. Closure implies finality, opensure means receptivity. Opensure is about remaining curious, responsive, and agile, ready to switch gears as opportunities emerge. Most importantly, given the theme of this compelling ensemble of imagination-centric essays, opensure is a necessary condition for imagination to flourish. Just as the "soil" of imagination must be fecund and generative to facilitate growth, so too must we make opensure our default rather than closure (Judson, 2021).

In full and humbling disclosure, I come to studying imagination in the context of leadership late in my career. I have held every formal leadership position there is in a large urban school district, from department head to superintendent. During these years, I also co-developed and facilitated leadership development programs, studied the leadership canon, and taught graduate courses on the subject. Ironically, I also supported the implementation of imaginative pedagogy initiatives in my school district, programs based on the pioneering work of Kieran Egan (1997) and the ongoing commitment of many educators involved with the Centre for Imagination in Research, Culture, and Education (formerly the Imaginative Education Research Group, or IERG) at Simon Fraser University. Just as the stories in this book describe so well, I have learned that imagination is absolutely essential to leadership and, indeed, holds the key to navigating our way through the unprecedented times we live in.

It would be unhelpful and inappropriate to reduce the insights in the preceding chapters to a set of "guiding principles" for cultivating imagination in leadership. The foregoing is a collection of essays that stand on their own, each one offering something valuable to ponder, to be inspired by, to learn from, and to inquire into more deeply. It is better to consider them as rich variations on the theme of reconceptualizing leadership—and indeed education more broadly—in a way that positions imagination as an essential element rather than an expendable frill. I conclude by reflecting on just how we might do that.

MOVING FORWARD

That the times we live in call out for imaginative leadership is a blinding flash of the obvious. In 1985, leadership guru Warren Bennis described the conditions leaders had to navigate as *VUCA*; they are volatile, uncertain, complex, and ambiguous (Bennis & Nanus, 1985). While leadership is, by definition, challenging, the conditions leaders navigate today are arguably several orders of magnitude more *VUCA* than they were 37 years ago. Social media, disinformation, climate change, eco-anxiety, epistemic crises, rising inequality, pandemics, opioid crises—the aggregate impact of these forces on those in leadership roles cannot be underestimated, nor can the need for more imaginative approaches to address them not be considered. To paraphrase the maxim often attributed to Einstein, the myriad challenges of today cannot be addressed using the leadership approaches that brought us to this juncture.

My view is that we desperately need to harness and apply the power of our individual and collective imaginations to lead us forward. That said, I also want to be clear that I believe that using imagination in leadership in and of itself will not bring about the necessary changes. Imagination is a necessary but insufficient condition for sustainable and transformative educational leadership. By this, I mean that we cannot reasonably refashion educational leadership without attending to other crucial factors, including the challenges of implementation, the role of followers, the inner lives of educators, and a reimagined conception of what leadership is.

In my 30 years in formal leadership roles in education, from department head through to superintendent in a large urban K–12 system, and for the past 12 years as a university administrator and adjunct professor, I have become acutely aware of the importance of implementation. Indeed, the educational landscape is littered with failed initiatives, not because they necessarily lacked merit but because insufficient attention was given to how to implement them (Cuban & Tyack, 1995; Fullan, 2020). Reforms in education are often piecemeal and overhyped, strong on promises but weak in delivery, and perhaps worst of all, simply introduced as if their inherent value is a sufficient rationale for their immediate adoption (Sarason, 1990). Attempts to introduce or increase imagination in leadership, therefore, in whatever form, need to attend to fundamental principles of design and implementation: transparency, clarity, validation of and link with current strengths, emotional impact, diversity, proactive, emergent and informed planning, celebrations of small breakthroughs, relentless communication, consultation, and contextual awareness (Fullan, 2020; Quayle, 2017).

In my 35 years practicing, teaching, and studying leadership, I've been struck by how rarely followers are mentioned. I find this ironic given that leadership cannot happen without them. It is also problematic because the influence of followers has progressively increased just as that of leaders has declined (Kellerman, 2012). In the educational context specifically, parental and teacher involvement in decision-making has increased steadily, as has the need for "student voice" (Groundwater-Smith, 2016). For leaders in education, listening to, consulting with, and collaborating with followers has evolved from an option to consider to an imperative to practice. This means that we need to consider how we prepare "followers" to optimize their agency and their pivotal role in the leadership equation; in my view, informed, engaged followers are a prerequisite to successful leadership.

The current movement to "Indigenize and de-colonize" the curriculum (Cote-Meek & Moeke-Pickering, 2020) represents an opportunity to both advance reconciliation and reconsider—dare I say *reimagine*—how we think about and practice leadership. The importance of being grounded in place and nature, the application of the 7th-generation principle of the Haudenosaunee (Ladkin & Spiller, 2013), learning and leading through storytelling, leadership *with* others rather than leadership *of* others, the importance of positive rituals—these values and practices, ways of being and knowing in Indigenous cultures for millennia, can make a transformative contribution to leadership. Considering the VUCA conditions referred to earlier, leadership that embodies and honors Indigenous wisdom in its relational, distributive, and collective qualities can significantly contribute to the sustainable model we need.

While I have frequently joined the chorus lamenting the school system's imperviousness to change (Cuban & Tyack, 1995; Fullan, 2020; Sarason, 1990), I believe a compelling, evidence-based claim could be made that public institutions like schools are undergoing a quiet transformation. The pervasive implementation of various "mindfulness" programs (Ergas, 2014; Kabat-Zinn, 2005) and the inclusion of social and emotional learning into the K–12 curricula—both now commonplace—would have been unthinkable even 20 years ago. This trend to acknowledge the pivotal role our inner lives play on the quality of our well-being can also be found in health care, business, and sports, as well as in higher education programs. In different ways, programs of this type have the same intent: validating that our thoughts, emotions, sensations, and self-talk hugely influence how we perceive and navigate the world (Bai et al., 2014). Moreover, that focused, nonjudgmental attention on the present moment (as opposed to ruminating over the past or worrying about the future) fosters clarity of thought, a grounded, relaxed perspective, and enhanced emotional regulation.

These conditions, intrinsic to a variety of contemplative practices, including but not limited to meditation, yoga, dance, and chanting, help make us more open to different ways of imagining and handling reality.

Franklin (2017) describes this connection with our inner lives as "imaginative mindfulness" (p. 93), a way to use contemplative practices to spark our imagination. Like the cognitive tools introduced through this text, contemplative practices enable us to access our imaginative capacity. Leaders who invest time and focus on both pathways—cognitive tools and contemplative practices—can shape an environment wherein the notion of what is possible is vastly expanded.

I would add that two structural features of formal education—a focus on "fixities" (Greene, 1995) and a studied avoidance of anything remotely spiritual (Bai et al., 2014)—also preclude the growth of imagination in leadership. There is an explicit bias in education toward knowing the answers, being in control, and avoiding risk (Greene, 1995), when in fact *not knowing* and thinking of "failure" in a different way are preconditions for imagination to flourish (Desmarescaux, 2022). The realm of what is possible dramatically and exponentially expands when we adopt a beginner's mind. Intellectual humility is a leadership attribute! Imagination can and must be cultivated. Seeing things not as they are but as they might be is more likely when the conditions for ideas to thrive are in place. The implications for schools and classrooms are clear: children will not cultivate their imaginative dispositions in the absence of open, supportive, and risk-taking conditions, and without bold leaders willing to push boundaries and encourage novel solutions. We need to ask ourselves if our places of learning support or sabotage the use of imagination.

Similarly, another epistemic problem, the artificial divide between the secular and the sacred, between religion and science (Bai et al., 2014), closes off a world of experiences that fosters new possibilities. Our failure to acknowledge the spiritual dimension of the human experience, particularly the role our inner lives play in our growth and development, closes off a myriad of imaginative possibilities (Palmer, 1993; Zajonc, 2009).

I have characterized *implementation, focus on followers, acknowledging the inner lives of educators, bias toward certainty and control,* and *the lack of attention to the sacred aspects of the human condition* as additional factors, beyond imagination, that leaders in education would benefit from considering. But perhaps each one of these elements is not discrete from cultivating imagination at the heart of leadership, but rather are different examples of the same dilemma: the fundamental failure to recognize how central imagination is to leadership, learning, and development. Returning to the soil metaphor, these factors might be considered elements in the soil that without our attention and cultivation stunt the growth of our imaginations. As the chapters in this book evocatively describe, imagination is the *sine qua non* of leadership. When we recognize that our imaginations are not dispensable extras but "the hard pragmatic centre of all human thinking" (Egan & Nadaner, 1988, p. ix), our capacity, as school leaders, to flourish and lead in these uncertain, volatile times will be realized.

REFERENCES

Bai, H., Eppert, C., Scott, C., Tait, S., & Nguyen, T. (2014). Towards intercultural philosophy of education. *Studies in Philosophy and Education, 34*(6), 635–649. https://doi.org/10.1007/s11217-014-9444-1

Bennis, W., & Nanus, B. (1985). *Leaders: Strategies for taking charge.* Harper & Row.

Burkeman, O. (2012). *The antidote: Happiness for people who can't stand positive thinking.* Farrar, Straus & Giroux.

Centre for Imagination in Research Culture & Education. (n.d.). www.circesfu.ca

Cote-Meek, S., & Moeke-Pickering, T. (Eds.). (2020). *Decolonizing and Indigenizing education in Canada.* Canadian Scholars.

Cuban, L., & Tyack, D. (1995). *Tinkering towards utopia: A century of public school reform.* Harvard Press.

Desmarescaux, F. (2022, February 23). The power of not-knowing. *Tricycle.* https://tricycle.org/trikedaily/not-knowing/

Egan, K. (1997). *The educated mind: How cognitive tools shape our understanding.* University of Chicago Press.

Egan, K., & Nadaner, D. (Eds.). (1988). *Imagination and education.* Teachers College Press.

Ergas, O. (2014). Mindfulness at the intersection of science, religion and education. *Critical Studies in Education, 55* (1), 58–72. https://doi.org/10.1080/17508487.2014.858643

Franklin, M. A. (2017). *Art as contemplative practice: Expressive pathways to the self.* State University of New York Press.

Fullan, M. (2020). *Leading in a culture of change* (2nd ed.). Jossey-Bass.

Greene, M. (1995). *Releasing the imagination.* John Wiley and Sons.

Groundwater-Smith, S. (2016, December 7). Why student voice matters. *EdCan Network.* www.edcan.ca/articles/why-student-voice-matters/

Judson, G. (2021). Cultivating leadership imagination with cognitive tools: An imagination-focused approach to leadership education. *Journal of Research on Leadership Education.* https://doi.org/10.1177/19427751211022028

Kabat-Zinn, J. (2005). *Coming to our senses.* Hyperion.

Kellerman, B. (2012). *The end of leadership.* Harper.

Ladkin, D., & Spiller, C. (2013). *Authentic leadership: Clashes, convergences and coalescence.* Edward Elgar Press.

Nazarian, V. (2010). *The perpetual calendar of inspiration.* Spirit.

Palmer, P. (1993). *To know as we are known: Education as a spiritual journey.* Harper.

Poetry Foundation (n.d.). *Matthew Arnold.* https://www.poetryfoundation.org/poets/matthew-arnold

Quayle, M. (2017). *Designed leadership.* Columbia Press.

Sarason, S. (1990). *The predictable failure of educational reform.* Jossey-Bass.

Wheatley, M. J. (2006). *Leadership and the new science.* Berrett-Koehler.

Zajonc, A. (2009). *Meditation as contemplative inquiry: When knowing becomes love.* Lindisfarne Press.

APPENDIX

Cultivate Leadership Imagination With Cognitive Tools

Table A.1. Use Imagination to Deepen Understanding and Generate New Ideas

Activity Name	Cognitive Tools	Use It
Identify the Story: Change the Story	The story form Revolt and idealism	What is the dominant story on the issue/topic? What biases, perspectives, or values does this narrative reflect?
		Does changing the go-to story support equity and inclusion? If so, what unquestioned "rules" or "commonsense" ideas in this story can be "broken"? What is one step you can take to "tell" this new story?
Seek Heroic Qualities	Transcendent heroic qualities	What transcendent qualities currently define the issue/topic (e.g., respect, hope)? What different qualities would support a more socially just school community?
Feeling: Naming (Mixed) Emotions for Understanding	Emotional responses Sense of incongruity Play The body's senses and movement	How do you feel about this topic/issue? What are your emotional responses? What is unexpected, playful, or incongruous in the issue/topic? How can the body's senses contribute to your learning?
Exploring Different Perspectives: Play and Puzzle	Change of context Extremes of experience and limits of reality Sense of mystery and puzzles General theories and anomalies	Try to understand this issue/topic from a radically different point of view. Engage in some *extreme* "what if'ing" from this new perspective—find the "boundaries" of the topic. What puzzles you? What doesn't fit in this new perspective with what you believe to be true? What do these anomalies reveal about the topic or about you?

(continued)

Table A.1. Use Imagination to Deepen Understanding and Generate New Ideas (*continued*)

Activity Name	Cognitive Tools	Use It
Making (and Breaking) Meaningful Metaphors	Metaphor	What metaphors currently reveal the meaning of the issue/topic? How can using different metaphors open space for new ideas or new perspectives? What new metaphor breaks apart the status quo?
Envision	Vivid mental imagery from words	What vivid mental images exemplify your current understanding of an issue/topic? What "comes to mind"?
		Envision what your ideal understanding *would be*. What/who is in this vision?
Identify the Rhythms and Patterns: Create New Patterns	Rhythms and patterns	What patterns contribute to the meaning of the issue/topic? What general causal chains, networks, or systems do you notice? How are current patterns limiting what is possible? What new patterns or processes might open up possibility?

Table A.2. Use Imagination to Engage Others in Meaning-Making

Activity Name	Cognitive Tool	Use It
Story-Shape Issues/ Topics for Faculty and Staff	The story form	Find the emotional significance of an issue/topic.
	Dramatic tensions	Frame an issue/topic around a dramatic tension.
	Transcendent heroic qualities	Reveal transcendent qualities within an issue/topic.
	Vivid mental imagery	Evoke a mental image to reveals the importance of an issue/topic.
	Metaphor	Share an analogy that extends/ conveys the meaning of an issue/topic.
	Humanization of meaning	Reveal the human angle. Identify how an issue/topic connects to someone's hope, fears, or passions.
Encourage Adults to Play	Extremes of experience & limits of reality	Do some "extreme" "what-if'ing." Encourage unusual responses. Aim to push past limits.
	Sense of wonder	Make the familiar "strange"—present the issue/topic in a new light. How would *X* policy or practice make day-to-day school life different? *Imagine if...*
	Incongruity/humor	
	Sense of mystery	
	General theories/ anomalies	Explore what is incongruous or puzzling about an issue/topic. Seek "unusual" combinations of ideas. Identify anomalies. What can we learn from the anomalies?
	Play	Encourage experimentation with ideas.
Encourage New Perspectives/ Outlooks/Insights	Humanization of meaning	Consider an issue/topic from someone else's perspective.
	Role-play	Engage in a role-play to think differently and generate ideas about an issue/topic.
	Change of context	Create a scenario to explore a topic in new ways and from different angles.

Table A.3. Use Imagination for Equity, Diversity, and Inclusion

Activity Name	Cognitive Tool	Use It
Seek Understanding: What's the Story Here?	The story form Rhythms and patterns	What or whose "story" dominates here? What or whose is missing? What limitations or constraints make it difficult to share experiences of ex/inclusion here? What are the rhythms or patterns of marginalization here?
Engaging in Extreme "What If-ing"	Extremes of experience and limits of reality The body's senses and movement	What is your ideal image of this community? What would it look, sound, feel like? Close your eyes and put yourself in this space: What do you notice? What do you feel? Who or what would be part of the conversation?
Evoke Wonder: Bring Uniqueness Into the Bright Light of Recognition	Sense of wonder Sense of agency	What is unique and inspiring about your school community? How does diversity enrich your community? What *glimmers with wonder* in this community? What action can you take with others to amplify what is wonder-full?
Practice Feeling Comfortable With Discomfort: Body Forth	Dramatic tensions	What are the tensions that different stakeholders feel in the school community (e.g., powerful/powerless; hope/despair)? What policies/procedures reproduce negative emotions? What can change?
Enact Care	Sense of agency	Deep transformation to support equity requires relationships based in *care*. Imagine an ethic of care infuses your organization. What does it mean to work from a place of *care*? Think about care as an *action*—what actions of care do you see/want to see in your school?
(Make) Metaphors Matter: Beyond Rhetoric (aka: Not Window Dressing)	Metaphor	Genuine inclusion is not rhetoric with little change. So, what *is* equity in action in your organization? It *is* ____ (fill in the blank with your goal—your metaphor for genuine change). In this organization we _____, we refuse to _____.

Activity Name	Cognitive Tool	Use It
"Picture" It: Snapshots of Equity and Inequity	Vivid mental imagery from words Revolt and idealism	What does equity/inequity look like in this community? Compare your community members' images of equity/inequity. Identify the procedures, processes, or relationships that reproduce inequity. Define measurable steps to address each inequity. What policies or processes can be ignored or changed in support of equity?

Judson, G. (2022). *Engaging and cultivating imagination in equity-focused school leadership.* This table was modified from a form originally published under a Creative Commons Attribution 4.0 International license (CC BY 4.0) for the International Journal of Leadership in Learning (https://creativecommons.org/licenses/by/4.0/)

Endnotes

Foreword

1. This foreword is dedicated in honor of Sir Ken Robinson, Dr. Maxine Greene, and Dr. Mihaly Csikszentmihalyi.

Preface

1. www.educationthatinspires.ca/imaginative-educational-leadership/
2. See www.educationthatinspires.ca/tips-for-imaginative-educators/ for the full list and an explanation of *cognitive tool*.

Imagination in Action

1. Quinn's story has been adapted from a previously published piece (Driussi, 2013).
2. Read more stories of imagination in action at www.educationthatinspires.ca/imaginative-educational-leadership/ and submit your own here: www.educationthatinspires.ca/write-for-imagined/.

Chapter 1

1. We invite you to add your story of imagination in leadership to the growing collection at imaginED! To do so, email **gillianjud@gmail.com** or submit through the QR code below, which leads to www.educationthatinspires.ca/write-for-imagined.

Chapter 6

1. Madeline Grumet, in a presentation in 1995 at the University of British Columbia, introduced the line "Tread gently, oh so gently" when speaking of being in the presence of children.

2. Performative inquiry is a way of being in research through theater and drama activities. Conceptualized and articulated during my doctoral studies, performative inquiry is a practice of noticing stop moments (Appelbaum, 1995) or what I have come to call "tugs on the sleeves," moments that call us to attention. Performative inquiry is pedagogical, a form of inquiry that seeks to reveal and disrupt what is, and ask what else might be possible. See Fels, 2020, 2016, 2015, 2012, 2010, 2004, 2002, 1999.

3. I am grateful for Karen Meyer, who introduced me to this way of questioning, and my son Marshall, who added, "Who cares?" from the back of his grade 4 classroom.

4. Noted theater director and activist Agusto Boal created a series of acting games for actors and nonactors that invite inquiry through embodied explorations and metaphorical connections with lived experience.

5. Another young man unexpectedly appeared in our midst during a high school musical production of *West Side Story*, and I asked the same question. See Fels, 2010.

6. See Levison (2001) for a thoughtful reading of natality and belatedness.

7. See *Little Girl Experiences Rain for the First Time*, YouTube, www.youtube.com/watch?v=mxmmvHsDeuI.

Index

Note: **Bold** type indicates chapter authors. Page numbers followed by "n" indicate numbered endnotes.

Affect
    affective mental imagery in poetry, 83
    in urban education, 163–165
Agency
    education policy and, 95
    shared agency in critical posthumanism, 154, 160
    sound as agentic actor in urban areas, 159–160, 163
Amador, A. G., 126, 128, 129
Anderson, Laurie, 10, 22, 23, 25, 27–28, **171–177**
Anthropocentrism, 136, 138–140, 143, 146–147, 153
Anti-oppressive research, 20–21
Appelbaum, D., 103n2
Arán Filippetti, V., 127
Archie, K. M., 129–130
Arendt, Hannah, 108, 109
Aronica, L., 125
Artful-mindedness mindset, 52–53
Asian communities, 156–163. *See also* Equity and social justice
Asikin-Garmager, A., 39
Asma, S. T., 2, 21, 52, 69, 87

Bai, H., 174, 175
Baldridge, B. J., 164
Ball, S. J., 5, 126
Barad, K., 154
Barnett, K., 39
Beeman, C., 143–144
Belliveau, G., 104
Benjamin, R., 86
Bennett, J., 154, 162, 163
Bennett, M., 21
Bennis, Warren, 172–173
Berghoff, B., 156
Best American Poetry, The (Glück), 73
Black communities, 79–80, 120, 156–163.
    See also Equity and social justice
Blase, Jo, 39
Blase, Joseph, 39

Blenkinsop, Sean, 9, **135–151,** 138, 143–145
Boal, Augusto, 106–108
Bolman, L G., 60
Bouckaert, M., 127–128
Boullosa, P., 25–28
Braidotti, R., 153–155, 159, 164
Brandon, Scott, xi–xii
Brass, J., 126
Broom, L., 73–74
Brown, G., 37
Brown, J. S., 2, 3, 6–8, 10
Brown, L., 20–21
Burkeman, O., 171
Burton, L., 164
Busch, S., 38, 39
Buswick, T., 76, 81
Buxton, C., 153

Camilli, G., 87
Cantú, Y., 124–125
Caring. *See* Empathy/caring
Carpe Diem, the Arts and School Restructuring (Greene), 54–56
Centers for Disease Control and Prevention (CDC), 5–6
Centre for Imagination in Research, Culture & Education (CIRCE), Simon Fraser University, 20–22, 172
Cerni, T., 39, 72
Change educator-leaders, 146, 147
Change process, 22, 26–29
    causing change, 28–29
    creative play and, 102
    educational reform and, 51, 68, 75, 81–82, 87, 125–127, 173
    education policy in, 91, 93–94
    Four Directions tradition applied to educational leadership, 145–148
    organizational change in cancer care innovations, 51–60
    poetic imagination in. *See* Poetry/poetic imagination

Change process *(continued)*
  preparing for change, 26–27
  responding to change, 27–28
Chapman, N., 67, 72, 81
Charles, A., 22, 23, 27–28
Cheng, E., 21
Child Development and Education Act (1989), 126
Clayton, P., 129–130
Cleverley-Thompson, S., 21
Coeur/care educator-leaders, 146, 147–148
Cognitive tools in IE, 179–183. *See also* Cultivating Curiosity, Conversation, and Imagination activities
Colmenares, E. E., 153
Common Core State Standards, 126
Community educator-leaders, 145, 147
Compassionate action. *See* Creative play
Conrad, D., 67
Contemplative practices, 174–175
Cote-Meek, S., 174
COVID-19 pandemic, 5–6, 20, 23–24, 37, 43, 68, 123, 124
Creative play, 102–113
  Boal's games for actors and non-actors, 106–108
  change process and, 102
  children in the world's renewal, 108, 110–112
  cognitive tools for implementing, 113
  examples of, 104–108
  here and now in, 102–104, 108, 109, 110–111
  joyfully interrupting the script in, 108–109
  nature of leadership in, 103–104
  performative inquiry and pedagogy in, 103–104
  play as pedagogical tool, 104–106, 113
  questions in framing imaginary worlds of possibility, 102–104, 110
  role drama, 104–106
  vulnerability in liminal dynamic space (Thomasson) and, 108, 109, 110
Creative Schools (Robinson & Aronica), 125
Creativity
  critical thinking and, 40–41, 127–128
  imagination vs., 2, 19, 69, 127–128
Crisis narratives
  institutionalism and, 68, 72
  poetry in reframing, 68, 83
Critical educator-leaders, 145, 146–147
Critical literacy (Muhammad), 120
Critical posthumanism, 152–156
  as collective re-imagining, 153–154
  in disrupting deficit-based perspectives, 152–153, 156–163, 166

implications of, 155
nature of, 153–156
nonhuman actors in the classroom and, 155–156, 159–160, 163
vignettes as entry point to, 156–166
Critical thinking, 40–41, 127–128
Cruden, L., 145–146
Cuban, L., 173, 174
Cultivating Curiosity, Conversation, and Imagination activities, 7–8, 33, 179–183
  for disrupting deficit-based perspectives, 167
  for eco-leadership in education, 149
  for equity and social justice, 132
  for implementing education policy, 86, 89–99, 100
  for implementing school culture, 48
  nature of, xiv, xv–xvi
  play as pedagogical tool, 113
  poetics and, 78, 79–81, 83
  "what if" approach and, 61
Culturally responsive leadership model (Khalifa), 125, 126, 127
Curiosity, in innovation, 52–53, 56–58, 60
Curtis, G. J., 39, 72, 77

Dantley, M. E., 123, 129
Daugherty, R., 39
Davies, B., 146
Davis, B., 109
Davis, L. P., 91
Daviter, F., 87
Deal, T. E., 60, 67
Deficit-based perspectives, 152–167
  cognitive tools for disrupting, 167
  critical posthumanism in disrupting, 152–153, 156–163, 166
  educational leadership preparation programs and, 163–166
  education policy and, 87–88, 91
  focus on human actors and, 152
  language and, 152
  methods of disrupting, 156–163
  others/othering and, 87–88, 91, 152–156, 165, 167
  vignettes in disrupting, 120, 156–166
Deleuze, G., 154
De Luca, F., 127–128
Dernikos, B., 158, 159, 164
Desmarescaux, F., 175
Dewey, John, xii
Dinishak, J., 91
Dougherty, Meaghan, 1–11, 171
Down, B., 4
Driussi, Lori, 15–18, 16n1
Duignan, P., 4, 5
Dunn, A. H., 152, 159
Dyke, E., 129, 130

Index

Earley, P., 86
Eco-leadership in education, 135–149
  anthropocentrism and, 136, 138–140, 143, 146–147, 153
  characteristic patterns of schooling as problem and, 135–138, 143
  cognitive tools for implementing, 149
  Four Directions tradition applied to educational leadership, 145–148
  Haudenosaunee/Mohawk tradition and, 135, 138–144, 174
  individualism in education and, 140–141
  nature as our first teacher, 141–144
Educational leadership
  alternative/social justice practices in. *See* Equity and social justice
  concept of leadership, 3–4, 31, 109
  culture building and. *See* School culture building
  entity vs. relational perspective on, 3–4
  followers and, 173–174
  Four Directions tradition applied to, 145–148
  imagination in. *See* Imagination in educational leadership; Imaginative Education (IE)
  impacts on others, 4
  nature of, xi–xii
  need for ethical and authentic, 4–6
  play as pedagogical tool in. *See* Creative play
  poetry and. *See* Poetry/poetic imagination
  preparation for. *See* Educational leadership preparation programs
  in relational perspective. *See* Relational leadership
  role in modeling characteristic patterns of schooling, 135–138, 143
  social justice values and. *See* Equity and social justice
  VUCA conditions in leadership (Bennis) and, 172–173, 174
Educational leadership preparation programs. *See also* Simon Fraser University (Vancouver)
  deficit-based perspectives and, 163–166
  equity and social justice skillsets in, 123, 125, 126–128
  Master's of Education (MEd) in Imaginative Education and, 40
  poetics in, 130–131
  professional development for educators and, 24–25
Education policy, 86–100
  cognitive tools for implementing, 100
  crisis of imagination in, 86–88
  engaging imagination in understanding, 88
  gardening cycle as metaphor for the policy cycle, 88, 89–99, 100
  importance of education and, 86–87
  phase 1: Context, 89–91, 97, 98
  phase 2: Initiation, 89–91, 97, 98
  phase 3: Formulation, 91–93, 97, 98
  phase 4: Adoption, 93–94, 97, 98
  phase 5: Implementation, 94–95, 97, 98
  phase 6: Evaluation, 95–96, 97, 99
  phase 7: Continuation, 96–97, 99
  policy, defined, 88
  reforms and, 51, 68, 75, 81–82, 87, 125–127, 173
  storytelling in IE and, 90, 92, 96, 100
  what if/what may be/what is possible evaluations in, 87–88
EDvent series, 25
Egan, Kieran, xiv, xv, 2, 8, 16, 21, 38–40, 86–88, 138, 146, 172, 176
Eliot, T. S., 81–82
Elmore, P. B., 87
Email communication, 65–66
Embodied imagination. *See* Creative play
Emdin, C., 120
Empathy/caring
  in cancer care innovation, 51–60
  and coeur/care educator-leaders, 146, 147–148
  ethic of care (Noddings), 141
  in relational leadership, 22–24
Engagement, 22, 24–26
  Friday Frenzy parent newsletter and, 24
  Ignite presentations and, 25
  "leaning in" and, 26, 32, 44
  nature of, 24–25
Enlow, B. K., 102, 123, 128–129
Eppert, C., 174, 175
Equity and social justice, 123–132
  cognitive tools for implementing, 132
  culturally responsive leadership model (Khalifa) and, 125, 126, 127
  deficit focus and. *See* Deficit-based perspectives
  eco-leadership and. *See* Eco-leadership in education
  ethical and authentic educational leadership and, 4–6
  family stories in, 119–121
  (re)imagining schools and leadership education for, 124, 130
  influences of imaginative practices on, 123–132
  skillsets in leadership preparation practices, 123, 125, 126–128
  Social Justice Education Movement, 130
  social justice values and, 128–130
Ergas, O., 174
Ethic of care (Noddings), 141
Evaluation, education policy and, 95–96, 97, 99
Evol, K., 129, 130

Family Community Learning Exchange
 (FCLE), 120–121
Fels, Lynn, 9, **102–115,** 103n2, 104–107, 109, 110
Fernández-Barrerra, M., 127–128
Fettes, Mark, 9, **135–151,** 138, 145
Fillol, J., 126
Formative evaluation, 95–96
Four Directions tradition, 145–148
  East/critical educator-leaders, 145, 146–147
  North/coeur (care) educator-leader, 146, 147–148
  South/community educator-leaders, 145, 147
  West/change educator-leaders, 146, 147
Franklin, M. A., 174–175
Freire, Paolo, 53, 54–56, 160, 163, 165–166
Froese, C., 26–28
Fullan, M., 22, 173, 174

Gaither, M., 126
Gandhi, A. G., 87
Gareis, C., 37–38
Gershon, W. S., 159, 163
Gilligan, C., 144
Giroux, H., 5, 126
Glück, Louise, 73
Gonzales, L., 68
González-Sancho, C., 127–128
Gopaul B., 105
Gorski, P. C., 152
Gorur, R., 87
Grace, B., 121
Green, G. P., 91
Green, T. L., 123, 129
Greene, Maxine, 10, 23, 53, 54–56, 58–60, 69, 77–78, 80–81, 108, 109, 175
Gregg, M., 165
Gross, S. J., 3–6
Groundwater-Smith, S., 174
Grumet, Madeline, 102n1
Guajardo, F. J., 120, 121, 124–125, 129
Guajardo, M. A., 120, 121, 124–125, 129
Guattari, F., 154
Guillaume, R. O., 126, 128, 129
Gun violence, school lockdown vignette and, 157–160, 163–166
Gutierrez, M., 127
Guyotte, K., 59

Haines, A., 91
Haraway, D. J., 154, 155
Hargreaves, A., 126
Hass, R., 146
Haudenosaunee/Mohawk tradition, 135, 138–144, 174
Hauserman, C. P., 37, 39
Hejinian, Lyn, 73, 77

Heyen, W., 78
Hollingworth, L., 39
Holloway, J., 126
Hopkins, R., 39
Hosking, D., 19
Hu, J., 21
Hughes, P., 121
Hume, David, 69–70
Hutt, E., 126

"I Am From" poems, in disrupting deficit approaches, 120, 160–163, 165–166
Iannuzzi, R., 26, 27
Ignite presentations, 25
Imagination (generally). *See also* Imagination in educational leadership; Imaginative Education (IE)
  cancer care innovations and, 51–60
  concept of, xii, xiii, 1–3, 19, 38
  creativity vs., 2, 19, 69, 127–128
  growth with use, 30
  innovation vs., 2, 19. *See also* Innovation
Imagination (Warnock), 69–71
Imagination in educational leadership
  in the alternative approaches of Indigenous traditions, 135, 138–144
  assumptions of, xi–xii
  change process and, 22, 26–29
  closure vs. "opensure" and, 171–172
  cognitive tools for implementing. *See* Cultivating Curiosity, Conversation, and Imagination activities
  conceptualizing imagination, xii, xiii, 1–3, 19, 38
  contribution to cognitive activities, 6–8
  development of, 27
  dialogue with the "new possible" in, 129–130
  education policy and. *See* Education policy
  engagement and, 22, 24–26
  equity/social justice practices in. *See* Equity and social justice
  "heart" in leadership and, 22–24
  importance of, xii, 2–3, 8–10, 25–26, 52–56, 153. *See also* Imaginative Education (IE)
  importance of understanding, 5–8
  innovation and, 2, 58–59
  as more than human, 136
  nature of, xi–xii, xvi, 68–71
  play as pedagogical tool in. *See* Creative play
  poetry and. *See* Poetry/poetic imagination
  positionality of authors and, 124–125
  Pragmatic Imagination framework for, 2, 3, 6–8, 10
  preconditions for flourishing, 175–176
  and professional learning in the research process, 22, 29–31

Index

relational leadership and. *See* Relational leadership
role of, 1
role of language in, 70–71, 72–73. *See also* Poetry/poetic imagination
school culture building and. *See* School culture building
schools as unpromising soil for, 135–138, 143
social imagination (Greene) and, 59, 69
soil-as-imagination metaphor and education policy, 88, 89–99, 100
stories of lived experience in. *See* Storytelling in IE
theory vs. praxis and, 124–125
vision and, 27, 39
"what if" approach to. *See* "What if " approach
wider context of, 5–6
Imaginative Education (IE)
closure vs. "opensure" and, 171–172
cognitive tools for implementing. *See* Cultivating Curiosity, Conversation, and Imagination activities
collaborative research study based on, 20–22
development of theory, xiv–xv
Master's of Education (MEd) in Imaginative Education, 40
nature of, xi–xii, xv
Pragmatic Imagination framework for, 2, 3, 6–8, 10
resistance to, 17–18, 107–108
stories of lived experience in. *See* Storytelling in IE
Imaginative School Symposium Series (ISSS), 20–21, 28–29
imaginED (website), 20n1
Improving American Schools Act (1994), 126
Indigenous communities, 110, 138–148. *See also* Eco-leadership in education; Equity and social justice
Four Directions tradition applied to educational leadership, 145–148
Haudenosaunee/Mohawk tradition and, 135, 138–144, 174
Individualism in education, 93, 140–141, 155, 158–159, 165
Ingold, Timothy, 15
Innovation
cancer care innovations and, 51–60
curiosity in, 52–53, 56–58, 60
imagination for innovation and, 58–59
imagination vs., 2, 19
mindset for, 52–53, 57–60
organizational support for, 57–58
paradoxes of, 52–53
resistance to, 56–57

"what might be" approach and, 15, 52, 53–54, 56–59, 71, 90
wide-awakeness in, 52–53, 56, 58–60, 109–110
Institutionalism
cultural scripts of, 75
nature of, 73–74
as obstacle to poetry in schools, 67–68, 72, 73–75
old vs. new, 67–68, 73–75
school improvement plans and, 75
Isabella (teacher), 156–163, 165

Jacotin, G., 127–128
Janson, C., 129
Janzen, G., 23–24, 27–28
Jenlink, P., 73, 75, 77, 81
Jickling, B., 143–144
Johnson, M., 58
Journal writing, in poetry journals, 78, 80–81
Judson, Gillian, xiii, 1, **1–11,** 2, 8–9, 19, **19–36,** 20–23, 26–29, 31, 38, 39, 52, 69, 86, **86–101,** 87–89, 91–96, 98–99, 120, 123, 138, 146, 153, 171, 172, 179–183
Jung, Carl, 59

Kabat-Zinn, J., 174
Kant, Immanuel, 70
Katz-Buonincontro, J., 127
Kayumova, S., 153
Kellerman, B., 173–174
Kelley, R. C., 39
Kelly, R., 31
Kennedy, John F., 77
Khalifa, M., 125–127
Kimmerer, R. W., 146
King, G., 39, 77
Kinloch, V., 121
Koschoreck, James W., 9, 102, **123–134,** 125, 132
Koyama, J. P., 87
Kretchmar, K., 152, 159
Krumm, G., 127

Labaree, D. F., 5
Ladkin, D., 174
Laitsch, Dan, 9, 86, **86–101**
Lakoff, G., 58
Landy, I., 23, 27–28
Lange, K., 76, 81
Language of Inquiry, The (Hejinian), 73, 77
Laruccia, M., 52
Laszlo, C., 110
Latinx communities, 120–121, 156–163. *See also* Equity and social justice
Leadership. *See* Educational leadership
Leander, K. M., 159

Learning in Depth projects, 16–18
Lee, Alaina, 120–121
Lee, Li-Young, 78
Leithwood, K., 39
Leland, C., 156
Lesko, N., 164
Levison, N., 108n6, 109
LGBTQIA+ communities, 125. *See also* Equity and social justice
Life of Poetry, The (Rukeyser), 75–76
Lincoln, A., 52–53, 55
Literacy
  alternative forms of, 159–160, 163
  critical (Muhammad), 120
Literary imagination (Nussbaum), 80
Literature and Existentialism (Sartre), 68–69, 70
Liu, E., 1–3, 19, 21, 69, 72, 78, 82
Locke, L. A., 129
Longboat, Dan, 135, 138–144, 146–148
Lorde, Audre, 68, 82
Lugg, C. A., 5

Machado, Antonio, 16
Machado, Moraima, 119–122
MacLure, M., 153, 156–157
MacNeil, A. J., 38, 39
Mah, Craig, 8–9, 19–36, 22, 24–31, 65–66
Mahoney, A. D., 21
Marion, R., 68
Martin, A. D., 153
Masterson, Jessica, 9–10, 152–170
May, Jamaal, 79–80, 83
McCall, S., 164
McCormick, J., 39
McDonnell, L. M., 86
McGovern, L., 105
McInerney, P., 4
McKenzie, B., 86, 88, 98–99
McLean, D., 21
Merchant, B. M., 5
Metaphor
  in education policy cycle as a gardening cycle, 88, 89–99, 100
  nature of, 86, 100
Meyer, John, 74
Meyer, Karen, 103n3, 109
Meyerhoff, E., 129, 130
Militello, M., 129
Milner, R., 152
Mindfulness programs, 174–175
Moeke-Pickering, T., 174
Moran, P., 126
Morgan, C., 76, 81
Moura, P., 126
Muhammad, G. E., 120
Murphy-Graham, E., 87
Museus, S. D., 91

Nachmanovitch, S., 119
Nadaner, D., 176
Nanus, B., 172–173
Nature and Madness (Shepard), 141–143
Nazarian, Vera, 171
Necessary Angel, The (Stevens), 72
Neoliberal ideology, 5
Nguyen, T., 174, 175
Niccolini, A., 164
Nilson, M., 105
No Child Left Behind Act (2001), 126
Noddings, Nel, 56, 141
Noppe-Brandon, S., 1–3, 19, 21, 69, 72, 78, 82
Nussbaum, Martha, 72, 80

Ogawa, R., 75
Okri, B., 18
Olivant, K. F., 127
Oliver, J. A., 124–125
Oliver, Mary, 67
Olsen, D., 39
Orr, K., 21
Others/othering
  deficit-focused approaches and, 87–88, 91, 152–156, 165, 167
  imagination in understanding, 23, 54–55

Palmer, P., 175
Participative evaluation, 96
Pazur, Sarah, 9, 67–85
Pedagogy of the Oppressed (Freire), 54–56
Pendleton-Jullian, A., 2, 3, 6–8, 10
Pereira, S., 126
Performative inquiry and pedagogy. *See* Creative play
Persaud, G., 39
Perspective-taking, in school culture building, 45–47
Peterson, K., 67
Petrosino, A., 87
Phillips, C., 67
Phillips, N. C., 159
Piersol, L., 144
Pillay, Rose, 8–9, 19–36, 22, 24, 25, 28–31
Play as pedagogical tool. *See* Creative play
Plóciennik, E., 127
Poetry Foundation, 177
Poetry/poetic imagination, 67–83
  cognitive tools for implementing, 78, 79–81, 83
  "I Am From" poems in disrupting deficit approaches, 120, 160–163, 165–166
  in (re)imagining schools and leadership education, 130–131
  institutionalism and schools, 67–68, 72, 73–75
  nature of imaginations, 68–71
  nature of poetics and, 71–73

Index

poetic practice for educational leaders, 75–77
poetic summation of the importance of equity and social justice, 130–131
poetry as leadership praxis, 73, 77–81
poetry in the current environment, 68, 72–73
poetry journals, 78, 80–81
Popa, A. B., 102, 123, 128–129
Potts, K., 20–21
Pragmatic Imagination (Pendleton-Jullian & Brown), 2, 3, 6–8, 10
Prater, D. L., 38, 39
Preston, Tara, 9, 37–50
Problem solving, in school culture building, 42–43

Quayle, M., 173
Quinn (student), learning outside the classroom, 16–18

Rasmussen, J., 21
Raven (student nature name), 144
Ravitch, S. M., 129–130
Reid, L., 26, 27
Relational leadership, 22–24
  empathy in, 22–24
  entity approach vs., 3–4
  nature of, 3–4
  risk-taking in, 22–24, 43
  in school culture building, 38–39, 40–42, 43–45
  storytelling in IE and, 22–24, 38–39, 40–42, 43–45
  trust in, 22–24
Releasing the Imagination (Greene), 69, 77–78
Renold, E., 157
Ringrose, J., 157
Risk-taking
  in relational leadership, 22–24, 43
  in school culture building, 43
Robertson, Courtney, 8–9, 19–36, 22–24, 27–31
Robinson, K., 2, 125
Rodríguez, G., 124–125
Roeper, G. A., 127
Role drama, 104–106
Roronhiakewen, 138
Rowan, Brian, 74
Rubin, S., 78
Ruff, M., 127
Rukeyser, Muriel, 75–76
Russ, A., 39, 77

Saizl, M. S., 126, 128, 129
San Pedro, T., 121
Sarason, S., 173, 174
Sartre, Jean-Paul, 68–69, 70
Schneider, J., 126

School culture building, 37–48
  Clara (school leader) and, 40–41, 42
  cognitive tools for implementing, 48
  embodying imaginative leadership in, 40–42
  Greg (school leader) and, 41–42, 43, 44–45, 46
  imagination and perspective-taking in, 45–47
  imagination and problem solving in, 42–43
  imagination and relationships in, 38–39, 43–45
  imagination and risk-taking in, 43
  Laila (school leader) and, 41, 42, 43, 44
  relational leadership in, 38–39, 40–42, 43–45
  research project on imagination for leaders, 39–47
  role of the principal in, 37–38
School improvement plans, 75
School lockdown vignette, 157–160, 163–166
Sclater, Jonathan, 8–9, 19–36, 22, 26–31
Scott, C., 174, 175
Sedgwick, E. K., 125
Seigworth, G. J., 165
Selznick, Philip, 73–74
Serres, M., 140
Servant leadership, poetry in, 81
Shapiro, J. L., 3–6
Sharma, M., 152
Shepard, Paul, 141–143
Sheridan, Joe, 135, 138–144
Shirley, D., 126
Shoto, A. R., 5
Simon Fraser University (Vancouver)
  Centre for Imagination in Research, Culture and Education (CIRCE), 20–22, 172
  Imaginative School Symposium Series (ISSS), 20–21, 28–29
  online collection of leadership stories (QR code), 10, 21–22
  SFU Faculty, 16
Simpson, L., 146
Sitka-Sage, M., 143–144
Slattery, P., 126
Slavin, R. E., 87
Smyth, J., 4
Social imagination (Greene), 59, 69
Social justice. *See* Equity and social justice
Sondel, B., 152, 159
Sonic affects (Gershon), 163
Spiller, C., 174
Spiritual dimension, 174–175
Steffensen, Karen, 9, 51–62, 52, 58
Steinbach, R., 39
Steiner, E., 129–130

Stevens, Wallace, 72
Stick, S. L., 37, 39
Storytelling in IE, xv. *See also* Poetry/poetic imagination
  cancer care innovations and, 51–60
  change process and, 26–29
  education policy and, 90, 92, 96, 100
  engagement and, 24–26
  family stories and, 119–121
  online collection of leadership stories (QR code), 10, 21–22
  parking/traffic problems at school and, 25, 65–66
  participant experience in learning through story, 29–31
  Quinn (student) and learning outside the classroom, 16–18
  relational approach to leadership and, 22–24, 38–39, 40–42, 43–45
  shift from hierarchical to horizontal relationships in, 120–121
  storylines in, 22
  value of leadership stories, 20–22
  vignettes in disrupting deficit-based perspectives, 120, 157–166
  "what if" approach and, 15–18
Strobel, B., 59
Strom, Kathryn J., 9–10, **152–170**, 153, 154
Students of color. *See* Equity and social justice
Styres, S., 146
Sumara, D. J., 109
Summative evaluation, 95–96

Tait, S., 174, 175
Takacs, D., 124
Tarlington, C., 105
Taylor, K. H., 159
Teemant, A., 156
Texas A&M AgriLife Extension, 99
"There Are Birds Here" (May), 79–80, 83
Thing-power (Bennett), 163
Thomas, Zachary, 9, 102, **123–134,** 132
Thomasson, Amy, 108–110
Thornton, B., 39
Timmerman, N., 143–144
Timpane, P. M., 86
Tooms, A. K., 125
Treatise of Human Nature (Hume), 69–70
Trust, in relational leadership, 22–24
Truth and Reconciliation Commission (Canada), 139–140
Tsai, K. C., 127
Tsao, F. C., 110
Tschann-Moran, M., 37–38
Turner, T., 39
Twitter communication, 66
Tyack, D., 173, 174

Uhl-Bien, M., 3, 4
U.S. Centers for Disease Control and Prevention (CDC), 5–6
Urban, W. J., 126
Urgel, J., 127–128

Valadez, M. M., 124–125
Vaquer, M., 76
Varela, F., 102
Verriour, P., 105
Vidal, Q., 127–128
Viesca, Kara, 9–10, **152–170**
View, J., 86
Vincent-Lancrin, S., 127–128
VUCA conditions in leadership (Bennis), 172–173, 174
Vygotsky, L., 127, 135

Wagoner, J. L., 126
Walker, K. L. H., 152
Wang, F., 129
Warnock, Mary, 69–71, 73
Watts, V., 148
Weiss, C. H., 87
Wharf, B., 86, 88, 98–99
"What if" approach (sense of wonder), 15–18, 61
  in cancer treatment, 56–59
  in disrupting deficit perspectives, 157–158
  in education policy, 87–88
  openness to, 27
  play and, xvi, 92–93, 103–104, 107, 111–112, 179, 181, 182
"What might be" approach, 15, 52, 53–54, 56–59, 71, 90
Wheatley, M. J., 171
Wide-awakeness, in innovation, 52–53, 56, 58–60, 109–110
"Wild Geese" (Oliver), 67
Williams, E., 39
Wilson, A., 21
Winn, K. M., 39
Witherell, C., 56
Woodard, J., 128–129
Wu, S., 21

Young, J., 146

Zajonc, A., 175
Zalipour, A., 71

About the Editors and Authors

Laurie Anderson, PhD, is the executive director of Simon Fraser University's (SFU) Vancouver campus, and an adjunct professor in SFU's Faculty of Education. Laurie has studied and practiced educational leadership for over 35 years. Laurie obtained his BEd, MA, and PhD at SFU.

Sean Blenkinsop, PhD, is a professor of education at Simon Fraser University in Vancouver, Canada. He is interested in eco-socially just cultural change education. Recent books include *Ecoportraiture* (an educational eco-research method), *Wild Pedagogies* (an exploration of changing pedagogies in the Anthropocene), and *Paddling Pathways* (a gathering of unusual Canadian paddling stories).

Scott Brandon is known internationally for education and complex systems organization. Scott spent 25 years as executive director at Lincoln Center, where he created the Imagination Conversations, a civic dialogue series. Scott co-authored *Imagination First* and continues to publish.

Meaghan Dougherty, EdD, is faculty at Douglas College in the Department of Child and Youth Care. Her research interests include educational leadership, the complex relationship between education and the labor market, relational practice, criticality, and teaching and learning encounters.

Lori Driussi, PhD, has been a passionate educator for over 30 years. She has held a variety of teaching and leadership roles and is currently a faculty associate with Simon Fraser University, living in the land of "what if."

Lynn Fels, PhD, is professor of arts education at Simon Fraser University and a former academic editor of *Educational Insights* (https://einsights.ogpr.educ.ubc.ca). Lynn's research engages performative inquiry, arts for social change, and performing mentorship. She is co-editor of *Arresting*

Hope (2015) and *Releasing Hope* (2019), exploring women's experiences inside and beyond prison gates.

Mark Fettes, PhD, is an associate professor in the faculty of education, Simon Fraser University. His work explores the intersections between language, land, imagination, experience, and practice. In British Columbia, he has worked with teachers and administrators, Indigenous educators, and knowledge-holders in a series of research collaborations based in place and community.

Gillian Judson, PhD, is an assistant professor in the faculty of education at Simon Fraser University. She teaches in educational leadership and curriculum and instruction programs. Her scholarship looks at imagination's role in leadership and learning (K–postsecondary).

James W. Koschoreck, PhD, is an associate professor and co-director of the Educational Leadership Programs. He earned his doctorate in educational administration at The University of Texas at Austin. His research interests include policy analysis and gay/lesbian issues in educational leadership.

Dan Laitsch, PhD, is an associate professor with the faculty of education at Simon Fraser University and chair of the Institute for Public Education, British Columbia. He co-edits the *International Journal of Education Policy and Leadership*.

Moraima Machado, EdD, is an elementary school principal in Northern California. Her work has focused on partnering with teachers, parents, and community members to create engaging and socially just learning environments for marginalized students.

Craig Mah, MEd, is a district principal in the Coquitlam School District, Imaginative Schools Network Member, and #BCEdChat co-moderator. He has written several articles for *Adminfo Magazine*, a publication of the British Columbia Principals' and Vice Principals' Association.

Jessica Masterson, PhD, is an assistant professor in the College of Education at Washington State University Vancouver. Her scholarship focuses on youth literacies and democratic education.

Sarah Pazur, PhD, is the director of School Leadership for the FlexTech High Schools. She holds a PhD in Educational Leadership from Oakland

University. Her work has appeared in *Phi Delta Kappan, English Leadership Quarterly, Principal Leadership Magazine,* and *Hybrid Pedagogy.*

Rose Pillay, MEd, is a former high school teacher and is now an educational consultant for the K–12 Catholic Independent Schools of the Vancouver Archdiocese (CISVA). In her current role, she supports the professional growth of classroom educators focused on curriculum implementation.

Tara Preston, MEd, is a middle school drama teacher in the Coquitlam School District. She completed her MEd in Imaginative K–12 Leadership at Simon Fraser University and is passionate about developing leaders.

Courtney Robertson, MEd, is a vice principal with the Langley School District. She completed her graduate studies in Imaginative Education at Simon Fraser University. Courtney began her career as a kindergarten teacher before moving into administration in 2016. Her primary research areas include dialogical thinking, leadership through relationship, and the "wonder" of teaching and learning for all.

Jonathan Sclater, MEd, received a master's in Imaginative Education in 2011 and was awarded a Prime Minister's Award in 2012 for his work as a classroom teacher. Now, as an elementary principal, he continues to use imagination to thrive as a school leader.

Karen Steffensen, MEd, has 40 years of experience in public education, from kindergarten to postsecondary education. Karen's leadership expertise brings insights from roles within the ministry of education, system-level leadership (supervisory officer/superintendent), school administration (principal and vice principal), university course director, and K–12 literacy and arts consultant.

Katie Strom, PhD, is an associate professor of educational leadership at California State University, East Bay. Her research employs critical, complex theories to study teacher development and advocate for different ways of thinking in education, with goals of disrupting inequities for minoritized populations.

Zachary Thomas is a doctoral student at Texas State University focusing on creativity practices in education. He earned his master's degree in education at Pepperdine University. His research interests include creativity in standardized classrooms and imagination in educational leadership policy.

Kara Mitchell Viesca, PhD, is an associate professor of teaching, learning, and teacher education at the University of Nebraska-Lincoln. Her scholarship focuses on advancing equity in the policy and practice of educator development, especially for teachers of multilingual learners.